THE SHARD

The Shard

The Vision of Irvine Sellar

Howard Watson

CONSTABLE • LONDON

CONSTABLE

First published in Great Britain in 2017 by Constable

1 3 5 7 9 10 8 6 4 2

A CIP catalogue record for this book
is available from the British Library.

ISBN: 978-0-34941-001-2

Typeset in Bembo by SX Composing DTP, Rayleigh, Essex
Printed and bound in Great Britain by Clays Ltd, St Ives plc

Papers used by Constable are from well-managed forests
and other responsible sources.

Constable
An imprint of
Little, Brown Book Group
Carmelite House
50 Victoria Embankment
London EC4Y 0DZ

An Hachette UK Company
www.hachette.co.uk

www.littlebrown.co.uk

For Alwyn and Brenda Watson

Contents

5 July 2012

The newcomer stands on the south bank of the Thames: it is 1,016 feet tall, 95 storeys high, and constructed of 11,000 panes of glass.

It is Western Europe's tallest building, and far taller than any other in London. It should be immense. It should threaten. It should loom.

The building is sharp, angular, and at a distance appears to be a singular structure, rising in pyramidal form until the point at which it should pierce the sky with determined intent. Instead, its apex is fractured, its numerous façades reaching slightly different heights and not touching, so the top of the building surprisingly feathers into the sky.

The wind swirls into the open upper spire, but that is only part of the building's conversation with the elements. Those 11,000 panes of glass are tilted back from the plane so they respond to the sky. Seen from the direction of the lowering sun, it is the reflection of light that gives form to the building and reveals its shape.

The structure diminishes upwards from its footing, helping the architect perform his magic trick: yes, the building is immense – so huge that it rises unexpectedly into view from many corners of London, providing a dramatic new axial point in the orientation of the city – but it does not threaten; it does not loom.

Yet it cannot be ignored.

This is the Shard, the most important work of contemporary architecture in Britain, and, at this moment, the most talked-about building in the world. Everyone from architecture critic to cultural historian, to philosopher, sociologist, Londoner and tourist, is in the process of forming an opinion on this gigantic structure of steel and glass, if their judgement is not already set in stone.

Across the river, on the northern bank, stands Old Billingsgate Market, which served as London's fish market for over a hundred years. As evening takes hold, members of the Qatari royal family, cultural figures and celebrities, and politicians including Boris Johnson and Ken Livingstone, current and former Mayors of London, are among a few hundred guests having coffee after the Shard's inauguration dinner.

Billingsgate may seem an unusual gathering place for the elite, but the smell of fish has long since gone. The building was refurbished by the architect Richard Rogers in the 1980s, and it is a fitting location for the Shard's inauguration dinner. Rogers is among the guests but, for today at least, he is in the shadow of his old friend and former practice partner, Renzo Piano. The enormous new building across the river is Piano's design. The Italian is joyful and still surprised that the building made it from his first sketch twelve years ago to stand, finally topped out and very nearly complete, on the opposite bank. Earlier in the day, Prince Andrew and Sheikh Hamad bin Jassim bin Jaber Al Thani, the Prime Minister of Qatar, officially inaugurated the building.

The dinner concludes with a speech by Sheikh Abdulla bin Saoud Al Thani, Governor of the Qatar Central Bank and a principal partner in the development, who has called the Shard 'the newest London landmark and a beacon of the City of London's resilience and expansion, even during tough economic times'. Now, he extends thanks to the thousands involved in building the Shard.

If Billingsgate were still a working market, one of the leading figures among the diners would have felt more at home than any of the glamorous guests. He came from the world of market trading, selling his wares from his own stalls when he was still a teenage boy. Now, as Sheikh Abdulla finishes his speech by saying he looks forward to strengthening Qatari–British relations, the ex-market trader is walking towards the stage with a slight swagger.

He is Irvine Sellar. He is the developer who masterminded the creation of the Shard: it was Renzo Piano's design, but it was his vision. Time and time again, highly informed commentators had predicted – with absolute confidence sometimes accompanied by a mocking tone – that his building would never be built.

As he walks towards the stage, he may remember his first dip into the world of commerce as a child. Not long after the Second World War had ended, he persuaded the children of the neighbourhood to part with their pennies, ha'pennies and farthings to play some rudimentary, homemade fairground games he had rigged up in his family's backyard. They included a marble game, in which the player could win a penny or tuppence if they shot the marble into the right hole cut out of a cardboard box, and a coin-in-a-bucket game. For this, young Irvine had dropped a half crown – worth a mighty two shillings and sixpence – into a bucket of water. The children queued up to drop a penny into the bucket, and if it landed on top of the half crown, they would win the prized coin. If it missed, Irvine would keep their penny.

He may have been no good at school, but he was a clever little boy who knew that the refraction of the water made it almost impossible to judge the drop correctly; he also knew that the lure of the half crown meant the children wouldn't be able to resist trying, and then trying again.

The day went well and the mini-entrepreneur earned a tidy amount of pocket money. That was until a boy whom Irvine did not really know decided to play the bucket game. To Irvine's horror, the boy's penny landed on the half crown at the very first attempt, cancelling out much of his profit.

Convinced it was a fluke and eager to make his money back, Irvine placed another precious half crown in the bucket. The little boy decided to try his luck a second time. His penny dropped through the water again and, with immaculate precision, landed right on top of the half crown.

Irvine couldn't understand it. All his earnings had been wiped out in a few seconds by a boy performing the almost impossible, twice in a row.

As he handed over the half crown, Irvine looked more closely at the victor: he was cross-eyed.

That day helped to spark the determination and willingness to learn and adapt that would become the overriding traits in Irvine Sellar's career – the traits that meant the vision of the Shard became a reality.

Almost seven decades after his homemade fair, Sellar reaches the stage and speaks to the guests, apparently off the cuff.

'What an extraordinary day. The tallest building in Western Europe is now physically complete. Though work still needs to be done within the shell, this remains a hugely significant step forward to realising our ultimate vision for London Bridge Quarter, a new dynamic district for our city with the Shard as its centrepiece, a new global landmark.' He looks at the audience with his customary mixture of intensity and humour. 'And I have now come to realise that the sky is certainly not the limit.'

Sellar then reveals a few details of the myriad obstacles that were placed in his way during the twelve years since he had decided to break the height barrier in London. He had faced huge planning, legal, financing, construction and even meteorological challenges, plus a massive global recession, but he had overcome them all.

'We've created a modern marker for London,' he concludes, 'a compass in our great city pointing towards a new financial era while serving as an elegant and powerful symbol of hope and prosperity. And Londoners will feel ownership of the Shard – they will be able to view from there, eat there, sleep there and work there – a new contour to London's skyline, a new mental geography, a way by which people relate to and interact with their city. As it has been said: "We shape our buildings – thereafter they shape us."'

Full darkness has descended and, speeches concluded, the guests pass out of the dining hall and onto the market's riverside forecourt.

A light show begins at 10.15 sharp, but this is no longer a private event for the privileged few. The body of the Shard is illuminated alternately in blue, purple, red and yellow, while a sequence of multi-coloured lasers shoots off from its spire and performs a choreography in the night sky to the tune of Aaron Copland's *Fanfare for the Common Man*. Thousands of Londoners are on rooftops and balconies, and some are having parties in top-floor flats as far away as Egham to the south and Golders Green to the north to celebrate the inauguration of the new building.

Thousands more are massed on Hampstead Heath and Primrose Hill; many line the banks of the Thames, the Millennium Bridge and Tower Bridge. The crowd on London Bridge, the crossing that reaches towards the foot of the Shard, is so vast it spills onto the road. In total, around 300,000 people have come to watch the show. The authorities are forced to make an emergency decision to block off traffic.

Viewers from Parliament Hill can see St Paul's Cathedral glowing white in front of a now reddened Shard, and the lasers playfully graze those newer symbols of London, the Gherkin and the London Eye.

Irvine Sellar had decided to change the skyline of London against all odds, but that was not the limit of his ambition: he wanted Londoners to feel proud of the change.

Now, as he stands outside Billingsgate and takes another sip of champagne, he doesn't look at the Shard. Instead, he looks at the reactions of the people lining the banks and bridges around him, and he knows he has succeeded.

Introduction

The currency of the word 'iconic' has been greatly devalued by overuse in recent decades – it is used to cover everything from a pop star with just one or two hit albums, to a building as trivial as the Trocadero, to a traffic bollard. The laziness of the label is signposted by its use in the *Boston Globe*, that venerable (some would say iconic) US newspaper, which printed the word 161 times between 1980 and 2000, and 2,976 times between 2000 and 2013.[1] In the latter period, the paper also used the noun 'icon' 6,674 times, and we can presume that the great majority of the references were not to Russian Orthodox paintings.

I am going to use the word only once in reference to the Shard for fear of making Jonathan Meades – the cultural commentator who wrote a sublime but vicious tirade against its overuse in 2009[2] – take off his trademark dark glasses and stab pins in his eyes. If there is a single iconic British building of recent times, it is the Shard. The word, in its pre-millennial and pre-clichéd usage, implies a representative symbol, and the Shard is truly that. Whether you are an admirer or a detractor, it is one of the most important buildings in the history of architecture in Britain.

London is a great ancient city, made unique by the simultaneous revelation of its multitudinous layers of history, but from the day of its inauguration in 2012 this new neighbour has become the establishing shot of London. It seems that a television viewer of anything from the local news to a crime drama cannot be sure that the setting is London unless an image of the Shard establishes the scene – the Houses of Parliament, Buckingham Palace and St Paul's Cathedral have been somewhat demoted despite their venerability. Simplified images of the

Shard's attenuated pyramidal structure are stamped on T-shirts, bags and mugs. As a cultural reference point, the Gherkin (or, more properly, 30 St Mary Axe) had its moment in the sun before it was overshadowed, literally, by other City developments. Partly for legal reasons – primarily height restrictions as directed by the Civil Aviation Authority – the Shard's Golden Age is unlikely to prove so short.

The depth of the Shard's cultural resonance is properly shown by its absorption into both the language and the psychogeography of London. The word 'shard', related to 'shear', comes from the Old English *sceard*, which in turn is of Germanic origin and meant gap or potsherd, much as it still does today – a sharp, broken piece of a brittle substance such as glass or ceramic. The British have become good at reducing any new attempt at adventurous architecture to a domestic, sometimes comic and pejorative word – Gherkin, Cheesegrater, Walkie-Talkie. Rather than just a belated label, however, the idea of a shard of glass was one of the focal reference points for the design of what was originally to be called London Bridge Tower. The connection of the word and the building is so entrenched that, while the word 'shard' was initially emblematic of the shape of the building, to some degree the building is now emblematic of the word.

The Shard has become part of our personal mapping of London. We look for it on the skyline to tell us where the south is, where the Thames is, where London Bridge is. We find other locations and destinations in relation to it, without resorting to GPS or paper cartography (reference to which tells us that we don't know our city, that we don't really belong). The knitting of this signpost into our own geography of London gives us some sense of ownership of the building, which is further fostered by the permeability of the Shard, principally through its viewing gallery. We can access the building, albeit for a fee, and see the city from it, and thereby better understand its shape and layers. The Shard is part of London's DNA, as is its developer, Irvine Sellar.

I have been absorbed by the twists and turns of the story of the Shard and the London Bridge Quarter right from the moment when first designs for the massive London Bridge Tower, at the time set to be the tallest building in Europe, were released in 2000. This has evolved into a book about the development of the Shard – how a single building came to change the skyline despite extraordinary problems and opposition – and what that story says about our relationship to very tall buildings, the totems of our age.

Tall buildings come with cultural and social effects, and their development should be imbued with a sense of civic responsibility. It is not just their effect on the horizon and therefore the city that should be the focus of any analysis, but their effect on the ground, on the locality – the sense of place. Consequently, it was essential to write about the new London Bridge Quarter in which the building stands. The ambition to change the skyline may be grand, but the same developer's ambition to create a new quarter, to change an ancient part of an ancient city, is no less aspirational even if it leads to fewer column inches.

Writing about a development also means writing about a developer. Almost simultaneous with the rise of the word 'iconic' to describe every form of building from a tower to a shed has been the rise of the caricature of the nasty developer. In popular culture today, the property developer is casually cast in the role of the evildoer, even outranking the banker, at least before the credit crunch. In several crime series in recent years, the developer has been stigmatised as the person who will go to any lengths, including murder, to protect or further their interests.[3] They are portrayed as a grotesque personification of Mammon, the egomaniac building phallic emblems of power with little regard for society, the architectural history of the city or the law; they will wipe out both homes and heritage in order to grasp even more extraordinary wealth.

Irvine Sellar, according to the portrayal of him by some of the UK's leading cultural commentators and historical institutions, fits the bill as the Dark Lord of Development: he is sketched as ambitious, direct, uncompromising and apparently ruthless; a jumped-up market trader driven by greed. Simon Jenkins regularly refers to Sellar's developments as monstrous and egotistical, and English Heritage claimed he was driving a spike into the heart of London. One leading architecture critic called him 'a stocky wheeler-dealer with rock-steady eyes who looks as though he could sell you a retail park with the one hand and deck you with the other if you stiff him on the deal'.[4]

Yet this man is also responsible for rejuvenating a truly hopeless part of London and bringing 12,500 jobs into the area, while pouring

£5 million into training local Southwark youngsters so that they could benefit from those job opportunities, and he frequently talks about his pride in the public accessibility of his building. This 'wheeler-dealer' is friends with one of the world's most eminent and culturally refined architects, and politically has a slight inclination to the left. A normally concise and curt speaker, Sellar will also talk at length about the fact that the Shard is a multi-use building that gives something back to London, rather than an inward-facing corporate monolith.

So, Dark Lord of Development or Left-Leaning Lily-Livered Liberal?

The question is not entirely facile: it is tied to whether the Shard is a good building and the London Bridge Quarter a good development – architecturally, economically, socially, culturally and ecologically.

On 4 July 2012, a day before the official launch of the Shard, Sellar told the *Financial Times*, 'I knew when I took on this project that it would be like going a full twelve rounds in the boxing ring. I might have a couple of bad rounds in there, but I have come back fighting every time and I will keep doing so.'[5]

Did he keep getting back up from the canvas and taking punch after punch just because he saw the development of the quarter as a cash cow or because he also genuinely cares about London?

In the early days of my research, I learn that, aside from the partly self-reinforced caricature as a pugilist, Irvine Sellar is genuinely a black belt in judo. I'm not much of a fighter, but I go to see him anyway.

Sellar is frequently portrayed as 'larger than life' and 'colourful'. Perhaps an inherent prejudice against the fact that he started out on a market stall fuels the talk of him as if he is a slightly threatening bookmaker. In the early days of the Shard proposal, there was intimation in the press that he was backed by Russian money – which has become tawdry shorthand for a suggestion of criminality – which was never the case.

Irvine Sellar was born in Finsbury in September 1934, and north London, including Tottenham, Wood Green and Winchmore Hill, was his territory. His father was in the rag trade, selling gloves to department stores, but Sellar started an apprenticeship at an accountancy practice and also tried insurance. He only lasted a few months in each profession before he veered towards market stalls, setting up a chain of them around the periphery of north London, including in St Albans, Watford and Bedford, selling mostly shirts. Despite that, and the fact that he clearly has a north London rather than East End accent, the media habitually refers to him as a cockney, and usually the only market that gets a mention is, of course, Petticoat Lane – somewhere he never worked.

In time, Sellar moved indoors from the stalls and dominated Carnaby Street; then he dominated the high street in the 1970s with his Mates chain; and then, when he stepped out of retail and into property development, he dominated the skyline.

To suit the stereotype, one might expect the office of the Jewish-market-trader-made-good to be heavy on gold, with dark oak panelling and a Moroccan leather-inlaid supersize mahogany desk for 'a touch of class'. In fact, when I meet him, the owner of a multi-million-pound business sits on a regulation black office chair behind a modular desk in a moderately proportioned corner office in a basement near Oxford Street. He is elegantly but modestly coutured and coiffured; he is fit and compact; and he looks so young for his age, but without any apparent intervention, that I make a note to re-check that he really was born before the war. He fizzes with energy. He has a near-permanent twinkle in his eyes that would seem friendlier if the directness of his gaze was not so unnerving.

His major achievement, the Shard, drew massive animosity from people who act as the defenders of our history and culture. Other obstacles – a huge public inquiry, the financial crisis, the ridiculous tightness of the site, the problems of building uniquely tall – were placed in front of the developer at every turn. Even close friends, allies and members of his own team thought the building would never rise from the ground. Yet there it is, a huge building that, on my way to meet him, caught the colour of the sky and returned an ice-blue sliver of a blade. Not only that, but it has become a symbol of the city – its confidence, its architectural daring, its future. The Shard has become the loved neighbour. And all because of this five-foot-seven, former market-trading senior citizen sitting opposite me – a man who had never attempted to do anything like it before in his life.

How on earth did he do it?

When I tell him that I have been commissioned to write a history of the Shard, and that I want to write about the developer behind it, he says, 'All these biographies and autobiographies about East End Jewish boys, sons of immigrants who became rich against the odds – I know most of them – it's all the same story and it's boring. If I'm interested in legacy, all I have to do is go outside and look up at the Shard. I don't want a biography. If that's what you're doing, I won't help you.'

Sellar is weary of the trite summations of his early years and he could set the record straight, but I am aware that he has recently resisted having a full, authorised biography as he says his upbringing does not explain what he has achieved. He is a man who is willing to talk about what he is doing, and what he has done in business – including his failures – but not about himself in terms of his personal life. He is not hiding anything: he just thinks it is dull and misses the point. He is forward-focused and says, 'You don't look in the rear-view mirror when you're doing a hundred up the M1.'

I explain that my purpose is to investigate how someone came to change the skyline of London and overcame the challenges involved, and that will necessarily involve understanding his past. To tell the story of the Shard, however, my focus will be on what he has done as an entrepreneur, not his favourite colouring book at primary school.

'You've got it,' he says. 'I'll talk to you. Okay?'

Over a series of meetings, I learn that 'Okay?' indicates that the subject is closed, that he means what he has just said and won't falter from it, and that it's time to move on – now.

I also learn that he will readily quote George Bernard Shaw and Oscar Wilde, while in the next breath play with the media stereotype of himself. During one early conversation, he says, 'You can write what you want about me. You can write horrible things. I won't try to stop you.' He then appears to weigh me up physically as if he is thinking about doing exactly that; my chances against him are dismissed with a smirk before his expression turns into a disarmingly charming smile.

During our conversations about the dramatic trials and tribulations of the Shard development, I realise that something his brother Maurice has told me is true: Irvine Sellar is at the very core a supreme salesman. He is now much more polished, sophisticated and knowledgeable than he was when he was working the stalls, but that is what he remains at heart: a salesman with unparalleled determination.

Sellar says about the Shard, 'We were told we would never get planning consent and we did. We were told we would never be able to fund it and we did. Then we were told we would never be able to build it and we did.'

William Matthews, who was an associate at the Renzo Piano Building Workshop and the Shard's project architect on the ground in London, told me, 'Until 2009, 2010, if Irvine Sellar had been run over by a bus, it would have been all over.'

He felt that no one except Sellar would have surmounted the hurdles placed in the way of the development in the first decade of the project; no one else could have kept selling the idea while the financial markets were collapsing around him. As the full story unfolds before me, it becomes obvious that Matthews is right.

I also realise that the building, although the product of Renzo Piano's imagination, is the architectural embodiment of Irvine Sellar.

The building is dominant on the skyline and may seem to impose itself on London, but in fact it both reflects the city and integrates with it; and, at a distance, few people realise that the Shard is made up of eight differently shaped façades. The developer, likewise, is more far complicated and nuanced than the view on the horizon suggests.

Chapter 1

Changing the Landscape

What is the first rule of salesmanship? Sell yourself. The buyer has
to like you and trust you. Then you'll be able to sell them something
of value because you've built up that trust.

Irvine Sellar

---

*I*n 1999, Irvine Sellar stood at the top of Southwark Towers, a reinforced
concrete, twenty-four-storey structure clad in glass and brick. It was designed
on a Y-shaped plan primarily by Stephen Furnell of the large architecture practice
T. P. Bennett. The building's greatest innovation was the use of sun-shading
balconies and reflective glass panels, along with natural ventilation, to save energy
consumption on cooling systems, but the Y-shape form was the most interesting
element of the building. It was also its downfall.

Almost as soon as the building opened in 1975, Southwark Towers was a
dinosaur, as it could not facilitate modern office layouts. The 1980s came with
sharper, more economical working practices in the form of large, open-plan offices,
but the distinctive Y-shaped footprint prevented their successful adoption.

Sellar, though, was not thinking of the building beneath his feet. He was
looking outwards, turning to take in the almost 360-degree view across the sprawl
of London and, not far over the river, the tallest buildings of the City, including
the distinctive Tower 42.

Looking down, his eyes followed the curve of the River Thames and its parade
of bridges, and he saw the arteries of the railway network coalescing into a thick,
dark band of tracks at London Bridge station, right at the foot of Southwark Towers.

He had made up his mind. The building beneath him was history. He was going to build the tallest skyscraper in Europe. He was going to change London's skyline, for ever.

Irvine Sellar is an unorthodox man. Any other developer, if they could find the right site, would have taken his grand scheme and tried to pitch it into reality in the heart of the City, just across the water. It might still have been the country's tallest building, but it would have been shouldered by existing giants. Sellar, though, saw the possibility of maximising value while reviving a uniquely historical but downtrodden and abused part of the capital. In doing so, he would recalibrate the very idea of building tall in London.

The origins of the Shard cannot be fully understood without understanding Southwark – and that points to the integrity of the building in terms of its relationship to its setting.

The history of Southwark begins with the history of London, just under 2,000 years ago. Londinium arose as a settlement almost immediately after the Roman invasion in AD 43, on the north side of the Thames at what would become the City of London. The siting was no accident. The water needed to be deep enough to accommodate large vessels, but the width had to be narrow enough to enable a bridge to be built, connecting the settlement with the south. The span of the wooden bridge linked the future City on the north bank and what is now Southwark on the south. Today's London Bridge is very close to the same spot.

As the architect and master-planner Terry Farrell explains, while writing of the shaping of London from its origins, the land on the north side of the Thames is slightly higher, and

> at the close of the bend near today's London Bridge, the river was fordable, which gave the Romans and their successors the ideal place to make the first crossing of the Thames inland from the sea. It is the combination of these aspects – such simple matters of natural terrain and geography, and the effect of the forces of nature working together – that meant London was founded here, just where it is.[6]

London, as I remorselessly point out to any visitors, is a city of layers. Effectively, the first layer of London is nature itself, including the shape of the river and its banks. The second layer is the fording of the river – the bridge – and the first roads and settlements on either side, followed by multitudinous layers of building and infrastructure laid down over the course of history. Southwark, even though historically it was outside the city, is elemental to the very concept of the capital.

On the south side – the inside bend – the water was slower and shallower. The land was flatter, making it a muddy marsh subject to tides, so it was less easy to form solid landing points. So began south London's reputation: less habitable; less desirable; a place for the wash of flotsam and jetsam while the north side prospered.

Unusually, London is two cities, Westminster and the City, but rather than sitting across the river from each other in the manner of Budapest, the cities are side by side on the north bank, which is illustrative of the attitude towards the south bank of the Thames.

The first bridge in London lay at the heart of the nascent economy in Roman Britain. As the Romans established a permanent settlement at Londinium around AD 47, the bridge provided the connection between north and south, so it was vital for communications, troop movements and trade, and its port prospered.

In AD 60 or 61, both Camulodunum (Colchester), the Roman provincial capital, and Londinium were sacked by Boudicca, Queen of the Iceni. During the less bellicose aftermath, Londinium, with its bridge, was considered the more strategically important of the two, and the town was rebuilt as a planned Roman city. London was the largest city in Britain by the end of the first century, and during the course of the second century became the effective capital of Roman Britain.

What would become the area of Southwark developed its own settlement on an island in the marshy flood plain, but it was firmly outside the Roman city walls that lined the north bank. Southwark was 'other', and that status of otherness has been ingrained in the area's relationship with London ever since. The Roman walls remained in place as part of the capital's defences for many centuries, meaning that the south bank would be the place of encampment for invaders, notably the Vikings.

After a succession of timber bridges, a more substantial bridge was built on almost the same location at the end of the twelfth century: the curve of the river at London Bridge was still considered to be the most suitable location for the only bridge. The new stone bridge, completed in 1209, was a religious undertaking, built by the 'Chaplains, Brethrens and Sisters of the Bridge of London' under the guidance of the parish priest/architect Peter of Colechurch.[7]

Detail of Old London Bridge from an engraving by Claes van Visscher, 1616 (© RPBW)

Old London Bridge, Southwark end, by E. W. Cooke, 1831 (RIBA Collections)

That bridge, over 900 feet long and consisting of nineteen arches, was a structural innovation, like the Shard would be eight centuries later: it was the first major stone arch bridge to be built in Britain. And like the Shard, its development was beset by unforeseeable problems and its form was born of an irregular site: the pointed arches were meant to be approximately equal in size, but the builders encountered hard surfaces and obstructions in the riverbed, so the span of the arches had to vary from 15 feet to 34 feet, affecting the intended harmony of its design.

The bridge was also, in modern argot, a multi-use structure. Homes and shops several storeys high ran along its length (it had 138 recorded trading premises in 1358): in today's property market-speak, it would perhaps be labelled as an 'integrated retail, residential, work and transport hub', which sounds rather like the Shard.

And like the Shard, Old London Bridge would become one of the great identifiers of the city. The bridge was so distinctive that it came to mean 'London'. It was used to illustrate the city on seals and other ephemera, and it was the subject of one of the best known of all nursery rhymes (although Old London Bridge never did fall down, and even survived the Great Fire of London in 1666). As well as defining the city, it acted as a barrier. Southwark was still a place of outsiders, as emphasised by the drawbridge halfway along the stone bridge's length: defending London still did not mean defending Southwark.

London Bridge remained the only London bridge for the next five and a half centuries. Westminster Bridge was completed in the middle of the eighteenth century, marking the starting point of the sporadic proliferation of crossings, which now number thirty-three between Dartford in the east and Hampton Court in the west, each in turn having an effect on bankside development and changing the function and status of surrounding areas.

The medieval London Bridge was replaced by the engineer John Rennie's less distinctive but impressive New London Bridge (free from the teetering parade of houses and shops), a few yards to the west. It was opened in 1831 and, famously, was shipped stone by stone to Lake Havasu City, Arizona, in the early 1970s. Its replacement, the current London Bridge, was more functional still, but it marked a further innovation in bridge building through the use of high-strength steel tendons tying together sections that cantilever from two piers.

In the sixteenth century, the area at the southern end of bridge came under the purview of the City but its name, 'Ward of the Bridge Without' (in contrast to the 'Ward of the Bridge Within' on the northern bank), reveals that Southwark, like the rest of the south bank, was still excluded and 'other'. Southwark's identity had been stamped by its status of being free from London's curfew, controls and statutes: the south bank had long been a place for wildness, revelry and the unorthodox, known for its taverns, theatres, brothels, pleasure gardens and gambling – Southwark was the home of England's first licensed brothel in 1161. It was a place of culture, however ribald, and it was the south bank, not the City proper, that was home to Shakespeare in the form of both the Globe and Rose theatres. Edward Alleyn, proprietor of the Rose, liked to spread his interests: he ran some local brothels, too.

This was a place for experimentation and transgression, literary or otherwise. Geoffrey Chaucer's pilgrims in *The Canterbury Tales*, written in the late fourteenth century, begin their journey towards the south from the Tabard Inn, just by London Bridge, among a clientele of wastrels, criminals and prostitutes. Bear-baiting and cock-fighting were the sports of choice in the inn's courtyard.

Southwark Fair by William Hogarth, 1733 (© Mashuk)

Southwark was the centre of bear-baiting in London (© Whitemay)

Southwark Towers and New London Bridge House (Sellar Property Group Archive)

In the 1660s, Samuel Pepys would visit Cherry Gardens in Bermondsey, not far away, to collect cherries, 'run wagers upon the bowling green', and go to Jamaica House, where he left the premises 'singing finely'. Pleasure gardens of greater fame were further to the west, including Cuper's Gardens, near the Waterloo Bridge of today but at the time serviced only by wherrymen. Decadent behaviour and sexual impropriety – it was nicknamed Cupid's Gardens – led to its demise; the authorities, finally attempting to fit a chastity belt on the libidinous south, denied it a licence in 1753. Longer lived was the more famous Vauxhall Gardens, which opened in 1661 and survived for 200 years.

As London's population exploded, the city turned its back on the river, even in architectural terms. The Thames became sick with pollution, and was associated with disease prior to the construction of Joseph Bazalgette's great sewer system, put in place partly in reaction to the Great Stink of 1858. Bridges were no longer a focal point for the city's life and trade, but a mere utilitarian tool for crossing, for passing through, and the surrounding areas suffered.

London Bridge station and Southwark Towers (© Gabriele Basilico)

The city blossomed north of the river, away from the water, while the south became a blackened industrial landscape of chimneys, prisons, brickworks, tanneries, warehouses, breweries, markets and eventually power stations – the sort of institutions, like the theatres and brothels, that were unwanted in refined areas of the capital. In the Victorian era, areas of the south bank were cut up and left marooned by the elevated railway lines serving destinations further from the centre. With travellers taking trains and new bridges providing other routes for pedestrians, passing trade for London Bridge's hostelries fell away. Even the famous Tabard, subsequently renamed the Talbot, fell into disrepair. It was demolished in 1873.

The Thames was no longer the heart of London. The London Bridge area was dirty and forgotten, a repository for the sprawl of burgeoning megacity infrastructure with little glamour or prettification required. London Bridge station, which opened in 1836, is the oldest railway terminus in London, but it did not bring prosperity to the immediate area. When Southwark featured in Charles Dickens' *Little Dorrit* (1855),

Tate Modern (© Godrick)

it was because of its association with destitution. It was home to the Marshalsea, the debtors' prison where the children of the Dorrit family are forced to live due to their father's penury, and where Dickens' own father had been incarcerated.

As the twentieth century progressed, Southwark still did not share in the commercial spoils of the City across the Thames. When George Orwell was researching dire poverty for *Down and Out in Paris and London* (1933), he rented a place in a tramps' dosshouse on Tooley Street at London Bridge, but he could not put up with such destitution for long, even in the quest for literary integrity. He wrote to his parents begging for money so that he could move. Southwark's fortunes were further battered when the docks started to close just down the river.

The area was unattractive both to potential residents and companies, despite its transport connections and proximity to the more glamorous parts of London. It was increasingly miserable, pockmarked by examples of poor post-war architecture and blighted by the dystopian jungle of Elephant & Castle and its huge Heygate Estate, routinely cited as one of the worst examples of post-war mass housing. The majority of Southwark's residential stock was social housing and it was regarded as one of the poorest boroughs in the country, with high numbers of struggling immigrants and unemployed.

It had the busiest railway station in London, but far from being a destination in itself, London Bridge was a place to be avoided. The area around the station – alien, chaotic, dark and unwelcoming – was the fulcrum of a hell in miniature.

Irvine Sellar bought Southwark Towers in November 1998 for £37.4 million, initially on a 125-year lease from Railtrack. At that point, he would be described as a mid-level property developer and, for such a big investment, he brought in partners in the form of interests linked to CLS Holdings Ltd and the Ironzar Trust, with Irish Nationwide Building Society also temporarily a shareholder before being bought out. CLS, a commercial property investment company, was established by the Swede Sten Mörtstedt in 1987 and was first listed on the London Stock Exchange in 1994. The Ironzar Trust was represented by Simon Halabi, the son of a wealthy Syrian businessman. He had become a successful property developer looking after his family's Jersey-registered companies, and he had just bought Mentmore Towers, the extraordinary nineteenth-century Buckinghamshire house built for the Rothschild family.

Southwark Towers had a reliable single tenant, PricewaterhouseCoopers, with a remaining occupational lease of 102 years. Sellar explained to me, 'Whatever I acquire in property, we as a team look at it and say "What's the angle?" Always. It's a dry investment but can we do more with it? Have I acquired at the right price so I can sell it at a profit? Or shall I improve it to maximise the value by extending the lease, adapting it or redesigning it?' He says of Southwark Towers, 'To put it into perspective, I acquired a building and I was going to sit on it. It was a good investment. I was going to sit there and allow the rent cheques to come in. Nothing to worry about. Then the White Paper got us excited.'

That document was *Planning Policy Guidance 1: General policy and principles*, which stated that, in order to promote sustainable development, the government was committed to 'concentrating development for uses which generate a large number of trips in places well-served by public transport . . . preferring the development of land within urban areas, particularly on previously-developed sites before considering the development of greenfield sites'. The paper went on to advocate mixed-use development as it 'can help create vitality and diversity and reduce the need to travel. It can be more sustainable than development consisting of a single use.'[8]

A close look at the title deeds for Southwark Towers revealed another factor crucial for plans for major development of the site. Barry Ostle, Sellar Property Group's development director who joined around the time Sellar and his partners were buying Southwark Towers, says, 'That was the most extraordinary piece of luck in this. The Southwark Towers building had a footplate of 25 per cent of the total site area – a 12,500-square-foot building footplate standing on a site that was almost 50,000 square feet. The original building was a Victorian hotel that was bombed in the war, but the red line was the site of the hotel and its grounds and it also extended underneath and above the station concourse. So at that point, possibilities opened up for Irvine's desire to do a major scheme, which coincided with the new White Paper.'

Sellar had his angle. 'I thought, "Christ, there's a chance of developing that tired building."' He completely agreed with the principles behind the policy guidance document: 'Most cities in the world that are globally recognised as power houses in the twenty-first century are dynamic and compact. I've always believed that you should be as close to transport hubs as possible because, as cities get increasingly congested, so the aggravation of travel is eliminated or reduced massively. People are working longer hours and, especially women, feel more secure if they are working close to a transport hub.'

Sellar recalls, 'I went to see the chap at PricewaterhouseCoopers and he said, "Irvine, we don't have any long-term aspirations for this building." And I thought, "Well, I do."' PricewaterhouseCoopers, in fact, had considered attempting to remodel the building to make it a more usable office but that plan was shelved.

Standing at the top of Southwark Towers, studying the view, confirmed to Sellar that the site of his new purchase fitted the brief of the White Paper perfectly, and it underlined how close London Bridge was to the commercial heart of London, but with few of the benefits.

Sellar made up his mind to build tall – very tall: four times the 328-foot (100-metre) high-rise on which he was standing.

When Sellar sets his course, there is little that can be done to persuade him to deviate from it – including, as it turned out, twelve years of what most other developers would consider to be a living nightmare.

It was not the White Paper and the red line in isolation that motivated Sellar. There were signs that the south bank to the east of the National Theatre was finally becoming somewhere rather than nowhere; the area had its own history and culture, and he believed that, despite the squalor of London Bridge, he could make it a destination rather than a point of departure.

The replica of Shakespeare's Globe had opened as a successful working theatre in 1997. The conversion of the Bankside Power Station, designed by Sir Giles Gilbert Scott and opened in 1952, was well under way, ready for its rebirth as Tate Modern in 2000, and Borough Market, almost on Southwark Towers' doorstep, was evolving into a specialist destination for food lovers. The massive More London commercial development was in its early stages along the riverbank. Two-bedroom apartments in Victor Wharf, a new residential development in Clink Street (named after the famous medieval prison), were selling for £470,000 and its three-bedroom penthouse was on the market for £1.4 million – prices previously unthinkable south of the river. Another three-bedroom apartment, right next to the Globe with a view of St Paul's, was on the market for £3.25 million. Bars and restaurants were cropping up. It was starting to become possible that London taxi drivers would not just be willing to drop a passenger over the river, they might also go there looking for custom.

There was a major problem, though. Southwark Towers was bought on leasehold from Railtrack, the owner of the national railway infrastructure of the UK, which was shortly going to be taken over by the government and renamed Network Rail. When Sellar made an initial approach to the railway company about developing the site, he was rebuffed. Railtrack had its own intended scheme to redevelop the station to incorporate the extension of the Thameslink service running north to south through London, and claimed that a development by Sellar would be an obstruction.

Nonetheless, a constructive dialogue about Sellar's proposed redevelopment of the site began, and eventually the rail company was swayed. Heads of terms were agreed for a new 150-year ground lease, which opened the door for the scheme.

Irvine Sellar's decision to push himself forward to play a leading role in changing Southwark – and changing London – surprised the property industry.

Giles Barrie, Editor-in Chief of *Property Week*, was blunt about Sellar's desire to build a massive building: 'I thought the guy was a complete joker. I didn't think he had a hope in hell. I thought he was a dreamer. It wasn't just me: everybody in property thought this was a loony idea.'[9]

Sellar was far from being a major player along the lines of Land Securities, which now manages a portfolio valued in excess of £14 billion.[10] He had enjoyed a sharp rise and suffered a shocking fall in his fortunes in the property industry in the 1980s, and was on his way back. In 1999, the Sellar Property Group's most notable project was the Pompey Centre in Portsmouth. The masterplan for the new, largely retail scheme on the site of the former Fratton Goods Yard had just been laid out. At 265,000 square feet (24,620 m²), the development, which is still owned by Sellar, is significant for a town the size of Portsmouth, which has a population of 200,000, but it was an unlikely preamble to erecting the tallest building in Western Europe. In fact, Sellar had never built a high-rise before – on any scale.

So why wasn't he daunted?

The seeds of his character as an entrepreneur were there from the beginning. Even as a young man, he was always looking for the gap in the market, for the opportunity, and when that opportunity came it was not in his nature to suffer from the self-doubt that afflicts most other mortals, even high-powered and successful ones. The standard questions, 'Do I know what I'm doing?' and 'Do I have the right experience?' have no place in the Sellar lexicon.

By contrast, if you spend half an hour in Sellar's company, you are unlikely to leave without hearing his adaptation of a quote from George Bernard Shaw's *Man and Superman* (1903): 'All hopes of progress lie with the unreasonable man. The reasonable man thinks it can't be done, and therefore doesn't try. The unreasonable man tries and often succeeds.'[11]

Flan McNamara, Sellar's construction director, framed the quote and it now hangs on his boss's office wall.

The developer's detractors may believe that the reference to 'unreasonable' marks Sellar's admission that he is pig-headed and, according to the *Oxford English Dictionary*, 'not guided by good sense'. Yet rarely are self-made multi-millionaires not guided by good sense, at least on some level. It may be a subtle distinction, but the unreasonableness of the Sellar that I unearth during months of investigation seems better understood by the *OED*'s second definition: he acts 'beyond the limits of acceptability'. That does not mean that he is crass or immoral – although he has been accused of being both – but that he constantly looks beyond the accepted way of doing things. He doesn't see the barriers.

There is another quote from *Man and Superman* that may have been recalled by Sellar, the former king of fashion retail, when both the development industry and the media were misreading his capabilities at the beginning of the twenty-first century: 'The only man I know who behaves sensibly is my tailor; he takes my measurements anew each time he sees me. The rest go on with their old measurements and expect me to fit them.'

Sellar was already a man capable of both personal reinvention and changing any environment in which he saw a commercial opportunity.

He would always remember his experience of the tough world of the markets as 'the thrill of my life'. It began when his father Joe Sellar arranged for a large order of gloves to be made for a department store. After the store rejected the gloves, which Joe thought were perfectly good, the Sellars ended up with their house full of boxes of unwanted stock. A friend suggested to Joe that he should take a market stall to clear it. The trick worked and Joe carried on running market stalls as they were so profitable. 'I was still a kid, still at school,' Irvine Sellar says, 'and I loved to help him because I was a natural salesman – I still am.'

After leaving school at sixteen and briefly toying with accountancy and insurance, he swore he would never be employed by someone else ever again – and he never has been. He wanted the freedom offered by the markets. 'My father bought me a little car and lent me sufficient money to buy my first bit of merchandise – fashion.' He was soon developing his sales technique and learning the psychology of leadership while expanding a chain of market stalls, mainly selling shirts.

Sellar had a small band of loyal people working for him. 'I had this leadership quality – people followed me, and they *liked* following me,' he says of those early years.

He would start work at five, driving his stock to the market sites and setting up the stalls. To make the early rise and suffering the cold, wind and rain worthwhile, he would ensure that any casual grazing of his wares would be turned into a sale. One of Sellar's favourite maxims, which was honed in this nascent career, is 'What is the first rule of sales-manship? Sell yourself. The buyer has to like you and trust you. Then you'll be able to sell them something of value because you've built up that trust.'

He fostered competition among his team to see who could get the most sales, but fed up with being subjected to the vagaries of the British weather and the effect that rain and snow would have on his sales, he started turning towards the idea of running shops. They offered a more regular income, a shorter working day without lugging stock from site to site, and shelter from the elements.

In 1957, he helped his father set up Sellar's Sports Wear in Wood Green, close to home, so they were familiar with the nature of the passing trade. Joe was appealing to the young by using the American term for casualwear within the name of the shop. Fashion design pioneers such as Claire McCardell were responsible for the sportswear revolution in the United States, using durable and comfortable materials such as denim and jersey for casualwear designs from the 1930s onwards. In the States, denim began to take hold in the early 1950s and was no longer just workwear for cowboys and labourers, but the United Kingdom was lagging behind.

When Irvine Sellar opened his own shop in St Albans in 1960, he expanded his stock from the shirts and windcheaters that were the core business on his market stalls; his venture was among the first wave of outlets in Britain to sell jeans as a fashion item. American brands such as Levi Strauss and Wrangler were being adopted simultaneously with that other American cultural import, rock 'n' roll, and Sellar's shop benefitted.

Despite the appeal of a roof over his head, Sellar would often leave the shop in the care of others while he still worked the markets. Even now, at an age at which most people would have retired, he likes to work at the coalface rather than feeling removed from the operation of his businesses.

The glamour of post-war American culture also fuelled his purchase of a blue Oldsmobile with white wheels, in which Sellar would ferry stock to the stalls – it must have been a peculiar sight in the market towns of Hertfordshire and Bedfordshire. A Buick and a Cadillac would follow, each bought from Lendrum and Hartman, London's only dealers in luxury American cars, who had a showroom at the suitably titled Buick and Cadillac House on Albemarle Street, near Hyde Park. Sellar was already looking the part of a young entrepreneur willing to shake up British reserve and the establishment. In time, his taste would turn to the slightly more reserved British elegance of Rolls-Royces and Bentleys.

David Hartwell, who worked in Sellar's St Albans store, remembers that Oldsmobile all too well. At the close of the day, after Sellar had returned from the stalls with the remaining stock, 'he would be weight-lifting in the back of the shop; I'd be washing the car'.

Sellar was still unwilling to give up on the possibility of a single sale. 'If there was someone looking in the window,' Hartwell says, 'I would be sent out with a broom, and would casually say, "Yes, isn't that a nice shirt? Why don't you come in and look at the others? They're terrific." If someone wouldn't buy a suit they'd be coaxed into buying a pair of trousers, or a shirt and tie. No one got out of that shop without buying something.'

Nonetheless, Sellar says that the early 1960s were 'hard days in menswear', at least in London satellite towns such as St Albans. He had overestimated the local youths' desire to break away from the conformity of their parents. Looking back, he says, 'Men, except for the Teddy boys and then the mods, of course, were not as fashion-conscious as they are today.' He dressed his windows with the latest trends, but discovered that some of the locals referred to his store as 'the spiv's shop'.

He pushed onwards in the belief that 'you have to keep your finger on the pulse and create something new'. He assessed his clientele in terms of leaders and followers, and concentrated on trying to convince people who were well-known figures in the neighbourhood to wear his fashion-conscious clothes and influence the people around them.

He also realised the benefits of channelling his energy. Still in his early twenties, he was also involved in both the nightclub business and car dealing when he received some pivotal advice from Clive Bowman-Shaw, a twenty-eight-year-old whom he calls 'one of the great influences on my life'. He met Bowman-Shaw, the founder of Universal Health Studios, a progenitor of the modern-day fitness chains, when he sold him a Cadillac.

Bowman-Shaw's instruction was to 'Stop pissing about with night-clubs. Stick to the retail business.' Sellar duly did, and he convinced his father to semi-retire and relinquish his role in the Wood Green shop so he could have greater control over the entire business.

The young entrepreneur worked even harder to make the most of his retail outlets, and he expected the same commitment from his staff. Hartwell says, 'We often worked very late. I remember being with him in his flash car at 10.30 one night on Christmas Eve. He'd come back late. I wasn't happy. I said: "You're Jewish, but I'm not. Christmas is an important time in my life." He gave me one of those great Irvine smiles. "I've got a present for you." It was a bottle of Scotch. With all his drive – ruthlessness, sometimes – he could be thoughtful and considerate like that. Mind you, I couldn't help wondering if that bottle came from one of our clothes suppliers.'

One of Sellar's team sensed his young boss's ambition. He describes Sellar coming into the shop and looking from side to side, saying 'Morning . . . morning' as if he were greeting the staff of a huge company. It is part of Sellar's make-up that he is always looking for bigger and better things.

And they came in the form of Carnaby Street.

Sellar was aware that something was going on in the West End. At the very beginning of the 1960s, some of the more fashion cognisant of Sellar's young clientele were implying that the stock in the St Albans store, outré though it was to the conservative majority, was a little dull compared to what was now on offer in London.

Sellar is by nature a boundary pusher. If there was a market for more colourful, more stylish and more radical clothing, he wanted to be at the heart of it. In 1963–4, he expanded into the West End, although the only rent he could afford was in Wardour Street – and at 'the wrong end' of that road, as he describes it. The shop was in Soho, the increasingly seedy den of vice that was becoming the playground of criminal gangs with a penchant for extortion.

One staff member who worked at the new Sellar outlet was unimpressed: it was next to a strip club and he had to share a washroom with the women artistes. He asked to return to the St Albans branch.

Sellar stuck it out and built up the shop's reputation, but the local atmosphere was edgy enough for him to ensure he had the means by which to defend himself if trouble crossed the threshold. He began to learn judo at a gym on Orange Street, at the bottom of Leicester Square.

There, he met Mel Morris, a future business partner, who says, 'Irvine became a black belt while I was only a blue belt – he always had to be the best in whatever he did.' Morris recalls that the Robinson brothers, who ran the judo club, put Irvine forward to fight a large man called Raymond Nash, a wealthy Lebanese who was an excellent fighter. 'I know there was some kind of aggravation between Joe Robinson and Nash,' says Morris. 'They got Irvine up and he fought a very, very long battle with Nash. Irvine won, of course.'

Morris describes the gym as a showbiz place populated by actors, including Albert Finney and Honor Blackman, who put her moves to good use in *The Avengers* (1962–4) and as Pussy Galore in *Goldfinger* (1964).

Sellar was beginning to move in interesting circles, and while drinking in a West End bar he met his future wife, Elizabeth Fitzpatrick, an Irish model whose interest in fashion had brought her to London at the birth of the Swinging Sixties.

The couple married in 1964 and had three children, Paul, James and Caroline. Sellar likes to have his family involved in his enterprises; Caroline is the commercial and operations director of the Sellar Property Group, and James is the chief executive of the sister company, Sellar Developments. Paul, meanwhile, has pursued a different path to become a critically acclaimed playwright. Writing is in the family, as Irvine's brother Maurice is a novelist, comedy writer and award-winning television producer.

Elizabeth, with an attuned sense of fashion, had a major impact on her husband's career. As she told the *Evening Standard* on 4 February 2010, she returned from a visit to Carnaby Street in 1964: 'I remember saying to him, "You've got to look at this street, you cannot move in it."' Within a couple of years, Sellar would buy up Carnaby Street's greengrocer's, grocer's and laundry and turn them into Irvine Sellars Menswear. (Sellar is known for his attention to detail, but an apostrophe was deemed surplus to requirements.)

Professor Amy de la Haye, who co-curated *Carnaby Street: 50*, an exhibition that celebrated fifty years of Carnaby Street in 2010, observed that the street has been linked to outsiders and alternative thinkers throughout its history. After the street was laid out in the mid-1680s, it became home to French Huguenots fleeing persecution in Catholic France, and the poet and artist William Blake was born on adjoining Broadwick Street in 1757. In the 1930s, Carnaby Street became associated with the Panafrican movement when Amy Garvey, wife of Marcus Garvey, opened a jazz club, the Florence Mills Social Club.

Carnaby Street as we know it today arose out of the underground gay culture of 1950s London. John Stephen worked as an assistant at the Vince Man shop in Newburgh Street, which sold flamboyant, tight-fitting clothes to an almost entirely homosexual clientele, and soon set up his own shop with his boyfriend Bill Franks in unglamorous Carnaby Street, hidden away from the main shopping thoroughfare of Regent Street. To attract attention, the partners painted the outside of the His Clothes shop bright yellow, blasted pop music out of the door and specialised in blue-and-white-striped matelot tops, Italian knitwear and coloured denim. The shop's success led Stephen and Franks to open more clothing shops along the street, selling outrageous clothing to an increasingly heterosexual clientele that had got in touch with its feminine side.

Post-war austerity had finally ebbed away, and teenagers and young adults now had more disposable income than at any point in British history. The new generation were not living in the shadow of the war, and were revelling in a new, throwaway consumerism and lack of stricture. Meanwhile, by 1964, the Beatles, the Rolling Stones, the Kinks and the Who had revolutionised the British sound and were just beginning to dominate the American charts. The miniskirt and the Mini became shorthand for the supposed new sexual and financial liberation of young women, even though in reality that freedom did not extend to many households.

By April 1966, *Time* magazine was christening the capital as 'Swinging London' and concluding that, 'In a once sedate world of faded splendour, everything new, uninhibited and kinky is blooming at the top of London life.' The focal point of the kinkiness was Carnaby Street.

By then, Elizabeth and Irvine Sellar had quickly emerged as leading lights in the fashion-retail adjunct to the creative explosion. In 1964, they had seen the potential to bring their own fashion ideas to the Carnaby Street clientele, and were early on the scene, but the rent was a big step up from the seedy end of Wardour Street. They had needed funding. Maurice Sellar, who at the time was producing programmes for Radio Luxembourg and was at the forefront of introducing commercial radio into the UK, introduced his brother to Alan Grieve, a young solicitor with Taylor & Humbert, whom he had come across in the course of his work.

Maurice Sellar recalls, 'Grieve said: "I think I know who Irvine would get on well with." There was a man called Roland Franklin, who was CEO of a noted merchant bank called Keyser Ullman. By then, Irvine and Alan were getting along great, and Alan was our lawyer in terms of whenever we wanted something sorted out. I asked Alan, after the meeting he had with Roland Franklin and Irvine: "How did my brother get on?" He said: "He absolutely mesmerised him. He got what he wanted."'

Sellar had effectively made his best sales pitch yet. Bolstered by the financial support, he outflanked Warren Gold, who was trying to rival Stephen as the King of Carnaby Street, to buy the remaining two and a half years of the lease of the grocer's on the street. It became Sellar's first Carnaby Street store at the end of September 1965, and the location soon proved a marked improvement on the threatening mood of Wardour Street.

Sellar was an ideal newcomer to Carnaby Street just as the Swinging Sixties were hitting their stride: he was unorthodox and interested in creativity and cutting-edge fashion, but he also had the steel of a man who had needed to turn a profit from a Bedford market stall at 7 a.m. on a cold, wet winter's morning.

He told *Men's Wear* newspaper on 2 October 1965: 'I'm not afraid of competition. You cannot compete with somebody who is doing something different. And I know that I can say with confidence to my customers that the only people they will come across in the street, clubs or dance halls wearing the same clothes as themselves will be other Irvine Sellar customers.'

Sellar was not interested in just repeating the Carnaby Street typology. He was designing his own clothes, having them cut in the East End, and eventually opened his own clothing factory in Neasden in north-west London so he could manufacture 80 per cent of his stock. He wanted to create clothes that were affordable, distinctive and quality, and that meant taking the entire process into his own hands. As Carnaby Street hit the peak of its fame in the late 1960s, becoming known across the world for its alternative fashions, innovation and daring – and seemingly intrinsic to the new creative liberty blossoming in Britain – Sellar was at the forefront.

What soon became a string of Irvine Sellar shops on Carnaby Street was a hit with celebrities, as Elizabeth Sellar recalled in the *Evening Standard* article in April 2010: 'We simply could not get enough stock . . . We had celebrities coming in all the time . . . You would see the Rolling Stones or the Monkees or the Beach Boys. They would turn up and buy stuff and tell me "If you watch *Top of the Pops* tonight I'll be wearing this shirt."' She says that 'the atmosphere was electric . . . It was a time of incredible freedom.'

It was not only glamorous bands that were drawn to Sellar's shops, but everyday mods. The largely working-class 'modernists' had a penchant for smart individuality, which for the men took the form of Italian-style, tight, three- or four-button suits, button-down shirts and distinctive shoes. The vehicle of choice was a Vespa or Lambretta scooter, which led them to wear old Army parkas over their precious outfits.

Sellar told *Men's Wear*: 'My type of customer is usually single, and in some type of job where appearance is important. He puts clothes at the top of his list. It is a Peacock Era we're living in, of course. There is no doubt about that. Young people take a tremendous amount of pride in their clothes.'

One of Sellar's radio adverts from the era features two men walking down a high street in the pouring rain. One of them says that he's bought a raincoat from Irvine Sellars.

'Why don't you wear it, then?'

'And get it wet? Are you mad?'

By the end of 1965, Sellar's life had already changed. He was still a young man, owned four menswear shops, lived in a Mayfair apartment and drove a black and grey Rolls-Royce. Sellar's ambition, however, was far from sated. On 9 November 1965, he told the *London Evening News*, 'I don't consider myself a success . . . At this particular stage I haven't proved to myself what I want to prove, but I hope to within the next few years. You see, I'm not easily satisfied. I drive myself very hard.'

Sellar, as it turned out, would never be satisfied. He would always be looking forward, studying the horizon – just as he was at the top of Southwark Towers, thirty-five years later – wanting to both innovate and push himself into unknown territory.

London beware.

Chapter 2

Tall Stories

We've only got one life and we should fill every minute to avoid regrets. Some people spend their time doing zero but a man can die at fifty and live the equivalent of two hundred years. Use – and treasure – every second.

Irvine Sellar

In the year 2000, the most outlandish thing that a developer could do was to announce plans to build very tall in the heart of London. The scheme was highly unlikely ever to make it beyond an imaginative rendering of an architect's dream. Announcing plans to build 'supertall' in Southwark, on the other hand, was sheer folly. (According to the Council on Tall Buildings and Urban Habitat's definitions, a 'supertall' building exceeds 300 metres [984 feet] and a 'megatall' building exceeds 600 metres [1,968 feet] at the 'architectural top', i.e. no cheating with flagpoles and antennae. Without wishing to be prescriptive or absolute, as height is relative to the urban grain, a workable marker in the twenty-first century for 'tall' is 100 metres [328 feet] and 'very tall' is 150 metres [492 feet].)[12]

In the period up to the new millennium, with National Lottery funding and a positive atmosphere fostered by the arrival of New Labour in 1997, there was a rash of construction in London – but none of the new buildings outside Canary Wharf was very tall. The only notable tall structure to be built on the south bank was the London Eye, and that was a Ferris wheel only 443 feet (130 metres) high and originally intended to be temporary.

Both history and the current climate were ranged against the ambitions of Irvine Sellar. No one thought he would win the battle.

London is not a planned city: its master-planner is merely the progress of time and the promise of fortune. The capital is built on the pursuance of profit – a patchwork, non-systematised city of individual entrepreneurial ambition. In its texture of buildings from across the centuries, London reveals the layers of this ambition, eras of hubristic confidence soon wilted, ideologies, pragmatism, depression and wild dreams; each epoch is full of its own ephemeral solutions for modern life, work, commerce and entertainment.

In contrast to London, in Paris there is an urban grain consistent to much of the city, created by the mass nineteenth-century clearing of the medieval streets by Baron Haussmann and their replacement with broad avenues, squares, parks and, typically, six- to eight-storey buildings. Many later metropolises across the world, and notably in the United States, have been planned and gridded from the outset, which should allow a cohesion of function and infrastructure, although one can easily argue that the failure of some American cities lies in an inability to alter the initial scheme in the light of social and economic change.

Planning does now have an essential role in London as the boroughs try to preserve the best of what they have and improve the worst with urban regeneration, but in terms of the long history and organic growth of the city, this is belated. The planning offices are dealing with often-disorderly existing street plans and mixed typologies, and rarely have a chance to create order from scratch or even knit together individual commercial developments with much sense of cohesion.

The lack of early planning means that Victorian roads intersect the haphazard medieval streets and alleys; villages have accidentally conjoined; areas have blossomed and shrivelled as a reaction to waves of commercial activity and social change. The process has been organic. The sense of the patchwork is reinforced by a lack of synchronicity in architectural style. The present, rather than prescribed adherence to a precedent, has dictated the form and aesthetic of new buildings in era after era.

London's patchwork can be seen on a single street, especially in old areas of the City, but different areas of London also have a distinct urban grain, partly a product of the time in which they were primarily built, partly because of topography, partly because of the mix of the functions of the architecture – residential, commercial, retail and industrial. The area around the Bank of England is a tight-knit chaos of narrow medieval streets; Grosvenor and Mayfair are more open and grand, and more obviously planned and controlled as part of a great estate; Hampstead is a village, with a principal intersection providing focus for a small, organic, rambling sprawl that peters into wilder terrain. All this can be seen from the air or diagnosed from the layout of streets on a cold, functional map. Such a map reveals that the London Bridge area's urban grain in the late twentieth century was born of transport infrastructure rather than a sense that this was a place to be experienced, to be trod.

Part of the more general urban grain of London is that it is surprisingly low-rise, except in a few localised areas, despite the fact that building tall is usually a typology of a major metropolis.

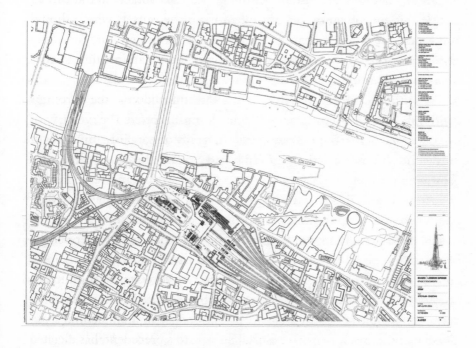

Plan of the London Bridge area, 2006 (© RPBW)

It is often claimed, especially when a scheme for a new high-rise first emerges and causes a wave of panic among cultural commentators, that London does not have a history of building tall. This is something of a fallacy: indeed, it is a tall story.

For its time, St Paul's Cathedral, declared complete in 1711, was monstrously large in both height and body. It is 365 feet (111 metres) tall and is still the second-largest extant church building in the United Kingdom in terms of area (only Liverpool's twentieth-century Anglican cathedral is larger). The late-medieval, spired cathedral that it replaced, however, was even taller and, standing at a height of 492 feet (150 metres), was briefly the world's tallest building when it was completed in 1314.

Victoria Tower of the Palace of Westminster – the tower that most people ignore when snapping Elizabeth Tower, home of Big Ben – was extremely tall for a secular building (323 feet/98.5 metres); it was the tallest square tower in the world when it was completed in 1860. The Midland Grand Hotel, which partially opened at St Pancras railway station in 1873, was born out of George Gilbert Scott's passion for Gothic-influenced monumentalism and was 269 feet (82 metres) tall.

At the end of the nineteenth century, the United States began to take the lead when it came to building tall. In 1885, Chicago's Home Insurance Building, designed by William Le Baron Jenney, became the first tall building to use a fireproof metal frame for the construction of both the floors and the skin of the building. It was twelve storeys, and only 180 feet (55 metres). The building survived a mere forty-six years, but this first skyscraper set in train a typology that would revolutionise metropolitan building and eventually transform skylines across the world.

As well as riveted metal framing, the electric elevator helped to make the form practical, as did advances in telecommunications: the humble telephone meant that people who worked in the same offices no longer needed to speak face to face. The metal skeleton of iron or steel, incorporating columns, would distribute weight evenly, in contrast to heavy masonry that had to be self-supporting: to reach 215 feet (66 metres), the northern half of the Monadnock Building, the world's tallest load-bearing brick construction when it was completed in Chicago in 1893, needed 6-foot- (1.8-metre-) thick walls at the bottom.

Old and new St Paul's Cathedral (*below* © duncan 1890)

The Home Insurance Building did not change architectural aesthetics – in form it copied load-bearing archetypes and held true to a classical influence with a broad cornice, bands of ornate masonry, regulated series of piers and a typical percentage of glazing. But the world had been transformed.

Within a few years Adler and Sullivan's Wainwright Building was constructed in St Louis and the Reliance Building was erected in Chicago. In 1902, the twenty-one-storey Flatiron in New York showed that skyscraper technology could allow an innovation in form: the skyscraper was no longer 'the same but taller'; it provided the possibilities for the wilder dreams of architects. In 1930, with the sublime Chrysler Building, designed by William Van Alen, and the Empire State Building, designed by Shreve, Lamb and Harmon, the skyscraper reached what some people still regard as its design apotheosis, and the tall buildings defined the aspiration of New York as it became the altar of Mammon. The development of the tubular steel construction system, the advent and development of computerised design and testing systems, and the lightweight glass-curtain façades that typified the hi-tech style in the later twentieth century, all allowed buildings to reach even greater height.

And what happened in London during this time, after it had given every sign of matching the United States? Nothing. Yet it was only royal intervention that prevented London from continuing to have high-rise aspirations.

Prince Charles's detractors may regard him as the royal who has had the greatest negative effect on the progress of contemporary architecture. That honour should perhaps lie with his great-great-great-grandmother. Queen Victoria, at five foot tall and with short arms and legs, may have been prejudiced by her own sense of the human scale, but whatever the cause she did not like tall buildings.

Victoria regarded the construction of the fourteen-storey Queen Anne's Mansions in particular as an affront. It was an apartment building in the Petty France area of Westminster, built by Henry Alers Hankey in 1873, and extended upwards to reach 154 feet (47 metres) in 1877. It survived partial bomb damage in the Second World War but was demolished in the early 1970s. At the time of its construction it was the tallest residential building in Britain and rivalled the scale of contemporaneous tall buildings in the United States. It was only 26 feet (8 metres) shorter than the Home Insurance Building in Chicago, and was completed eight years earlier.

Queen Anne's Mansions, also known as Hankey's Mansions, was controversial but had kudos and attracted notable tenants such as the composer Sir Edward Elgar, the explorer Sir Harry Johnston and the Irish writer Augusta, Lady Gregory. The building's principal offence was that it had the temerity partially to block Queen Victoria's view of the Houses of Parliament from Buckingham Palace.

Queen Anne's Mansions in 1966 (© Architectural Press Archive / RIBA Collections)

The monarch's ire was a catalyst for Section 47 of the London Building Act, passed in 1894, which limited the height of new buildings (except chapels and churches) to a mere 80 feet (24.4 metres) 'exclusive of two storeys in the roof and of ornamental towers, turrets, or other architectural features or decorations' (i.e. if you wanted to build a ridiculous Puginesque fantasy castle, you could still break the 100-foot barrier).[13] London has always been an evolving city, steeped in history but absorbing waves of the new. It is highly possible that, without that regally initiated banning order, London, at least to some degree, would have shared Chicago and New York's passion for grand adventures in the sky. Rather than a naturally low-rise city, London was unnaturally low-rise, the organic growth that had made it unique having been stunted by a legally administered anti-growth hormone.

At the time that Irvine Sellar was beginning to make waves on Carnaby Street, the law had recently been relaxed and London was starting to build tall again, but those sixty-odd years had changed the character of the city so skyscrapers would be at odds with the low- to mid-rise urban grain as it now stood. While in the later twentieth century legion estates of often poorly built box-houses were allowed to flood out from the peripheries of cities and towns and pour over the countryside, changing the nature of much of Britain, and not for the better, a tall building is treated as an unusual, culturally alien object, and thus subject to extraordinary scrutiny, planning constraints and criticism. As a nation, we seem far more upset by changes to the skyline than by changes to the land itself.

London's skyscrapers may be comparatively few, and comparatively new, but they are emblems of the mood and indulgences of their times. The Shell Centre (1962), designed by Sir Howard Robertson, was the first office building in London to be taller than Victoria Tower at the Houses of Parliament and broke the 100-metre barrier (352 feet/107 metres). Architecturally, it was a tentative step back into building tall. It lacks a confidence of its own and harks back to the art-deco-influenced Golden Age of the American skyscraper, with its use of stone cladding and bronze-framed perpendicular windows.

The Shell Centre's immediate successors were more individual and forward-looking. The 1960s, with the race for space in full flow, gave

Shell Centre (© future Galore)   Centre Point (© Iain McGillivray)

us the sci-fi BT Tower (1964); the modernism of Ronald Ward's Millbank Tower (1963), Richard Seifert's Centre Point (1967), and Sydney Kaye and Eric Firmin's Euston Tower (1970); and the brutalism of Ernö Goldfinger's extraordinary residential Trellick Tower (1972). The latter two were completed in the early 1970s but it is clear that they were designed in the 1960s, with their nods towards otherworldly cities of the sci-fi-obsessed imagination.

These were standalone buildings and they were monumental in their siting. As Peter Murray, the writer and leading authority on building tall in London, says about the siting of the Shard away from the twenty-first-century City cluster, 'You have to see the Shard in the context of the post-war thinking about the planning of tall buildings and what tall buildings do to cities. When we started building taller buildings in the 1960s and 1970s . . . there was a thought that tall buildings provide individual icons as locators to places.'

For example, Centre Point marked the east end of Oxford Street, while Marble Arch Tower, designed by T. P. Bennett and completed in 1966, marked the west end of the street.

Murray explains, 'They were thought to have value in the same historic way that Big Ben and St Paul's mark the passage of the river. And you can see that being replicated by the Vauxhall Tower down in Nine Elms, and now, of course, the Shard at London Bridge.'

Each of these buildings, from Centre Point to the Shard, has faced sharp criticism because of its solitary siting.

There is an unofficial lobby of interests that is not against tall buildings per se, but dislikes standalone buildings. This may be a reaction to a perceived disharmony with the social grain, and a view that standalone buildings are more obviously monumental, attention-seeking and arrogant.

The idea of clustering – or of making a set of tall buildings part of the urban grain of an area – naturally emerged in the City, where there was an obvious need for a high density of office space as the banking and finance industries bloomed. While not the tallest of tall buildings, schemes such as CityPoint (1967, originally named Britannic House), St Helen's (1969, formerly the Commercial Union building) and the Stock Exchange Tower (1970) announced the City's intent through a first wave of skyscrapers.

This wave reached its apogee with the NatWest Tower, now called Tower 42, which was completed in 1980. Standing at 600 feet (183 metres), it was the tallest building in the United Kingdom. The building was designed by Richard Seifert to have a structural quirkiness that his Centre Point building lacks: seen from above, the building is in the shape of the NatWest bank's logo – a hexagon comprising three chevrons. The shape means that it has a difficult floor plate, and some people will never be drawn to it in aesthetic terms, but Tower 42, in its sculptural character and ambition, is the direct forebear of the post-millennial wave of City building.

In between those two eras, a second high-rise cluster emerged to threaten the City's position as the financial centre of London. The 1980s, when the London of the Thatcher years adopted a new corporate and financial aggression, were marked by the birth of Canary Wharf, and the architecture mirrored the ballsy, financial hardness that stood

NatWest Tower (Tower 42) (© Douglas Freer)

at odds with the old City and its medieval chaos. César Pelli's pyramid-topped One Canada Square, with its cold monumentalism and touches of art deco, harked back to the financial excess of New York and Chicago in the late 1920s, and is almost a copy of his own design for Three World Financial Center (1985) in New York. It drew little from London's architectural typologies and announced the new order: London finance was global finance.

One Canada Square (© Tony Baggett) and Canary Wharf (© Dynasoar)

One Canada Square, constructed in 1988–91 and standing at 770 feet (235 metres), took the NatWest Tower's crown as the tallest building in Britain. Not only was its architectural impulse quite foreign to London; the grander scheme that it signposted was unlike anything London had known.

Set on the Isles of Dogs in east London, Canary Wharf was a massive, master-planned commercial development, supported by the state in the form of both funding and huge tax incentives – firms would forgo having to pay business rates for ten years – but with little interference from local government. The development was more or less self-regulated in terms of planning and had great control of the overall infrastructure and space between the buildings – areas that a Londoner would normally expect to be in the public realm and in the care of the local authority.

In 2001, One Canada Square was joined by 8 Canada Square, known as the 'HSBC Tower', which was designed by Norman Foster, and 25 Canada Square, given the similarly exotic title 'Citigroup Centre 2', another César Pelli design, which became the joint second-tallest buildings in the UK. All three buildings, even the Foster, look like they could have been dropped into Toronto or the burgeoning financial centres of the Far East. That the buildings have never been given interesting if pejorative nicknames by the London public shows its disinterest if not disaffection for these hulks. Within a couple of years, the triumvirate was joined by a parade of other 500-foot (150-metre) plus towers.

While Canary Wharf sprouted tall shoots from the wasteland of the Docklands, the City was already reinventing itself by tearing down some of the uninspiring slabs that had gone up just a couple of decades earlier. While toy-town Canary Wharf could offer function and symmetry, the City would offer individualism and character.

This was aided by the City of London's chief planning officer, Peter Rees, who saw the City's uniqueness in its layers of history and was not scared to add another. This new phase of building, reliant more on groundscraper squatness than height, strove for the fresh and unusual, but some of the developments have not stood the test of time well: the neo-Gothic Minster Court, designed by GMW and completed at the beginning of the 1990s, and the postmodernism of No. 1 Poultry, designed by James Stirling and featuring pink and yellow limestone stripes, never settled into their environment and have always looked like they were trying too hard for attention. Other buildings from this phase have already disappeared.

Towards the end of the twentieth century, the City had another go at building tall, and now fully bought into the romance and cultural impact of the skyscraper, a typology to which Rees, it appears, had become increasingly sympathetic.

In 1996, following the Provisional IRA's destruction of the Baltic Exchange three years earlier, outrageously ambitious plans were submitted for the Millennium Tower, a 1,266-foot (386-metre) scheme on the site. The proposed building would have been more than twice the height of the NatWest Tower, which remained the tallest building in the City.

The 1.5 million square feet (140,000 m²) building was designed by Norman Foster to have a highly unusual asymmetrical floor plate comprising two ellipses. The scheme's height was reduced after consultation with the Civil Aviation Authority for fear it would be a danger to planes, and the development eventually folded in the face of continued opposition, even to its reduced height.

The mooted tower was, however, a taster of the post-millennial attitude of the City when it came to building tall: the hiring of the cream of world architects to make an impression with strident architecture in an unusual form.

The Millennium Tower was nicknamed the 'erotic gherkin' in a *Guardian* article of September 1996, and a de-sexed version of that name stuck for the built scheme, in a new design by Foster, that replaced it. Permission for the 591-foot (180-metre) 'Gherkin' – or 30 St Mary Axe as it is more formally known – was granted in 2000. Construction began in 2001 and the building opened in 2004, beginning a new chapter for building tall in the City. The Gherkin, the Cheesegrater and the Walkie-Talkie are quirky and experimental in form, expressing the confidence of the deregulated City and the idiosyncrasy of London. The trading floors may have gone, but the buildings are the trader's urgent shout for attention and the twist of his eccentric bow tie.

The twenty-first-century City (© Borchee)

Into this world stepped Irvine Sellar in the year 2000. In an environment that was historically against high-rise, his intention was to build the tallest tower in Europe. And while the City and Canary Wharf could offer some level of acceptability for a skyscraper, he had no intention of adding to either cluster. For him, it was poor, downtrodden Southwark or bust.

Sellar was about to make a leap skywards from a retail park in Portsmouth and other retail developments in Belfast and various provincial towns. That he would even consider beginning the journey reflected his strength of character and self-belief. He also had weapons in his arsenal, namely his charm; his capacity to understand how other people's needs could be aligned to his own goals; and his ability to pinpoint the right person to help him.

The person to whom Sellar knew he should speak was Fred Manson, the London Borough of Southwark's director of regeneration and environment. In the end, the planning decision would be made by elected councillors rather than the council officer, but without Manson's support for the enterprise, there would be little point in pushing forward.

Manson, a lean, sharp North American who combines great intelligence and a strong personality, felt that Southwark had been unfairly overlooked when it should have had a promising future. It was he who had encouraged Tate to take over Bankside Power Station; Tate Modern now attracts around 5 million visitors a year to an area that had been regarded as decrepit. His ambitions for the borough and those of the developer were in sympathy.

Peter Murray says that Irvine Sellar would not have been able to build the Shard 'without as strong a planning person at Southwark as Fred Manson'. He had been director of regeneration at Southwark since 1994, and knew what the borough had to offer in terms of infrastructure and location. Looking north across the river and east towards Canary Wharf, Manson was all too aware that both areas had been given investment that would never be afforded Southwark if the status quo remained unchallenged.

Tate Modern was just about to open when Irvine Sellar came to see Manson in early 2000. Manson was still having trouble bringing investment into the borough despite the advent of the huge gallery, and some of the responsibility for that lack of investment lay directly with the massive development of Canary Wharf.

'Because of the staggering subsidy going to Canary Wharf,' Manson explains, 'we could never get a bank to come to Southwark. The government gave Canary Wharf forgoing business rates for ten years and then they extended it another ten years. Bank after bank came to us and said we love this site, we would like to be along the river near London Bridge, and then they would do the calculation, and they would say, "It would cost us 50 per cent more than in Canary Wharf." I think I was quoted a figure that £40 billion in tax was forgone because of Canary Wharf during this twenty-year tax break. Now, that's a lot of money. And the amount of money the government put into Canary Wharf was, I think, something like £10 billion. We kept on saying, give us just five, four, three billion, and we can transform this borough.'

Manson reflects on the frustration. 'Developers are funny. They run in a herd, and the first one never seemed to get there . . .'

'Until Irvine Sellar . . .?' I ask.

'Yes. He seems to have his own way of doing things. He doesn't follow the herd.'

He says that, in the lead-up to the new millennium, 'I thought Southwark had a value as an employment centre, and I thought high-value employment was better than low-value employment. I thought that the borough needed to establish itself as a business centre in an impressive way. I wasn't wedded to the idea of a tall building, but I certainly wasn't opposed to it. If there was going to be a tall building it should be on top of a transport hub, and there's not many better than London Bridge.'

He was fed up with the City relying on Southwark's transport infra-structure to feed its offices across the water while there was no net benefit to the borough in terms of jobs and investment. He would see tens of thousands of people coming out of London Bridge station in the morning and crossing the river – and the border of the borough – to get to their City jobs. 'I think the thing that really amazed me was when the huge tower design by Norman Foster was proposed on what became the Gherkin site: they did a transport analysis and it was going to take all the spare capacity of London Bridge station to serve their building. I thought, why do all the people have to schlep all the way from London Bridge over to the centre of the City? Why can't their jobs just be there, at London Bridge?'

Sellar has a high opinion of Manson: 'Fred is a quirky character, but good, and he said something along the lines of "Southwark Towers is a crap building. I will support your building if it is great architecture." He said, "Why don't you test the public appetite with some concepts?"'

Shortly after the news broke of Sellar's prospective scheme for a huge tower, Manson was invited to attend a dinner held by the City of London. 'At about the time this was being considered, I was being invited to a number of City dinners. I always found out what the issue was when I found out where I was sitting, and on this occasion I was sitting opposite Peter Rees.'

Even before they had been given their appetisers, Rees, according to Manson's memory of the event, said, 'You must agree that all new tall buildings must be in the City and not in Southwark.'

'I said, "No, I don't agree with that at all,"' Manson recalls. 'I told him that I would do everything within my power to ensure that Southwark kept the City on its toes. Peter was absolutely taken aback when I didn't agree that the City was the centre for all office development.'

As Sellar points out, the logic for a geographically prescribed City of finance was rapidly diminishing: 'The idea of the Square Mile is dated now because it was just based on messengers running around feeding information on bits of paper. That's gone now because at a click of a button you can reach all areas of the world.'

Nonetheless, Peter Rees's dismissal of Southwark when it came to ambitions to build tall as part of a commercial development was based on what was accepted at the time as sound logic. The borough, and London Bridge and its SE1 postcode in particular, may have been central, but the river was not just a historical barrier. Manson recalls that St Martins Property Investments, which owned sites along the south bank of the river, went to the City to ask if they could have an EC postcode because SE1 carried such a stigma. In the standard psychogeography of London, the area was still 'across the river' and therefore in no man's land, miles away from the corporate heart of London and unable to sustain major commercial development. Big business was not part of Southwark's urban grain, nor were very tall buildings.

Southwark Towers, the building that Sellar and his partners had purchased, was one of three relatively high-rise buildings, but London Bridge was hardly a cluster to rival the ongoing development at Canary Wharf or the grouping of major financial institutions in the City. The tallest of the three buildings at London Bridge was not even an office block, but a hospital, and a fairly grim one at that.

Guy's Hospital has been on the St Thomas Street site since it opened in 1721. Its founding purpose was worthy but, even in the context of eighteenth-century hospitals, dire: it was established to help patients with incurable diseases who had been discharged from nearby St Thomas' Hospital as they were beyond the help of known medicine. The hospital expanded and became a leading London institution, which now has 750,000 patients per year. The site was redeveloped in 1974 with the addition of two conjoined structures: the twenty-nine-storey

Guy's House and the thirty-four-storey Guy's Tower, which at 440 feet (134 metres) was initially the tallest hospital building in the world.

As Guy's is a state-financed hospital building, it is fair to presume that architects Watkins Gray were more concerned with function than aesthetics, and it shows. The principal tower is actually the shorter of the two, and it's a dull grey, rectangular block of a building. The taller, narrower tower was improved in 2014, with architects Peynore & Prasad recladding the building in folded, anodised aluminium in a £40 million makeover. A light sculpture by Carsten Nicolai was added, and the height of the building extended to 487.7 feet (148.65 metres), which meant that it regained the top spot as the world's tallest hospital tower.

The wider principal tower, however, has remained largely unaltered. Thomas Heatherwick's *Boiler Suit*, made of woven steel panels that undulate to give an otherworldly appearance, has encased the large ground-floor boiler room at its foot since 2007, and there has been some prettification of the façade on the lower floors, but the building remains something of an eyesore. I once heard a leading architectural critic, who is immune to the delights of the Shard, say that its main feat has been to block out the view of 'that fucking hospital'.

As Guy's Hospital was cheek-by-jowl with the similarly maligned 328-foot (100-metre) Southwark Towers, London Bridge's mini-cluster was regarded as an architectural atrocity. There were problems at ground level, too, as their proximity across St Thomas Street, coupled with Southwark Towers' unusual Y-formation, created a blasting wind that pedestrians had to endure even in fairly mild conditions.

The third tall building at London Bridge, New London Bridge House, did little to raise the aesthetic profile of the mini-cluster. Sited close to Southwark Towers, the 1967 building was built on the former grounds of ancient St Thomas' Hospital, which neighboured Guy's before it was moved to Lambeth in 1871. New London Bridge House, twenty-five storeys and 308 feet (94 metres) tall, was the product of the most notable architect involved in the triumvirate – Richard Seifert. The Swiss-born architect became the king of the British high-rise after height restrictions were lifted at the beginning of the 1960s. He was later responsible not only for Centre Point and the NatWest Tower, but Drapers Gardens and King's Reach Tower and 500 other office blocks across Britain and the rest of Europe. In terms of adventurous architecture, New London Bridge House was no NatWest Tower, and ranks towards the bottom of those 500-plus buildings. The best that can be said about it was that, due to its incurve, it was reminiscent of Millbank Tower, which predated it by four years.

Although London Bridge had a mini-cluster, it was one that most people preferred to ignore for aesthetic reasons, if nothing else, and hardly suggested that London Bridge was the right location for the tallest tower in central London, never mind Europe. Fred Manson and Irvine Sellar may have been the only two people who saw it as a credible location, and even Manson thought that Sellar, due to the difficulties of building tall in the wrong part of London, stood no chance in fulfilling his ambition.

But, as Sellar says, 'If you don't have self-belief, you should not be in the property business.'

In April 2000, Irvine Sellar announced his intention to build a supertall building at London Bridge. It would be a co-development on the site of Southwark Towers by its new owners: Sellar Property Group, CLS Holdings and the Ironzar Trust. Sellar, in typically robust style, announced: 'This provides an opportunity to create a global landmark. We believe that our proposals for London Bridge Tower will complement the planned redevelopment of the station complex, and will continue the renaissance of London's south bank.'

The 1.3 million square feet would replace the 214,000-square-foot Southwark Towers at an estimated cost of £600 million. London Bridge Tower was to be the sixth-tallest building in the world after the Petronas Towers, Kuala Lumpur (1,483 feet/452 metres); the Sears Towers, Chicago; the World Trade Center, New York; the Jin Mao Building, Shanghai; and the Empire State Building, New York. The request for planning permission would be lodged with the London Borough of Southwark in summer 2000, for building completion in 2005, at which point the London Bridge Tower would be the tallest building in the whole of Europe: 1,400 foot (420 metres), including its spire.

The building was to be a round pipe with a roof height of 1,200 feet (366 metres) that furled, corkscrew-like, into a spire reaching a further

200 feet (54 metres) into the air. Set close to the southern bank at a spot where the River Thames bends, it would be visible from almost all of London. The huge office scheme was a provocation to the City, and the tower's name underlined its bold setting across the water.

The architect for the scheme was a young man named Peter Vaughan of Broadway Malyan and the prospective engineer was Arup. The latter had already established itself as one of the leading architectural engineering practices in the world. Broadway Malyan, on the other hand, was an unknown quantity when it came to building tall. Although it had been practising in the UK since 1958, it was yet to gain the global profile it enjoys today, with sixteen offices worldwide. In 2000, the practice had just completed work on phase one of BP's Research and Technology Park in Sunbury, Surrey, but that development cost less than a tenth of the proposed London Bridge Tower scheme, and had none of the profile.

Sellar says, 'We worked very closely with Broadway Malyan on some concepts – very brave, very tall, because the only way you can go on a small site is up. It wasn't on a freehold – it's on a long lease, so I had to work with Railtrack at the time to get them to agree to what we wanted, which wasn't easy.'

As far as the press was concerned, a largely unknown developer wanted to use an unknown architect to build Europe's biggest tower in a totally unsuitable location – while plans for the Millennium Tower, a similar-sized tower by one of the world's leading architects in the highly suitable cluster area of the City, had been driven into the ground just a couple of years earlier. Even proposals for Foster's much-reduced replacement scheme were heavily criticised.

The scheme for London Bridge Tower appeared to some commentators to be a piece of cynical manoeuvring by a speculator: an attempt to pimp the value before 'flipping' the property. Increasingly as the late twentieth century had progressed and property prices had escalated, often the easiest way for a property developer to make money involved no genuine attempt at development at all: purchase the property at the lowest possible price, build up its worth by promising development and gaining planning permission, and then sell it on for an inflated price.

When I asked Tony Leyland, who worked with Sellar during his first move into property in the early 1980s and remains a close confidant, whether he was surprised that Sellar went through with the development of what would become the Shard, he replied, 'I thought he was just doing what we did, what everybody did at that time, to build up the value before selling it on. When he went ahead and built it, I was astonished. I didn't think it could be done.'

Fred Manson smiles wryly when I mention the prevalence of flipping, and he quotes Peter Stewart, who was director of design review at the Commission for Architecture and the Built Environment (CABE) at the time: 'All development in London is a failed property deal.'

Sellar, as reported by the BBC, attempted to cut off any assumptions at the pass: 'I know that there are a lot of plans announced for skyscrapers which turn out to be completely speculative, but we are very confident about this. It is not going to be a quick process but we are willing to commit a lot of money, time and effort to getting the tower built. There's a shortage of office space, but more than that I think London deserves a global landmark of this sort.'

Saeed Shah countered in the *Independent* on 10 April 2000, 'Developers say that there is a growing demand for large buildings in central London. But its sheer size and its impact on the cityscape, particularly views of St Paul's Cathedral on the opposite riverbank, seem certain to trigger objections from environmentalists.'

Sellar said that the Sellar Property Group had already commissioned research into sightlines, which proved that the views of St Paul's would not be overly affected, but, as he would learn, that issue was not about to die down. London's latest guidelines on height were laid down in a review by the London Planning Advisory Council (LPAC), which had concluded that tall buildings should be restricted to outlying areas such as Canary Wharf and Croydon, or City fringe areas.

While Manson was supportive of plans to develop the London Bridge site, he confirmed after seeing Broadway Malyan's renderings that he did not think the scheme had much chance of ever seeing the light of day.

He recalls the meeting with Sellar and his architects: 'I said something like, "The likelihood of this going forward is 5 per cent, and the likelihood of this going forward with Broadway Malyan is zero. I may as well say this in front of you because I will say it outside the room.'"

Even if Southwark did wish to grant planning permission, the borough was going to pass the decision on to the first Mayor of London, who would take up office in the new post in May 2000.

Rowan Moore, one of the United Kingdom's leading architecture critics, savaged the scheme in the *Evening Standard* on 10 April, and alluded to problems Sellar had encountered as a property developer a decade earlier: 'Oh spare us. A property developer with a bumpy history has joined forces with some mediocre architects to stick an upraised digit into the London air. Few places in London will escape its dismal machismo.'[14]

He objected to any claim that the London Bridge Tower could be called 'a world-class landmark, something to make London walk tall . . . there is nothing world class about a tower not quite as high as the Empire State Building, which was built 70 years ago'.

He went on to dismiss the design of the scheme, referring to 'the meritless and graceless glass blocks they are erecting' in Vauxhall and asking, 'Do we really want the same thing writ enormous?'

His argument was more considered than some of the critics venting their ire at the prospective pole. He dismissed the blanket claim that tall buildings were inappropriate, and did not suggest that London Bridge was the wrong place for a skyscraper. Instead, he emphasised the fact that, as tall buildings have such an impact on the city and its skyline, people have a right to expect them to be inspiring in architectural terms, and to give something back to the city.

'This tower does neither,' he concluded. 'It is a developer trying out his luck. It is a poke in London's eye with a sharp stick. Please, future Mayor, save us from it.'

Moore was not finished. Two days later he was bashing at his keyboard again, decrying London's existing skyscrapers: 'If someone could double the height of the apologetic huddle around the NatWest tower, our spirits would be proportionately raised . . . There is, on the other hand, everything wrong with the 1,378ft tower that the developer Irvine Sellar wants to put over London Bridge station. It lacks sense or grace . . .'[15]

As Moore pointed out, tall buildings that only exist for the sake of their private owners and occupiers are the genuine problem, not the idea of the skyscraper itself. Corporate tall buildings can loom over the minion worker ants and threaten with their dominance, and are unlikely to encourage civic pride merely by their blocking presence on our skyline. 'They should earn their right to invade our airspace by truly inspiring us,' Moore wrote. 'They should give something back to the public, whether by creating great spaces at ground level, or giving genuine public access to their best views.'

He was personally damning of Sellar's ambition. 'There's something, in short, horribly Peter Stringfellow about the urge to be tallest . . . Someone should tell Mr Sellar and his kind that it's not size that counts, but what you do with it.'

Moore was not going against the tide when he lambasted Broadway Malyan's London Bridge Tower. For a couple of weeks, it became the piñata of the press. It was struck from every angle – its height, its design and its position were all criticised. It was held up as a symbol of the architect's unfettered ego and the developer's unbridled greed.

Sellar had at least drawn attention to his site, and to the possibility of having a large-scale development on the wrong side of the river. Despite the criticism, the press coverage would only increase the property's value when the time came to sell. In the meantime, Southwark Towers was a moneymaking building anyway. Most developers would have put the scheme to one side and retreated into the shadows.

Irvine Sellar didn't. He went to Berlin.

Chapter 3
A Lunch in Berlin

Finding the gap in the market is what makes an entrepreneur successful. Some of them are blindingly obvious; some of them are not.

Irvine Sellar

O n 30 May 2000, two men sat down for lunch on wooden benches in a hotel restaurant in Marlene Dietrich Platz in Berlin. The men were of a similar age, in their sixties, with long, successful careers behind them. It could be expected that the conversation between two such men would turn to the past and imminent retirement plans. Rather, they were there to discuss the future.

The two men were Irvine Sellar and the architect Renzo Piano, and neither had any intention of retiring. They were both men whose careers consisted of challenging themselves and going against the grain, and they were willing at least to discuss a new adventure.

Sellar and his London Bridge Tower scheme had taken a battering, but he was not about to throw in the towel. He was unwilling to lower his ambitions or the height of the building in the face of opposition; instead, he had decided to up the stakes in terms of design. He had already taken note of what Fred Manson had said about the need for the scheme to have great architecture. He had read Rowan Moore's damning articles in the *Evening Standard*, too.

I ask Sellar whether Rowan Moore had a direct influence on his scrapping of the original design.

'Put it this way,' he replies, 'I wouldn't say that I took his advice. I already had my own thoughts. But I listened.'

This particular phrasing is key to understanding Sellar, and key to his success. Sellar may be a strong character, regarded as bullish and entrenched in his opinions even by those who have worked closely with him, but when someone talks sense he listens, analyses their point, matches it to his own ambitions, and adapts. He is always in pursuit of an absolute – the best as he sees it – and he will take on board anything that helps that become reality.

Sellar says of the Broadway Malyan scheme, 'It wasn't that bad a design really. Worse towers have gone up since then. They were just very conceptual designs. We had not refined the scheme at all.' He had his own reservations, however. He has always been interested in creativity and innovation, ever since his early days in fashion retail, and thought that London, certainly at that point, had not been brave in its new architecture. He was willing to test the waters.

The man who had aligned the stars in Berlin was Tony Fitzpatrick, a charismatic forty-eight-year-old structural engineer at Arup who had worked with Richard Rogers and Norman Foster. His high-rise projects with Foster included the Century Tower in Tokyo and the abandoned Millennium Tower scheme in London. It was he who, in 2000–1, would take the wobble out of the 'wobbly bridge', leading the team that brought stability to Foster's Millennium Bridge across the Thames. Barry Ostle of the Sellar Property Group says, 'The chemistry between Tony and Irvine was extremely good. He spoke fluent Italian, and although he was a Londoner he was brought up in Italy. He put in a call to Renzo to arrange a meeting and off we went.'

Fitzpatrick was at the table in Berlin, as was Ostle, Piano's wife Emilia and very young son Giorgino. Fitzpatrick, though, was never to see the progeny of his matchmaking. In July 2003, by which time he was chairman of Arup's Americas Division, he died in a cycle accident in California.

For a moment, Piano was unsure what to make of Sellar. According to the *Sunday Times* on 1 July 2012, he thought Sellar was 'like a man wearing sunglasses. You don't know if he's going to smile at you or kill you.'

Sellar says that Piano quickly dismissed the Broadway Malyan design: 'I showed him our scheme, which he didn't like.' The developer told Piano that he wanted to create a tall building that had genuine architectural merit.

Piano said, provocatively, 'I don't like tall buildings . . . They are like fortresses.' It was not a good start.

Renzo Piano was born on 17 September 1937 in Genoa, Italy. He told Dominic Bradbury of the *Telegraph* on 19 November 2011, 'Genoa is a city of the sea, and the harbour is a magical place, full of ships, like a moving, floating city. But my real love was the building site. Eventually you become an architect but at heart you are still a builder – it's under your skin.'

He comes from a family of builders, which makes him a practical architect even if his designs are elegant and imbued with a sense of poetry. When he decided to become an architect rather than a builder, his father was mystified, since he saw an architect as having a lesser role in the profession of building.

Piano's relationship with the water and sailing ships in Genoa would be evident in his design for the Shard, but he had also enjoyed a long relationship with London – even though he had never had a major design commissioned in Britain. Having worked with Louis Kahn in Philadelphia, in 1969 he came to London with his first wife Magda and their children in the hope that the move would allow him to pursue hi-tech architecture – light structures with an emphasis on steel and glass, and free from traditional ideas of heavy, stolid buildings of authority.

'I was travelling to salvation,' he told the *Telegraph*. 'I still see London like this. It was my second love, and the place where I spent the most intriguing years of my life.'

Piano says that he 'grew up professionally' in London, where he attended the Architectural Association School of Architecture (AA) in Bedford Square. The AA, established in 1847, is the oldest independent architecture school in the United Kingdom, and in the 1960s it became rich territory for radical thinking. He set up a small office on Brook Street with the similarly progressive high-tech architect, Richard Rogers, who was also in his thirties. Language was never a barrier between the two men: Rogers, despite his English name, was born in 1933 in Florence to Italian parents and did not move to England until the Second World War.

The young partners suddenly became famous when they won the competition to design the Centre Georges Pompidou in Paris. Piano told Steve Rose in the *Guardian* on 14 June 2010, 'I'm still surprised we were allowed. We were bad boys. We were teenagers . . . Richard was the more intellectual, more brilliant. I was more like the *bricoleur* [handyman].'

They were idealistic and provocative architects, who had almost blithely entered the public competition to design the cultural centre in the Beaubourg area of Le Marais, the ancient heart of Paris, close to Notre Dame Cathedral.

The Centre Georges Pompidou, which houses the Musée National d'Art Moderne, an enormous public library and a home for music and acoustic research, was commissioned by the French president Georges Pompidou and constructed between 1971 and 1977.

The two men devised a building that revolutionised expectations of a public building. Piano has called it, 'a middle finger raised at academicism, but also a parody of the technological imagery of our times'.[16] They wanted the maximum possible area of the 1.1-million-square-foot (103,305 m²) site to be reserved for the building's cultural functions, so they designed a seven-storey, 150-foot (45.5-metre) white steel exoskeleton with the building's services on the exterior and made them a dramatic element of the design. The different services, on the west front, were categorised through bright colour coding: yellow for cables, green for plumbing, blue for air ducts, and red for circulation and flow, including the external escalators.

The effect was a playful boiler house, completely at odds with expectations of traditional architecture. As Robin Pogrebin stated in the *New York Times* in March 2007, when Rogers won the Pritzker Prize, the building 'turned the architecture world upside down', or perhaps more accurately, inside out.

The judges had a choice of 681 entries in the open competition, and went for the most radical of them all. The building was extraordinarily controversial, and there was an extended public outcry about the desecration of ancient Paris. Yet many Parisians soon came to love the Centre

Centre Georges Pompidou (© Marc Dufresne)

Georges Pompidou. Before long, it was referred to as simply 'Beaubourg', as it identified the area, and it became one of the most important cultural sites in Paris. It was expected to receive 8,000 visitors a day, but it attracted 40,000, and research revealed that 20 per cent of them did not even go into the art museum. They were drawn there to experience the building, ride its external escalators and see the view.

The balance had shifted. From that point on, cultural commissions, particularly for museums and galleries, would be pursued with a view to creating a shell that was in itself a cultural lure, rather than forbidding and elitist.

Sellar was aware of Piano's reputation as he contemplated overhauling the scheme for the London Bridge Tower. He says, 'I knew that Renzo had lived in this country but he hadn't built anything here. I thought he would be right for this building because he knew London.' Sellar wanted his building to be innovative and did not mind if it was controversial, but he also wanted it to be loved. Piano had pulled off that trick in the centre of Paris, and Sellar wanted him to do just the same in an ancient part of London.

• • •

The Centre Georges Pompidou commission was a prestigious calling card for both Richard Rogers and Renzo Piano, and they continued to work together until its completion in 1977. While Rogers then pursued the inside-out idea again with the Lloyd's of London building in the City, and went on to create the Millennium Dome and Terminal 5 at Heathrow Airport, Piano worked with engineer Peter Rice before setting up his own practice in 1981. The title, the Renzo Piano Building Workshop, points to his sustained attachment to hands-on building rather than abstract architectural theory.

He soon earned major commissions, many of them for museums and galleries, across the globe. He designed the Menil Collection building (1977) and the Cy Twombly Gallery (1987), both in Houston; the NEMO Science Museum in Amsterdam and the Beyeler Foundation Museum in Basel, which both opened in 1997; and in 2000, at the point that he first met Irvine Sellar, he was designing the Centrum Paul Klee in Bern.

His ethos, though, is not to be restricted by a signature style, which has become both the calling card and curse of many internationally renowned star architects – or starchitects, as they are known in a world where four syllables are too many.

In May 2012, in an interview with Marcus Fairs, the editor of the online architecture and design magazine *Dezeen*, Piano said: 'the *griffe* [maker's label or signature], the recognizable gesture . . . I believe this is part of the star system of architects but it's not a good story for architecture because it doesn't celebrate architecture but celebrates the architects. I think in the end it is not good for architecture because in the end it limits the freedom. You as an architect – let's assume you have a certain success; you are always pursued to repeat yourself.'[17]

He added, 'Everybody talks about a lack of freedom but probably the most difficult freedom to keep is not from other people, but yourself. You fall in the big trap, which is the one of recognizable signature . . . I hate this idea of being trapped by the need to promote your *griffe* – your label.'

That is not to say that Piano does not have what he has referred to as an 'internal coherence' through the following of certain rhythms and preference for particular materials – the use of terracotta, for instance, is a sporadic theme in Piano's designs. When you view his designs together you may detect a similar perspective, a way of seeing, but there is no sense of factory production or similarity of form in the manner of Frank Gehry's metallic curves or César Pelli's towers.

Richard Rogers summed up Piano's approach in the *Telegraph* in November 2011: 'He is not a formalist and doesn't do shapes for the fun of doing shapes. He makes poetry, but it comes out of a deep-rooted belief in the function of a building and a sense of where that building is. He has a very good feel for the site itself. Nothing is abstract in the sense of being unrelated to the site or the client's brief. He is both a scientist and an artist.'

Consequently, if Rogers is correct, he is a developer's dream – if that developer wants to marry artistry, distinction and, of course, a decent return.

Piano is willing to pursue diverse projects on hugely differing scales, ranging from pavilions to the Ferrari wind tunnel (1998) at Maranello, the Padre Pio Pilgrimage Church (2004) in San Giovanni Rotondo, which can accommodate 30,000 people, and the 58,000-seater San Nicola football stadium (1989) in Bari. The Jean-Marie Tjibaou Cultural Center (1998) in Nouméa on the remote Pacific island of Grande Terre in New Caledonia is a collection of ten ribbed huts that pays homage to the local Kanak culture. With New Caledonia's history as a French colony, Piano says that he went to great effort to ensure that the homage was not 'an Occidental interpretation'.

The Jean-Marie Tjibaou Cultural Center may have been one of his smaller projects but it emphasised that, as an architect, he wanted to respond to the particularities and locality of a site, rather than swamp it with an off-the-shelf design.

This was relevant to Sellar, who, after the anonymity of the Broadway Malyan design, was keen to develop a building that responded to the unique London Bridge location. Also relevant was Piano's dexterity with glass, prevalent in many of his buildings from the Beyeler Foundation Museum to his own practice (1991) at Punta Nave, near Genoa. The latter building, poised on a clifftop on the Ligurian coast, is a spectacular timber-framed glasshouse. Glass is a major element in Piano's 'interior coherency'.

Also notable for Irvine Sellar's future ambitions of creating a London Bridge Quarter around the Shard is Renzo Piano's great interest in

The Jean-Marie Tjibaou Cultural Center (© EQRoy)

city-making and densification. The Italian architect was responsible for master-planning the huge Daimler-Benz development at Potsdam Platz in Berlin.

Potsdamer Platz had once been at the very centre of Berlin's cultural life, but it was destroyed during the Allied bombardment of Berlin in the Second World War. Following the end of the war, when the Berlin Wall was erected it split the platz, turning it from a vibrant meeting place to a desolate, severed landscape symbolic of the divisions between East and West. Piano helped to sew the city back together again.

The eight-year, nineteen-building project had just been completed as Sellar and Piano sat together at lunch in Marlene Dietrich Platz, right in the hub of the development.

With this interest in placemaking, together with his ability to make ground-breaking buildings that become new cultural signifiers for a city, Piano seemed to be the perfect partner for the London Bridge development.

Except for one thing: in his career spanning thirty-plus years, Piano had little experience of building tall – the tallest of his buildings was the recently completed Aurora Place, a forty-four-storey, 655-foot (200-metre) building in Sydney, half the size of the prospective London Bridge Tower. And on top of that, he had just said that he disliked tall buildings. At that moment, Sellar thought he had made a wasted journey.

Piano has a genial, humorous and informal bearing, but he is also thoroughly professional. At the lunch with Sellar he was being deliberately provocative. He wanted to ascertain quickly whether he and the developer in front of him could share the same vision. Tall buildings that arrogantly and stolidly fill the skyline without giving anything back to the city are anathema to him. If he was going to design an immense skyscraper, the developer would need to have a far more nuanced ambition than merely depositing the largest possible slab or pole on the site.

Piano has an extraordinary reputation. When I was travelling from Genoa airport to see the architect at his studio, the randomly selected taxi driver told me that Piano was 'the true visionary of Genova' (Christopher Columbus did not get a mention). The driver explained that, whenever he learns that Signor Piano has designed a new building, he spends hours at home trying to create his own model of the design. It would be nice to think that, somewhere on the outskirts of London, a cabby has a garage full of handmade scale models of Norman Foster buildings, but I'm not holding out hope.

The esteem in which Piano is held worldwide means that he is able to run offices in both Paris and Genoa, and is offered hundreds of commissions every year. If he did not already have some interest in Sellar's development, the discussion would not have even got as far as lunch.

As he had lived in London and later often returned to stay with his friend Richard Rogers, he knew a little about the area but, before that lunch, it was highly unlikely that his curiosity was going to transform itself into a thousand-foot tower.

Then, when Sellar showed him images of the exact location of the development – it's position by the Thames with the railway tracks sweeping together to form a thick sheaf at its foot – Piano's interest became evident.

As Sellar gave him further details, Piano's enthusiasm grew for the concept of a skyscraper in Southwark. He says about Sellar, 'Sometimes you have people in a parallel life who you have something in common with. When we met, it was clear immediately that we have affinity. He started to talk about his idea of a tall building and I could tell we shared something.'

Piano began to match Sellar's vision with his own associations of the city in which he had lived as an aspiring young man. He thought of London as a city of spires, including those by Christopher Wren in the rash of church building in the seventeenth century. He was more than familiar with his fellow Italian Canaletto's paintings of the Thames in the eighteenth century, particularly *The River Thames with St Paul's Cathedral on Lord Mayor's Day* (1747–8) with its multiplicity of spires in the background and a smattering of tall ships on the river, their sails and masts creating triangular, similarly spire-like shapes. Canaletto's *London, The Thames from Somerset House Terrace towards Westminster* (c. 1750–1) features a spire that could be seen as a direct forebear of the Shard. Piano was also animated by the sense of motion and the confluence of the river and the railway lines at London Bridge. He immediately saw the site as a fulcrum for the energy flowing through the city, which could be lifted upwards through the building.

His enthusiasm was such that he needed to start sketching out his ideas there and then. With no sketchpad, he started drawing on the menu card.

Piano said that he would want the building to have public access. As William Matthews, who worked on the Shard for Renzo Piano Building Workshop, told me in 2016, 'One of the mantras of the Renzo Piano office is how the building is seen by the public. You might think, "Why does the architect care about that? He should be concerned about the aesthetics, the colours, the materials." But Renzo does care about how people use the building.'

Matthews went on to explain, 'Most tall buildings were private, corporate edifices with no public access. But if you look at the best-known buildings in the world – the Eiffel Tower, the Empire State Building, the Burj – the boy from Burnley or Burundi can think "It's slightly mine because I can go up it." This makes them icons.'

It also adds a further layer of problems for a developer, as public access means giving up valuable space.

'It was also clear that this tower was sitting in the centre of a crossing system of different transportation – trains, buses and all that,' Piano explained in *Dezeen*. 'So it was typical of work we have done in the past about brownfields [post-industrial sites] – how to intensify life in the city . . . Growth of the city from inside: filling the holes, filling the industrial sites, railway sites.'

Importantly for Piano, the siting of the tower and its integration with the public transport system meant that the office workers based at the building would have no need to drive cars to work, thereby both congestion and pollution would be reduced. 'It was an excellent chance to show that you could provide life in a city without increasing the traffic – by using public transport.'

In raising the prospect of a publicly accessible, eco-friendly building with no car parking, Piano may have expected Sellar to finish his lunch quickly, fly home to London and begin looking for another architect with a more commercial vision. Perhaps a straight up and down fridge was not so unappealing after all.

Sellar stayed seated. He already shared Piano's views on density and transport, and he started to explain that the idea of public access was a perfect match to his own desire to create a multi-use building.

As Piano sketched, Sellar said that he wanted a tower that would include offices and apartments, but there would be public access to a hotel and restaurants. Piano also started to mark in where there could be a viewing platform, and soon the two men were using the phrase 'vertical city' to describe the scheme.

Piano tells me, 'We had immediate affinity over this idea of mixed use and public access. I don't know who first started talking about mixed use. If it was me, he immediately said yes; if it was him, I immediately said yes. I don't remember precisely who said what because we already had affinity.' As he recalls the conversation, he again picks up a pen and starts sketching in green ink. 'I was drawing. If you want to make offices, you need a bigger plate at the bottom, then if you want a restaurant, you need a smaller plate, if you want to make a hotel you need a smaller plate and smaller again for apartments, and I liked the idea of a viewing platform at the top. Then we say, "Why don't we do this?"' He draws the tapered Shard. 'That was me drawing just because I was the one with the green pen in my hand – it was my job – but we were both talking.'

He says of the process of developing ideas with Sellar: 'Architecture is a kind of mix of practicalities and dreams. They come together at the same time. Creativity is like playing ping-pong, and Irvine is a good ping-pong player. He doesn't cheat, you know.'

Mixed use is often used to describe a single-use building such as an office block with merely a publicly accessible shop, bar or restaurant at the foot. The building that the architect and developer were already beginning to conjure in their minds was more genuinely mixed use than that, and perhaps better described as multi use, a term Sellar himself prefers.

Many architects, planners and theorists see multi use as the way forward for city building. Clusters of sole-function office blocks can close down an area of the city, making it a ghost town in the evenings and at weekends, as is typical of financial districts across the world. Mixing the likes of office, residential, retail, hotel, leisure and entertainment can bring vibrancy and make the surrounding area a 'place', i.e. one that reflects the breadth of human activity through work, rest and play, rather than being focused on an individual function, and thereby brings identity and texture to the urban grain.

Multi use is also the coalescence of a typical commercial developer's nightmares. Buildings with a single purpose are cheaper to build, as you have limited functionality and services to consider and can simply repeat the floor plate, maximising revenue. A multi-use building requires different orientations in terms of both services and construction, while taking up valuable space with a variety of escalators and lifts and reception areas servicing the various functions. The architect is likely to specify the need for different design elements and materials. At each point of variance, the developer's return diminishes.

Joost Moolhuijzen, Renzo Piano Building Workshop's partner-in-charge of the Shard, explains a further problem, 'The London commercial property sector considered that a mixed-use tower with different uses (commercial, residential, etc.) stacked on top of each other was bad business sense and impossible to manage as the leases run over different periods and are difficult to combine.' On 16 July 2000, two months after Piano and Sellar's Berlin meeting, Hugh Pearman wrote in the *Sunday Times* that 'financiers tend to lend money only to projects of a kind they are used to. It is difficult enough even getting funding for apartments and offices in the same building – something that is commonplace in the United States.'[18]

Consequently, while Piano was sketching away and the two men talked, there were no multi-use skyscrapers in Europe. Not a single one.

Matthews says, 'In a way, Irvine wrong-footed Renzo. Renzo said, "I want to do a publicly accessible building, a mixed-use building." No other developer would have said yes to mixed use. No one had ever done mixed use in Europe. It is becoming more popular but developers only do it because they have their arms twisted by the authorities. Irvine just said, "Yes, we can do that."'

Irvine Sellar already had a history of saying 'Yes, we can do that' when faced with a creative and innovative proposition. Renzo Piano was known for turning architecture inside out but, from the mid-1960s onwards, Sellar had been similarly avant-garde when it came to something as elemental as the way we shop. His years in fashion retail were characterised by creativity, breaking new ground, influencing taste and understanding the importance of location, all qualities that he would take into his later career as a developer.

In an interview in *London Magazine* in June 2016, Sellar directly linked what was happening in architecture and fashion in London from the late 1960s onwards:

> I have lived in London most of my life, first in the Manor House, Wood Green and Southgate areas. Post-war London was a dark, miserable, grey place. The buildings were never cleaned and the air was thick with smog and cigarette smoke. Industry used to operate in the docks and residential buildings faced away from the Thames. The big change in the last thirty to forty years is that now we are attracted by water and by river views. It wasn't until the 1960s that new creativity emerged [in all aspects of design].[19]

Christine Spooner, Irvine Sellar and Kinna the Cheetah (Irvine Sellar Archive)

Sellar's great innovation, which marked a momentous change in fashion retail, arose during his Carnaby Street years. In the mid-1960s, he noticed that an increasing number of young women were coming into his menswear shops along with their boyfriends. The expectations of a young man to be a 'dedicated follower of fashion' were on the rise, and their partners were playing an increasing role in helping them look the part. The women were interested in the cuts, the cloths, the quality and the patterns, and some, in the increasingly androgynous Swinging Sixties, were selecting items such as men's tailored trousers for themselves.

In April 1966, at the launch of Tom Cat, another new Sellar store on Carnaby Street, model Christine Spooner was dressed in clothes from Sellar's male range. She was accompanied by Tom Jones, the young Welsh heartthrob who had recently had hits with 'It's Not Unusual' and the Bond theme song 'Thunderball', but he was upstaged by the animal on the end of Spooner's lead: a five-year-old cheetah named Kinna. The stunt ensured that Sellar's new shop gained free publicity in the newspapers.

Men and women mix it up in one of Sellar's stores (Irvine Sellar Archive)

A month or two later, his wife Elizabeth had what he describes as 'a flash of genius'. She asked Irvine if she could use the basement of another of his shops, at no. 27 Carnaby Street, for womenswear. He agreed.

He sensed that there was a ground-breaking retail opportunity in having both menswear and womenswear in the same store. More men would be drawn into the store if they were shopping with their partners, and would naturally gravitate to the menswear, and vice versa: in sales terms, it could lead to a double hit.

'The idea of men's and women's being under one roof was unique in those days – everybody does it now,' Sellar says. 'A man wouldn't walk into a woman's shop to save his life. It was a huge barrier, it was effeminate. It was just not a thing we did as men. So that's where we broke the gender barrier.'

Until that point, with the exception of large department stores, male and female fashion was entirely separate, and seeing men standing and smoking outside women's clothes shops, waiting for their partners to come out, was a feature of high streets up and down the country on a Saturday. The Sellar store at 27 Carnaby Street revolutionised the concept of the shopping experience. While acknowledging Elizabeth's inspiration in 1969, Sellar told the *Evening Standard* on 8 July 1969, 'Mind you, she'd have heard about it if it hadn't worked out!'

Sellar called the store Mates, and it is often referred to as the original 'unisex' store. Sellar, though, disparages the term, even though it is sometimes claimed that he invented it: 'It wasn't unisex,' he tells me. 'I don't like that word. There was a men's area and a women's area, with different clothes, but in the same shop.'

As he told the *Financial Times Weekend Magazine* in March 2001, 'We went to a great deal of trouble to avoid the sexes actually mixing and spent an enormous amount of money building wide staircases so that the men could get past the women's clothes quickly. They were easily intimidated.'[20]

Soon the national newspapers were reporting on the phenomenon. On 7 October 1966, Shirley Flack's article in the *Daily Sketch* had the headline 'ANOTHER BARRIER FALLS: with a boutique for Him and Her TOGETHER'. Sellar explained the principle to Flack: 'It works like this. A couple are window-shopping together. She comes in to buy a plastic mac. While she is trying it on, the boyfriend sees a tie he likes, or a suede jacket, or a pair of trousers . . . It is all very informal – the old conventions don't hold any more.'[21]

The shop may not have been unisex in the purest sense, but it was novel, and even more women were taking the opportunity to graze the men's section. Despite his protestations in the press, Sellar was receptive to the cross-gender interest in his clothes. When he put frock-coat suits designed for men on sale, 300 of them were bought by women in just forty-eight hours, pairing them with purple satin shirts and flowered cravats. He would run out of size 32-chest jackets so he started to increase the number of smaller sizes, and also supplied bowler hats and silver-knobbed canes with the girls in mind.

He told Flack,

As a sales gimmick it's quite effective. Put a girl's trouser suit among a bunch of boys' clothes, and even if she wasn't looking she couldn't fail to notice and want that trouser suit. It's the psychology of proper display. Having the boys and girls buying their clothes doubles the atmosphere. You couldn't do it everywhere. You couldn't do it in the high-road, Wood Green, for instance. They're not ready for it yet. But it's the pattern for the future.

Irvine Sellar and one of his stores on Carnaby Street (Irvine Sellar Archive)

He was personally negotiating every property deal in his growing empire, storing up experience for his later career. By the end of 1966, Sellar had four outlets on Carnaby Street as well as stores on Earls Court Road and the King's Road. In the 1970s, the King's Road would take Carnaby Street's crown as the place where alternative youth would seek out avant-garde fashion, and Sellar was far ahead of the game. He was not particularly enamoured by the clientele in the early years, though, telling Nik Cohn, 'The King's Road? A lot of pseudo-intellectuals, that's what they are; but they're spenders, I'll give them that.'[22]

Among the clothes Irvine was manufacturing and selling at the beginning of 1967 were 'Donovan' caps as worn by the pop-singer Donovan himself, the Beatles and the playwright Joe Orton. The extent to which young men were becoming fashion conscious was emphasised when the headmaster of Castle Derg County Secondary School placed a large order of caps with Sellar 'because boy pupils refuse to be outdone by the girls'.

Sellar was constantly innovating styles or finding a new angle for ongoing trends. When the craze for bright red, blue and green military jackets took off, bolstered by Peter Blake's cover for the Beatles' *Sgt. Pepper's Lonely Hearts Club Band* (1967), the supply of originals was scarce. Sellar, through a piece of left-field thinking, negotiated a deal with Courtaulds, manufacturers of carpet furnishing fabrics, to supply their Evlan tweed materials so he could make new military-style suits, for both men and women, that had the weight and durability of the originals. He told the *Evening Standard*, 'It will go to show that garments bought in Carnaby Street are not in the least disposable. We've tested the clothes for non-creasing in a jammed wardrobe by rolling them up and stamping on them.'

Also in 1967, Irvine introduced the 'maxi' dress into his stores, anticipating the fashion world's fatigue with the miniskirt. Sellar told a newspaper in January 1967, 'In dropping the hemline I'm being both practical and sexy too. Practical because in our chilly, wet English weather, the wintry blasts hit hardest where the skirts are shortest, so to speak.'

Two years later, Leyland, who made the Mini car, announced that its larger Austin 1500 saloon would be called 'the Maxi', which seemed more than a coincidence.

In the late 1960s, by which time Westminster City Council was initiating plans to turn Carnaby Street into a pedestrianised zone due to the constant volume of shoppers and sightseers, Sellar had seen enough. John Stephen, the original King of Carnaby Street who peaked at having fifteen outlets on the street, had thought about trying to buy out Irvine Sellar, but as Sellar's profile grew he asked the young entrepreneur if he wanted to buy him out instead. Sellar was not interested. While the media still heralded Carnaby Street as the capital of cool, he thought that its creativity and edginess were being subsumed by a rise of tatty commercialism.

He says, 'By then Carnaby Street was just a tourist trap. All the real excitement, the real creativity, was gone. They killed the goose that laid the golden egg. It became cheap and it was just for the tourists. It had trashy retailers like Lady Jane – and it lost all its uniqueness.'

He was still making money, but money itself has never been enough for Sellar: he wants the excitement of change and innovation, and overcoming challenges is his opiate. He told Stephen that he had other plans, far bigger plans: he was going to take over the high street.

Sellar has always had an eye for a marketing opportunity (Irvine Sellar Archive)

By 1968, Sellar had decided that the high street was ready for his cross-gender shopping concept. In that year, as well as opening large Mates stores in both Regent Street and Oxford Street, Sellar started to fulfil his ambition to have a store on every high street in prime locations across the country. He opened in twenty-four locations in the Home Counties and the provinces in that single year. 'My name was in lights, on bags,' he remembers. 'The back of our vans used to say: "You are following the fashion: Mates by Irvine Sellars."'

The stores were getting larger as well as more numerous. The early Mates stores were typically around 1,500 square feet (140 m²), but the first Oxford Street store was 5,000 square feet (465 m²) and by 1973 many of the other stores were 4,000 square feet (372 m²).

By 1971, Sellar was prominent enough to feature heavily in Nik Cohn's cultural survey, *Today There Are No Gentlemen: The Changes in Englishmen's Clothes Since the War.* The stereotyping of Sellar as a ruthless cockney wheeler-dealer was already well under way, and Cohn felt the need to counter: 'He was not villainous. It would be pleasant to depict the Carnaby Street operators as bloodsuckers, ruthless exploiters, milking innocent kids of their very last dime; but Sellar wasn't like that.'

Sellar told Cohn, in one of his more revealing and introspective interviews, 'I'm in business, and when you're in business, your personal tastes come second to your profits, or they should do. People try to get at me but I'm not a monster – I'm human, like everyone else.'

The entrepreneur explained his drive:

I run a chauffeur-driven Rolls but it isn't the money that matters to me, it's the feeling of achievement. Sometimes I get a feeling of uneasiness, but then I reason it out and think, What the hell, what do I have to worry about? I'm riding the crest of the wave. I'm in this for just two reasons. One is to make money so that I can go public, and the other is to serve the public and give them better value for money. That's the truth. I'm idealistic in my way.[23]

Around the same time, on 21 November 1969, he told *The Times* that he was partly motivated by jealousy of other people's achievements. 'I like to just do things very well. I like success. I believe it's the people with the complexes who are the successful ones, it's overcoming those feelings that helps to make one drive oneself.'

The Mates brand had become a household name by the early 1970s, but the expansion into new territory had come with losses, a lack of stock control and inadequate management systems as he wrangled with the rapidly growing beast. In 1972, Sellar, in a seemingly untypical moment of self-doubt, asked consultants at Cooper Brothers Ltd to objectively assess whether he should step down as managing director of Irvine Sellars Ltd and take a non-executive director role.

Neil Boggon of Cooper Brothers noted:

(a) You have personally established a business and built it up to its present size in less than 10 years.

(b) You have demonstrated ability in selecting good sites for your business – sometimes identifying these in advance of your competitors.

(c) Your ideas on display and your abilities in selling are both good.

Boggon wisely maintained that a non-executive role 'is not one which comes naturally to a young man full of energy'. He believed that the systems Sellar was already putting in place would correct the issues, and concluded categorically that he should remain as managing director because he was the best person to overcome the temporary challenges.

Any doubts were eradicated. A year later, Sellar acquired the forty shops of the Noel Fashions subsidiary of Dorothy Perkins for £1.8 million, immediately selling on eighteen of the stores to Clarks shoes and opening the remainder as Mates by Irvine Sellar. To maintain control of his company in the prospect of going public, he also bought out the interest of Keyser Ullman, the merchant bank that had invested to help him open his first London shop on Carnaby Street a decade earlier. By 1978, Sellar's profits were exceeding £1.2 million (an income value today of £11.2 million).

Irvine Sellar with his private aeroplane in the 1970s (Irvine Sellar Archive)

On 5 October of that year, he told the *Men's Wear* trade publication:

In the line-up for a race you can have a number of superb, Olympic standard athletes, but at the finishing line there is only one winner. He's the one with something undefinable, some drive, some persistence, which forces him to go just that bit faster than all the others, to beat them. I feel I want to do that. I won't be satisfied unless I can do better than the rest. I want the best merchandise, the best sites, the best displays, the best figures. If you aim at perfection, it keeps you going on and on, because nobody can ever be perfect so you never reach perfection.

Sellar continued to innovate, organising a Mates fashion show in 1979 with a theme inspired by *The Deer Hunter* film and set, unusually for the time, to music. In much of what he does, Sellar reminds me of a theatre impresario setting out to surprise an audience.

Sellar expected his staff to share his high standards, and despite the growing size of his retail operation he continued to have a hands-on approach. His lawyer Alan Grieve, who had joined his board, would do regular spot checks on stores, and every Saturday – the busiest day of the week – Sellar himself would pick up one of his area managers, each of whom was responsible for eight stores, and assess every detail of their stores from window dressing and display to the noise levels and customer service. 'There were certain stores where they just didn't get it,' he says, which would lead to warnings or sackings for members of staff.

His forthright approach could lead to embarrassing incidents: 'I went to one store. Customers were pouring in – we were very busy. I noticed that women were looking at the merchandise and walking out. They were not being attended to, so I said to one of the assistants, who was just standing around, doing nothing: "You see these customers? Your job is to attend to them and serve them." She replied, "But I am a customer."'

By the end of the 1980s, Sellar had over ninety stores on the most prominent high streets in the country, and, at one point, seven stores on Oxford Street. He had brought the idea of cross-gender shopping and branding to a small clothes shop on Carnaby Street and then exploded the concept so that it became a standard typology for high-street shopping. It was the model for many successors, most notably Next.

It was typical Sellar behaviour: see the opportunity, seize the opportunity, and become an innovator and leader in the field. Add a touch of poetry, and you have got Renzo Piano.

Thirty years later, Sellar drew on his Mates experience when he was thinking about his future tower. 'What I thought,' he says, 'was that it has to work commercially, and to work commercially it's not going to be just one huge office building. A bit like my old Mates days, I needed to get balance and spread the risk. At Mates, I was offsetting risk because when the men's goes down the tube, the women's doesn't necessarily go down at the same time. If you've got multi use in a very tall building, you've spread the risk. I liked the idea of that.'

At the restaurant in Marlene Dietrich Platz in May 2000, Renzo Piano completed his sketch and handed it to Irvine Sellar.

Renzo Piano's first sketch of what would become the Shard, 30 May 2000 (© RPBW)

'I thought, he's got it,' Sellar says about his reaction to that first sketch. 'I liked his thought process – the fact that it was like a sail coming out of the Thames, the elegance of it, the beauty of it. I could see it working. It had star-like quality even at that point. You could just see that this would be different.'

The design was of a slender tapering form, born out of the proposition for a multi-use building. The office space was at the bottom of the building, because it would require the biggest possible floor plate to attract corporate tenants. Above that were public floors, which initially would include a viewing gallery, followed by a hotel, where guests could benefit from the higher view but where there was no need for such a large floor plate. At the narrow top was the residential accommodation because the apartments, if they were to occupy a whole floor each, would still have a substantial living space. At the apex was a second viewing gallery.

Piano had followed the elemental modernist principle of design: 'form follows function', a phrase that Louis Sullivan, early pioneer of the skyscraper, had coined in his essay titled 'The tall office building artistically considered' (1896). Piano's love of the poetical is already prevalent in that functional drawing through the sweep of the pen strokes and overall balance of the design, rising from the confluence of transport infrastructure.

Piano explained in *Dezeen*, 'In some way this idea of something starting fat and becoming small was a rational and instinctive process. Rational because it made sense from the beginning. Instinctive because it became clear that the only way to make something elegant was to not fill the sky – to make something slim.'

In his book on designing the Shard, Piano described the ongoing conversation that he and Sellar had that day:

> The vertical city was a good metaphor, because we like the idea of a place that would be alive 24 hours a day, just like a part of the city: a well-built district that through a mix of residential and commercial spaces would be used around the clock. And that same day we also began talking about a meeting place for people, after all, we were in Marlene Dietrich Platz, a small square where east and west were reunited.
>
> We talked about the social and political significance of belonging to a polis like London, with its abundance of historical buildings along the banks of the River Thames. And we even talked about poetry. We asked ourselves how it would be to site such a tall tower so close to the river, where less than a century ago sailboats moored.[24]

Moolhuijzen recorded that Sellar's ability to see the benefits of a multi-use building was 'proof of his astute instinct to know what could work'. Whereas other developers would have shied away, 'Irvine Sellar however saw it as reducing risk; the subsequent tumultuous economic years and shift of value from office to residential property has probably proven Irvine right.' More than that, Sellar saw multi use and a mix of tenants as positive: 'Being in a building that has a variety of uses and people is far more exciting than a dull, single office building let to either an accountant or a business, or law practice. And it's more exciting for the area, obviously, because you've got a multitude of use.'[25]

Looking back on that day, Piano said, 'A client must be illuminated . . . Sometimes they say they are illuminated because they are very

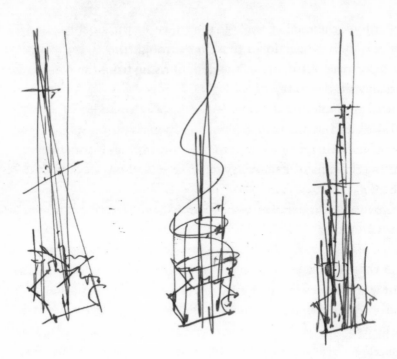

Early Renzo Piano sketches for the Shard (© RPBW)

sophisticated. He doesn't look very sophisticated. But it was in his eyes. The eyes mean a lot. He has previously done quite mad things. He really felt the sense of adventure.'[26]

Matthews believes that a building the size of the Shard would not have been built on the London Bridge site if the two men had not found such common ground at that lunch meeting and if Sellar had rejected the idea of multi-use and public access: 'I have no doubt that all the things put on the table that day, and that Irvine Sellar said yes to, are why it got through planning. That fact that Irvine was saying yes meant that we could do something radically different here. Europe had never driven that type of car – it was more common in the Middle East and Asia. It would open up London and be beneficial to the city.'

When Piano shook Sellar's hand over lunch, sealing the deal to work together, 'It was,' says the developer, 'one of those magic moments.' He knew he had found the right architect: someone who could share his vision of changing London Bridge – and London's skyline – for the better.

Sellar took the menu card away with him, and it is now framed on his office wall. A tremendous number of refinements to the design would occur before the Shard was completed, but the sketch that lunchtime is remarkably similar to the final building – a reflection of the strength of the initial principle and the two men's absolute confidence that they had found the best way forward.

Piano and Sellar may seem to be a strange pairing: the erudite Italian aesthete and the former market trader from north London, but the former is more pragmatic and the latter more creatively driven than one might expect. Out of this came a collective idea and a friendship, one that would have to endure over a decade of seemingly insurmountable challenges that neither could have foreseen as they rose from the table at the conclusion of lunch.

The agreement they made that day would change both of their careers.

Chapter 4

Big Thinking in a Little Space

Design can be complicated and fussy and I don't like that.
In fashion and architecture, stay with the simple line of good
design.

Irvine Sellar

O n his return to London, Irvine Sellar was in a positive mood about
the prospects for building tall. 'There is something in the air,' he
told the *Estates Gazette* on 17 June 2000.

With a positive economic climate taking hold, the tower block was
beginning to look like a strong commercial proposition in London.
Tower 42, the renamed NatWest Tower, had been refitted in 1998 and
was achieving the highest rents in the City. The developer Gerald
Ronson had recently revealed plans for a skyscraper of his own, the
Heron Tower, although his ambition did not match that of Sellar.
Ronson was initially planning a thirty-seven-storey tower – designed
by Kohn Pedersen Fox, the leading American architecture firm that
had been involved in Canary Wharf – in the safer high-rise territory
of the City.

As the *Estates Gazette* reported, 'Towers are back because developers
and planners have recognised their value in an urban environment.
British planners, their noses put out by the success of Bilbao and
Barcelona, have recognised that the odd landmark, even a controversial
one, is not always a bad thing.'

Irvine Sellar, it seemed, would be pitching his new scheme into a positive market where the mood was growing for tall buildings and innovative architecture.

Soon after Sellar returned to London, he went to see Fred Manson at Southwark Council again. Sellar had managed to secure the interest of one of the most esteemed architects in the world, and was now proposing a multi-use development which he thought would be beneficial to London and to Southwark, but if he believed that this news would send the wily Manson into raptures, he would have been disappointed.

'When Irvine Sellar came back to me and said he had got Renzo Piano involved – he didn't have a scheme at that stage – I said it improved the chances to only 10 per cent from 5 per cent.' He believed that prejudice against building tall, and against Southwark, was still more than likely to castrate the scheme. 'The subtler way we went through it was I told him he had a 99 per cent chance of building something that was the same height as the building that was already there. Whether it was mixed use or not wasn't really a factor for me. My concerns were the height of the building and getting development and investment into the area.'

Sellar has an optimistic disposition and a can-do demeanour. Whereas others may have translated Manson's words to mean a 90 per cent likelihood of failure when it came to building supertall, Sellar focused on the fact that he had just doubled his chances.

Rowan Moore, the *Evening Standard* architecture critic who had been so derisive about the Broadway Malyan scheme, was impressed by Sellar's choice of architect, writing on 18 July 2000:

> It's very possible that his tower is still a stunt, but he couldn't have chosen better. Renzo Piano is not only one of the world's top 10, but he is also famous for qualities like subtlety, delicacy and craftsmanship which, if a tower like this is to work, it will badly need.

His praise came with a note of warning:

> Whether his genius is enough to justify 1.5 million sq. ft of offices being hoisted into our airspace remains to be seen, but if he can't do it, nobody can.[27]

If Sellar thought he had scored a killer blow by hiring a stellar architect, he would have been disappointed when the leader writer in the same newspaper, without seeing the prospective scheme, wrote on the same day,

> The gullibility of local councils, allied to the ambition and greed of architects and developers, could push these proposals through, unless Mayor Livingstone, or the Environment Secretary John Prescott, have the courage to stop them in their tracks . . . However beautifully designed such isolated towers may turn out to be, they will represent the kiss of death to London's skyline.

Sellar was just at the beginning of what would turn out to be a long and sometimes vicious campaign against his building.

In summer 2000, Irvine Sellar took Renzo Piano and his team up to the top of Southwark Towers. The uniqueness of the site was immediately evident to the architects. Joost Moolhuijzen, the Dutch partner-in-charge of the project at Renzo Piano Building Workshop, recalls looking down from the twenty-five-storey building: 'A river of water (the Thames) and a river of steel (the railway tracks) were at our feet.'[28] Being there in person meant that Piano could see that his first instinct was right: the building could rise as if it was generated by the energy of the rail tracks and the water.

Seeing the skyline from the vantage point of Southwark Towers gave Moolhuijzen cause to note that London stands in contrast to the 'forest' of vertical towers in New York, and instead is 'dense, even chaotic at times and largely mid to low-rise, especially south of the river. Evidently designing a very tall building for London demanded a completely different approach.' Moolhuijzen was right to think that sensitivity to height would be a major issue in London. After a long career almost exclusively building low to mid-rise, Renzo Piano agreed to design another skyscraper, the New York Times Building in New York, eighteen months after agreeing to design the Shard. The complications of building in London would mean that the fifty-two-storey New York building would be up and running five years before the Shard was completed.

Moolhuijzen's solution to distinctly English problems was to bring on board Englishman William Matthews, who became the practice's associate-in-charge of the tower project. Matthews had studied at Sheffield University and worked at design engineers RFR in Paris before joining the Renzo Piano Building Workshop. He was taking a sabbatical, driving a VW van down to South Africa, when Moolhuijzen got in touch to say that Piano was going to build a skyscraper in London and asked him to come back. Matthews abandoned the trip even though, he now says, he assumed that the scheme would never get built. The Shard would dominate his life, day in, day out, for the next dozen years. He says, 'My relationship with Irvine – and our shared trait of stubbornness – meant that I stayed on the project until the end.'

He left the Renzo Piano Building Workshop soon after the Shard was completed in 2012 and set up his own practice to undertake projects such as an apartment in nearby Borough Market and an innovative footbridge for Tintagel Castle, Cornwall. It is only now, he says, that he is thinking about becoming involved in designing a tall building again, 'but hopefully it wouldn't take twelve years'.

Standing at the top of Southwark Towers next to Irvine Sellar allowed Renzo Piano to determine that the site itself would give rise to some of the extraordinary challenges that accounted for those dozen years.

The location was extremely complex in terms of topography. Effectively, the site was initially created by the Luftwaffe when, during the Second World War, a German bomb, no doubt aimed at London Bridge station, the bridge or the band of railway tracks, destroyed the station hotel. Southwark Towers was built in its unusual Y-shape in a failed attempt to make best use of the irregular, derelict plot. The site for the prospective thousand-foot skyscraper was penned in by St Thomas Street, Guy's Hospital, New London Bridge House, the railway station and its infrastructure, the railway tracks, an Underground station and a bus station. To make matters even more complicated, the site partly sat on top of London Bridge station, which would mean building into its airspace, and was split onto two different levels.

Part of the reason why skyscrapers have a bad reputation concerns their relationship with the immediate locality and the public realm at ground level: to judge a skyscraper, it is essential to look not just at its sculptural impact on the skyline, but at its footing and its effect on the street and the sense of place.

All the problems with the Southwark Towers site would need nuanced architectural resolutions but also, on a practical level, would undoubtedly lead to tremendous problems in construction as there would be such little leeway around the base of the tower.

Many developers would not have considered building supertall on the site for practical reasons, and many a star architect would have walked away and put their name to an easier, more instantly gratifying project instead.

I ask William Matthews if he feels that the Shard was partly built out of the naivety of both architect and developer, and whether, if either of them had been more experienced in building tall, they would have walked away.

'I now associate naivety and bravery,' he says. 'They can be the same thing. We set about asking "Why not? Why not? Why not?" The practice had not done a tall building before. We were not a sort of César Pelli who could say, "I do skyscrapers – have this one."'

The likes of Pelli might well have thought that the site did not suit their building and backed off. To solve the problems, both Irvine Sellar and Renzo Piano were forced into innovation, which, after all, was both men's calling card. If either one of them or their teams had followed a more traditional approach, and had stopped asking 'Why?' or 'Why not?' at every turn, then the Shard would never have been built.

The role of guest and host were soon reversed, and in September 2000 Irvine Sellar found himself just outside Genoa in the Renzo Piano Building Workshop for the first design workshop on the project.

Piano made a joke about a shard-like splinter when Sellar came into the workshop (the architect later framed the splinter and gave it to Sellar) and gestured towards a model in which a simple, tapering piece of wood arose from the surrounding site. That was the first time that the word 'shard' was used to describe the London Bridge Tower project.

Sellar remembers the workshop process, drawing comparisons to fashion retail: 'To use clothing as an analogy, it was not like buying either a Canali or a Brioni suit off the peg; it was like being in a workshop in Savile Row and having the suit made and designed for you piece by piece.'

The architect and the developer agreed to seek planning permission for a 1,313-foot (400-metre) skyscraper, but in October 2000 altered their plans to comply with the Civil Aviation Authority's recommended height restriction of 1,000 feet (305 metres). The built Shard is a little taller at 1,016 feet (310 metres) only because it has a split-level footing and its height is measured from the lowest ground-floor point.

Having been to the site, Piano was assured that the pyramidal, multiuse structure he had sketched out over lunchtime at the Marlene Dietrich Platz would be elemental to the success of the project.

The early design was finessed through workshops, sketching, modelling and computer-aided design (CAD), pursuing the idea of a tapering tower with diminishing floor plates to suit the needs of the proposed different components. The area of the base was only approximately 43,000 square feet (4,000 m²) – not large for a huge skyscraper – while the space on the top floor (what would become the viewing gallery) was less than 3,800 square feet (350 m²). Fortunately, Piano had ongoing experience of working on a small and unusual site. Maison Hermès, which was commissioned in 1998 with phase one completed in 2001, is a ten-storey building in Tokyo that has 65,000 square feet (6,000 m²) of floor space and is 148 feet (45 metres) long. The compression of the site, however, means that the structure is a mere 36 feet (11 metres) wide.

At the heart of Piano's thinking, given the historical setting for the scheme and the lack of other very tall buildings in the immediate vicinity, was his wariness that 'we were building a tower that could appear arrogant, a challenge to the city itself'. The tapering form would make the building a more delicate presence than a rectangular tower or slab of the same height. The architect again returned to thoughts of Canaletto's spires and the masts of ships. He eventually decided that the glass façades should not rise sheer but be broken into a series of elevations diminishing in size like the mainsail and topsail of an eighteenth-century sailing ship. He noted in 2012, shortly after the building opened, 'We're talking about completely different sizes and scales. But the idea of rendering the building increasingly thin until it disintegrates into glass slivers in the sky is certainly reminiscent of these landscapes.' He told Edward Simkins in the *Sunday Telegraph* on 12 November 2000, 'Architecture is about telling stories and expressing visions, and memory is part of it. Our memory is permeated by history. That is why this design alludes to spires.'

He wished to ensure that the tallest building in Western Europe was not a hulking, dark totem of power, alien to its environment. The fracturing at the top of the spire, with the apexes of the façades never quite touching, was a conscious attempt to express some hesitancy and humility – a hard thing to achieve in a building over a thousand feet tall.

Piano wants to make buildings that seem light: he wishes to put air into the design and to make them diaphanous. He has, in a sense, been seeking immateriality ever since his and Rogers' designs for the Centre Georges Pompidou shocked the world in the 1970s. The nature of the glass that was going to form the huge façades of the Shard was going to be essential to the 'disappearing act' that Piano wished to perform.

Piano and his team would be reliant on the latest advances in glass technology to create the right effect, but a theoretical precedent for his building lies in the work of Bruno Taut shortly after the end of the First World War. Taut was influenced by his friend, the writer Paul Scheerbart, whose works such as *Glasarchitektur* (1912) reveal an obsession with glass and light. Taut himself, through his 'Crystal Chain' – a chain-letter correspondence with other expressionist architects and artists – influenced both Walter Gropius of Bauhaus and Hans Scharoun, architect of the Berliner Philharmonie (1963), in their approach to the use of glazing.

Taut's *Alpine Architektur* of 1919 featured a crystal, spired utopian city of contemplation in the Alps with the glass reflecting and becoming one with its environment. The designs were consciously antithetical to the darkness, aggression and hard machinery of the First World War. This philosophy was imbued in Bruno and his brother Max's design of a huge tapering glass tower for the Chicago Tribune Tower competition of 1922 (the design was far too adventurous and lost out to John Mead Howells and Raymond Hood's neo-Gothic fantasia).

As architecture professor Francisco Martínez Mindeguía notes, Bruno Taut's designs were consciously linked to notions of transparency, transformation, movement and dissolution.[29] These are all words that align with Piano's ambitions for his stalagmite, which itself would not have seemed out of place in Taut's Alpine city. As Piano said in 2012, the windows of the Shard were deliberately tilted so 'the building would be sensitive to changes in weather and light, like a sensor for the sky. And the London sky is one of the world's most interesting, the clouds pass by quickly, it rains and then the weather changes and the sun peeks through the clouds again. It's a fluid northern sky, and the tower somehow manages to harness its soul and reflect it.'[30]

In years to come, during the long development process of the Shard, much attention would be given to the glass. Tall buildings often have what Piano defines as a 'defensive attitude' in their architectural relationship with their locality. This is obviously borne out by façades that seemingly cannot be breached – a physically realised, hermetically sealed corporatism and lack of permeability. Piano, though, is particularly referring to the need for towers to protect themselves against the elements, notably the sun. This often leads to the use of tinted glazing, which in turn makes a building appear aggressive and almost antagonistic in its corporatism. To create a 'tower that plays with the effects of light', Piano would require glazing that was environmentally friendly in terms of both ecology and the relationship with the locality.

Piano and Sellar's desire to diminish the power and threat of the building was carried through to its base. As the Shard scheme progressed, the developer would continually seek coherency between the building and its environment. He would take responsibility for integrating a new station concourse into the architecture of the Shard, and Renzo Piano would even design the bus area in front of the station. The lower street and concourse levels of the building would be as small as practical to free up public space.

No external space was given over for car parking, so the anticipated 8,000 office workers would be dependent on the three different forms of public transport – bus, train and tube – surrounding the scheme. The building's lower level would be parallel to St Thomas Street, while the upper ground floor would adjoin the railway station concourse. This would make the building's interaction with the public realm all the more important. It was essential that the building was not an oppressive presence for either the 50 million passengers passing through one of

London's busiest stations every year, or the workers and patients at Guy's Hospital. Consequently, Piano wanted the building to be 'light on its feet' despite its immense size. Even at this early stage of the design, the team at the Renzo Piano Building Workshop were playing with ideas to cut the building as far back to the core as possible at ground level, with the structure supported by open outer columns rather than having a blanket façade on the perimeter. This would free up public space and make the building seem more permeable.

Renzo Piano has an obsession with density, and this was a principal motivation for wishing to design what both he and Irvine Sellar frequently call a 'vertical city'.

One of the architect's most significant works, at least in my reckoning, is also one of his least glamorous: it does not even feature in Wikipedia's list of over fifty Renzo Piano projects, perhaps because it is a low-cost housing development.

The project, commissioned for Rue de Meaux in Paris in 1987 and completed in 1991, says much about Piano: his sustained belief that the solution to accommodating population growth lies in densifying the city; his ability to respond to history and topological texture; and his desire to create a good environment for living. His five- and six-storey housing blocks densified the city by providing 220 affordable dwellings per hectare but he also found the space in which to create a communal garden between the blocks. The façades are graceful and still look contemporary, with terracotta cladding and glass-fibre-reinforced concrete. The blocks may be modern, but they are respectful to the grain of the nineteenth arrondissement in which they are situated, and, more broadly, to the similarly sized buildings in the Baron Haussmann boulevard plan.

Piano's interest in density persisted after the completion of that little-known project. In 1999 to 2000, a significant exhibition, *Living in the City: An Urban Renaissance*, was curated by the Architecture Foundation and shown at the Design Museum in London. The exhibition was the result of an open competition for designs and, somewhat unusually for the practice, the Renzo Piano Building Workshop participated because Piano wanted to investigate further ideas about urban regeneration,

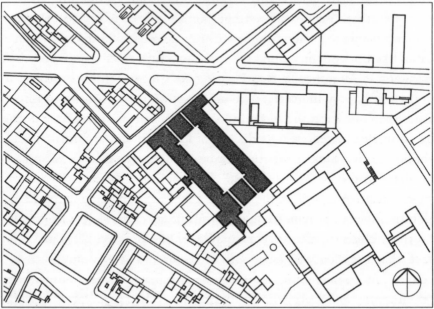

Piano's densifying design for Rue de Meaux (*above* © Michel Denancé *below* © Fondazione Renzo Piano)

mixed use and densification. It was no accident that Piano accepted Irvine Sellar's invitation to build very shortly after the exhibition closed in March 2000. The development gave him the opportunity to realise some of his ideas about densification and city-making.

The world population stood at only 1 billion (a thousand million) in the nineteenth century and now exceeds 7 billion, while by the end of the twenty-first century, it is expected that 90 per cent of the world's population growth will be in cities. London, the most populous city in Western Europe, had a population of 6.6 million in the 1981 census. The current projection for 2021 according to the Greater London Authority's London Datastore is for a population in excess of 9.2 million.[31]

There are benefits – in terms of use of space, environment and transport infrastructure, and the prevention of urban sprawl – in high densities in cities, but only if the buildings are well designed and their placement is sensible. In Paris and Barcelona, where there is greater availability of suitable sites, density can be increased to a high degree with six- to eight-storey buildings. In central London, as Peter Murray points out, 'What you have is smaller sites where, I would say quite naturally, developers want to maximise the value by building tall and in some cases planners are willing to provide them with permission to do so. Clearly those areas have to be carefully chosen.'

Piano wants to 'defend the earth' through architectural solutions. 'Cities like London must stop growing by explosion', he told the *Sunday Express* on 17 August 2003. He returned to his theme of using brownfield sites – largely post-industrial plots and wasteland – to densify the city, rather than allowing the metropolis to sprawl outwards and threaten the countryside and the character of more rural towns and villages around the city. He believes that, unlike the period of densification in the 1950s to the 1970s, which saw an explosion of high-rise council housing featuring poor architecture and careless siting, contemporary tall buildings can provide a solution while respecting the environment and the architectural history around them. Piano says, 'The city is a place that breathes and has a life of its own and without surprise the city cannot live. Cities also need beauty, new and old. Beauty is a right for cities and their people.' By contrast, suburbia is 'the disease of the peripheries'.

Sellar also sees densification as a solution. 'In central London, you have to build tall. Where else can you go?' he was quoted as saying in the *Financial Times* in 2002. 'If the city is to keep growing, it has to go upwards. And it has to keep growing otherwise it will die.'[32]

In 2000, while Sellar was developing plans for the Shard, London was the most sought-after city worldwide for commercial property, and office rents had risen by 30 per cent in a single year. He believed that building vertically rather than horizontally, and thereby not scraping up quantities of land to meet the demand for office space, made both commercial and ecological sense.

The lack of densification and high number of abandoned brownfield sites in London remains an issue, especially as the city has a seemingly endless and growing crisis in affordable housing. Perhaps we could learn from the Pinnacle@Duxton development in Singapore, a city that has much greater density than London, with seventy-five people per hectare compared to London's seventeen. The Pinnacle is a high-rise public residential development of seven towers of affordable housing, with public gardens on the twenty-sixth and fiftieth floors. The development, with its views, setting, aerial gardens and quality of build, offers associations of luxury living in an affordable environment.

Social housing is not Sellar's main area of interest. The developer may have a surprisingly altruistic strain layered within his more obvious ambitiousness and talent for deal-making, but the Shard is a commercial development and should always be understood in that context. That is not to say that Sellar does not have a solution for the affordable housing crisis – he is a constant thinker who appears to hold a forthright opinion on almost everything under the sun. He believes that massive investment in affordable housing could be brought about by the issuing of special bonds, an approach that has been taken in other countries.

More pertinent in 2000, though, was his wish to ensure that his own plan to densify the city would gain all the support it could muster in the corridors of power.

On 4 May 2000, Ken Livingstone arose from the dead. The left-wing Labour politician had been leader of the Greater London Council from 1981 to 1986, where he was such an irritant to Conservative Prime

Minister Margaret Thatcher that she contrived to abolish the GLC altogether. Leaving one of the most important financial and cultural centres in the world without any form of democratically elected overarching authority was perhaps one of the most churlish and cynical manoeuvres of the Thatcher era. The GLC was not without its problems and inefficiencies, but, fundamentally, she wiped out a tier of democracy when the people within that democracy inconveniently failed to vote in tune with her own beliefs.

'Red Ken' did not quite retreat into the shadows and he remained a key figure in the left of the Labour Party, but he was diminished without a platform. Thatcher's actions were soon generally acknowledged as disastrous when it came to both the representation and promotion of London – especially during this era when even a city seems to need a brand identity replete with a slogan and a logo. Consequently, the Greater London Authority, with an elected London Assembly, was created in 2000. When Londoners were given the chance to select the first elected Mayor of London in May of that year, they returned Livingstone to power in an easy victory. He began his acceptance speech, 'As I was saying before I was so rudely interrupted fourteen years ago . . .'

One of the first things that Sellar did when Piano agreed to design the Shard was take him to see the new mayor.

Sellar and Piano may seem an unusual partnership, but Sellar and Red Ken were an altogether more bizarre match-up – a commercial property developer and a man who had once twinned London with Managua in Nicaragua in support of the extreme socialist Sandinista government, and was now accusing his formerly beloved Labour Party of being fervently right wing.[33] Livingstone, however, would be a long-term devotee of the Shard. Sellar, in turn, thought that Red Ken's policies were good for the capital, and even made a donation to his successful mayoral re-election campaign in 2004.

In the run-up to the 2000 election, Livingstone had been occupied by the future of London and how bold architecture could both help the city's standing on the global stage and resolve some of its entrenched problems. Livingstone, in fact, had been among the attendees at the *Living in the City: An Urban Renaissance* exhibition at the Design Museum, and had seen the ideas posited by the Renzo Piano Building Workshop.

Left-winger though he is, Livingstone was worried that there were signs that London could be losing out to Paris in attracting major corporate headquarters. With little direct funding in the hands of its boroughs to attempt to regenerate run-down areas, London needed commercial investment, and a key way to achieve that was to allow the development of further tall buildings. *Property Week* on 24 November 2000 reported Ken Livingstone quipping: 'I had Gerald Ronson in my office the other day. He told me he wanted to build 41 storeys at his Liverpool Street site. I told him to go away and come back with something bigger.'

Livingstone was very much in favour of the regeneration of Southwark in particular. Piano recalls, 'Then we talked to Ken Livingstone, and it became clear that something like the Shard, in that location, was about bringing the attention of London to that deleted part, a part that was right in front of the rich City but was badly treated and a bad environment I used to call "the kingdom of darkness".'

When interviewed about the Shard development, Livingstone explained his thinking: 'In the late summer of 2000, Irvine turned up with Renzo Piano to talk about what later became known as the Shard. Here, I thought, was the potential to transform an area that had been completely forgotten. London Bridge transport connections were crap; the Northern line connection was a difficult one – but when the extension of the Jubilee line came in, suddenly there was scope to get a lot more people in and out, making it a vibrant area with a lot of work for people. It was not an area where most of the kids had been to university: it would provide the jobs that they had the skills to do. Irvine Sellar and Renzo Piano thought the same as me, that it had the potential to transform one of the most run-down areas in London.

'At the time, we were talking about a taller tower than the Shard. I said: "I shall abolish all restrictions on height and density; each thing will be judged on its merit." Some of the best housing I've seen has been really high density – for example, in Amsterdam. But the tall building has got to be architecturally impressive.'

Livingstone's thoughts about density were completely in tandem with those of Sellar and Piano: 'And this is the other thing – the misconception that London is a dense, overcrowded city. It has the same population as

New York and Paris, and twice the space. We are the least dense major world city.'

There remains some truth in this, and despite the governmental planning guidance, there is a notable lack of density around transport infrastructure. In 2015, London First and Savills, the international real-estate services provider, released a report that showed that if low density around well-connected areas of London was raised to the level of similarly connected but higher-density areas, 1.4 million homes could be built.[34]

When asked about his reaction to Irvine Sellar, Livingstone says, 'I just recognised instantly that here, in Irvine, was a man who wanted to leave a legacy, something really world-renowned. One of my planning advisers said: "It's all a scam, He'll get planning permission for this; then Renzo Piano will be dumped; they'll come back with some horrible slab; and, having granted permission, you'll never be able to unravel it." I thought: "This is just rubbish. This man really wants to leave a legacy his kids and grandkids will be proud of."'

Sellar knew that Livingstone's support was critical: even if the borough council gave unconditional planning consent for a major development, the mayor could overrule it and refuse planning permission, killing the project stone dead.

Later in 2000, on seeing the plans for Sellar's skyscraper, Livingstone said publicly, 'I support the scheme. It will be a great pity for London if it is not built. The London Borough of Southwark, which is the planning authority, is also likely to be enthusiastic.'

With the designs of Renzo Piano, and with Mayor Ken Livingstone and Fred Manson of Southwark both on board, Sellar re-entered the media fray in early November 2000 and released images of his new scheme, still called London Bridge Tower rather than the Shard. He knew there would be opposition, and he was well aware that even if he surmounted all the hurdles to come, it was possible that he would not gain the necessary investment to build the tower. But, as Sellar said to *Sunday Business* at the time, 'To be an entrepreneur, you have to be prepared to take a little more risk than the average guy.'[35] He was confident in his new scheme but prepared for the worst, as he told the *Sunday Telegraph*:

Computer rendering of a very early Shard design, before the
apex became more obviously fractured (Sellar Property Group Archive)

'I'm back with a smile, but you remain anything but complacent. If you've seen it all before you keep your eyes open.'[36]

Following his enthusiasm for the appointment of Piano, Rowan Moore in the *Evening Standard* was not disappointed now that he had a chance to view the design. He praised the lack of car parking and reliance on public transport and said that the building would not obstruct the protected views of St Paul's. 'It is, in short, the nicest skyscraper you could hope to meet,' he concluded. 'It has the makings of being an inspiring landmark, several leagues above the dull clodhoppers permitted in the past.'[37]

On 18 May 2001, the *Daily Mirror*, in a rare foray into architectural commentary, attempted to demean the scheme by calling it 'a folly, Ken's equivalent to the Dome', implying that the building would be an inflated white elephant.[38] The Millennium Dome, reborn as the O2, is now one of Great Britain's most successful entertainment centres and the Shard one of its most notable landmarks, so the claim proved unwittingly correct.

There were more notable detractors, including a parade of cultural commentators taking the opportunity to vent their thoughts on arrogant architects and greedy developers. Simon Jenkins, the former editor of *The Times*, is not an antagonist to modern architecture, having helped found the Thirties Society (which became the Twentieth Century Society) to protect recent adventures in British architecture. He has, however, consistently spoken out against changes to the London skyline, and on 18 January 2001 referred to the London Bridge Tower as a 'monster': 'These gigantic buildings have no respect for the existing skyline . . . If planning means anything, it must have some regard for the dominant Georgian and Victorian scale of London.'[39]

Sellar has come to expect such comments. On 19 July 2016, Jenkins was still calling Sellar 'egotistical' and Piano 'vain' for proposing a building of a more modest eighteen storeys in a ragged area of Paddington that is in obvious need of development.[40]

Perhaps more surprising was the criticism of Deyan Sudjic, who has long been linked to progressive architecture as the founder, with Peter Murray, of *Blueprint*, and who in November 2000 had recently taken over the forward-looking international architecture magazine *Domus*. In his article in the *Observer* on 19 November 2000, he praised Renzo Piano as 'brilliant, innovative and sensitive', but continued, 'Unfortunately, to judge by the sketches that have so far emerged, the Sellars [*sic*] tower is none of these things. The jagged pyramid with which Piano now proposes to skewer the London skyline would transform the look of the city permanently and not for the better.'[41]

He was completely against the siting of the London Bridge Tower: 'So far London's tallest towers are being clustered, which makes them

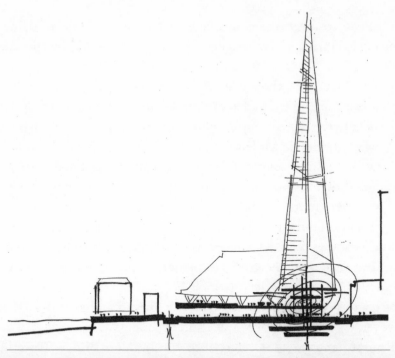

Images released to the press in March 2001 (Sellar Property Group Archive)

far less aggressive. Sellars wants to go out on a limb on his own. And that is what makes his scheme so damaging.'

Sudjic implied that Irvine Sellar was not the right man for the development: 'Maybe it is the sheer implausibility of Irvine Sellar, a one-time boutique owner who kept Swinging London in bell-bottoms, trying to build Europe's tallest skyscraper that has made the response to London's single most gargantuan project since Canary Wharf so muted.'

When I read that sentence to Sellar in 2016, he flared: 'I hate the word "boutique" and I've never sold a pair of fucking bell-bottoms in my life.'

Sudjic, though, had a point relevant to future investment in the project. As the *Estates Gazette* reported on 27 January 2001, 'the scheme has yet to gain credibility in the market. "If it had been proposed by Land Securities, everyone would believe it was going to be built," says one commentator, adding: "Even if Sellar gets consent, he has still got lots of negotiating to do before construction starts."' The article suggested that his reputation as an outspoken and aggressive entrepreneur was at odds with the cautious property market at the beginning of the millennium. The article concluded, '"He's a hard-nosed son of a bitch," says one associate. With planning consent secured, Sellar and his partners will probably sell the scheme, but then again, he might just decide to build the tower.'

Sellar was still having to counter claims that he was just puffing up the price with a view to selling the site and that a man with his inexperience of building tall could not possibly have any serious intention of going through with the project: 'This is not a speculative venture,' he stressed to Edward Simpkins in the *Sunday Telegraph*. 'Substantial sums of money are being spent and we are not talking hundreds of thousands, we are talking millions of pounds. The only people working on spec are us.'[42]

Despite the latest round of abuse thrown at the building's siting, its design and the developer himself, Irvine Sellar was still fully committed to taking the scheme through to its planning application in March 2001.

William Matthews tells me, 'There are a lot of faceless people in property, and he is certainly not faceless. He has got a sense of humour and a sense of commitment. He likes commitment. He has told me a joke a hundred times: "What's the difference between a chicken and a pig in an English breakfast? The chicken was involved. The pig was committed."'

Chapter 5

The Fear of Neighbours

Analyse the deal upfront and think of every single reason why you should or shouldn't do it, and what could go wrong. Have the post-mortem before the death.

Irvine Sellar

I've said to people who criticise me for being tough and uncompromising, 'When I was a baby in a pram, I was as innocent as the next baby in a pram. It's people like you who have made me what I am.'

Irvine Sellar

In March 2001, when Irvine Sellar placed his planning application for the London Bridge Tower with the London Borough of Southwark, he took the step of giving a cast-iron guarantee that he would not sell on the scheme once planning permission had been granted, and that the design would not be dumbed down. The guarantee was unprecedented. As well as puffing up land value, developers had a history of using top architects for the initial design of a scheme and then using lesser-known architects literally to cheapen the development after it had gained clearance, jeopardising its architectural integrity. Not so the London Bridge Tower. Sellar signed a contract with Renzo Piano agreeing that the Italian would have final say on every aspect of the design.

'There is no reason why it shouldn't be built now,' Renzo Piano was quoted as saying in *Property Week* in March 2001, 'except fear of the unknown.'

• • •

'Love your neighbour as yourself'; 'Do to others as you would have done to you.' This fundamental religious principle, common in different forms to Islam, Judaism, Buddhism and Christianity, is also known as the Golden Rule or the law of reciprocity. It is a cross-cultural tenet of civilisation, and appears to be natural to the evolution of society: in the interests of harmony, a gathering of people requires each person to treat others as they themselves wish to be treated.

Sigmund Freud pointed out in *Civilization and Its Discontents*, however, that the motor for the tenet is negative because 'Civilization has to make every effort to limit man's aggressive drives', and suggested that it is a failure:

> For all the effort invested in it, this cultural endeavour has so far not achieved very much . . . There comes a point at which each of us abandons, as illusions, the expectations he pinned to his fellow men when he was young and can appreciate how difficult and painful his life is made by their ill will.[43]

The religious principle is born out of our natural animosity to each other; effectively, it sets a rule of law to protect one another from the lack of trust and the hatred, aggression and war that can emerge from the fear of otherness, the sense of threat and the staking of territory. Rather than loving our neighbours, our inclination is to hate them.

The problem with a tall building, especially one that changes the skyline, is that it is everybody's neighbour.

Architecture is a multi-layered narrative – social, cultural, aesthetic, topological, spatial and textural – and, as every A-level English or film student knows, narrative is fed by conflict. Space can be defined as the area of conflict between the resident and the newcomer: the stranger who fills the void. The new neighbour who wishes to fill space evokes in us not love but hostility and fear of dominance. Rather than being welcomed unconditionally with open arms, they are viewed with fear and suspicion, and their every move is subjected to the most intense scrutiny.

If the new neighbour is made in our own image – in that they take our shape and seem to be born of the same culture – we feel less fear. No matter how liberal and open-minded we might be, it is the obviously new and different that threatens.

Britain's history of dislike for not just new buildings but entire new waves of architecture is long. London's cultural guardians sometimes protest against new buildings because they go against the grain of what they regard as a largely Victorian and Georgian city. It is as if those eras of grand building themselves did not meet resistance from naysayers using the same arguments about the aberrational change (on a greater scale than is possible today) to the character of London.

Many Georgian architect-builders and their clients disliked the late medieval and wished to return to the classical; the Victorians disliked the new-fangled neo-classicism of the Georgian and Regency periods and sought inspiration in medievalism; modernism draws more from classicism than it does from the Victorian Gothic; and the denouncers of modernism and its bastardisations wish to return to the Victorian and Georgian. We seek validation in the new by looking for the past, but the very recent past is too fresh.

As Jonathan Meades has said: 'It is evident that if an audience is asked what form a new housing development should take, it will reply like a) or like b) – something with which it is already familiar, something extant, not something new, not something which is yet uninvented. The consensual cannot help but be feeble.'[44]

New adventures in architecture take time to settle, be understood and win our affection – the Tour d'Eiffel spoiled the view until it *became* the view. The neighbour must prove themselves to be a valuable component of society rather than a threat, but the period required for acceptance is shortening. In Britain, we are now protecting 'new' architecture that is only forty or fifty years old – even that punchbag brutalism has its admirers beyond the architecture cognoscenti – and we more readily fall in love with contemporary design. This is tied to the design revolution of the 1960s through the democratisation of avant-garde fashion, in which Irvine Sellar played a significant part, and the birth of Habitat – the bringing of interesting contemporary design into the standard home. Latterly, a spread of television programmes has further helped to introduce us to the value of new design, while the speed and range of communication mean that we are more aware of fashion in architecture and the work of leading architects. We are quicker to understand that the new neighbour may not be the enemy, and that their presence may be culturally enriching rather than destructive.

Nonetheless, there remains a great level of fear when it comes to the tall building, the new neighbour whose presence is so inescapable. The desire to build tall is ancient, from earthworks in Neolithic Britain to the pyramids of Giza to Pharos, the Great Lighthouse of Alexander the Great, pagoda-style temples in the Far East and the Gothic cathedral in Ulm. As Philip Johnson, the father of the skyscraper, said, 'I think the interesting question is why does man want to build to the sky. What is there about the desire for domination, or to reach God, or for private pride? . . . Every civilization is touched by that desire.'[45] Humans are hard-wired, in a primal sense, to want to build tall, to mark out their territory and blast upwards so they can be the biggest and the best – to be the aggressive neighbour in Freudian terms. Lord Rogers points towards building tall as a natural phenomenon: 'If our ancestors had taken the same attitude to new buildings as those who now foolishly resist the march of the skyscrapers, we would never have moved out of caves.'[46]

As a society, however, we fear change and we fear being dominated by the aggression of others, and a thousand-foot tower can both change and dominate our city. We feel we own our skyline as it is sewn into our sense of identity, it is part of our *terroir*, and the person who changes it has changed our sense of self without our personal permission.

The fear also relates to safety, in both a social and a structural sense. The fear of the high-rise has been channelled into media coverage and popular culture. A mugging that happens in a high-rise is yet another crime in a lawless tower block; a mugging that happens on a Victorian street is just a mugging.

The fear of tall buildings found a place in the Bible through the tale of the Tower of Babel, and some latter-day heavy hitters of the literary world have preyed on the uneasiness. Aldous Huxley's *Brave New World* (1932) and George Orwell's *Nineteen Eighty-four* (1949) to some extent lean on the high-rise, while Anthony Burgess and J. G. Ballard more obviously used the residential tower block to create a dystopia and gave it a role in the abasement of humanity.

Burgess's *A Clockwork Orange* (1962) made the link between residential tower blocks and the almost amoral, extreme violence of the sociopathic droogs. Alex, the fifteen-year-old anti-hero, lives on the tenth floor of the indecorously named 'Municipal Flatblock 18A' but his victims, in what is perhaps the most frightening scene of the book, live in a more typically English cottage called 'Home'.[47]

Richard Wilder, the main character in J. G. Ballard's *High-Rise* (1975, and the 2016 film) thinks: 'Living in high-rises required a special type of behaviour, one that was acquiescent, restrained, perhaps even slightly mad. A psychotic would have a ball here.'[48] Set in a tall building in the hinterland of London – precursor to the development of the Docklands but inspired by Ernö Goldfinger's recently completed Trellick Tower (1972) in North Kensington – the clean, cutting-edge modernist design cannot hide the cancer of social hierarchy and the savagery of the human beast. Ballard called his dystopian totem a 'small vertical city'. Both Irvine Sellar and Renzo Piano innocently use the same term to describe the Shard but, of course, they do not share Ballard's fear of urban density and its effect on human interaction.

The time in which Ballard was writing is notable: by then the failure of the high-rise experiment in social housing was acknowledged. Housing estates built in the UK were, at least according to the standard characterisation, crime-infested to the point of lawlessness and badly maintained, with the lift more likely to serve as a urinal than a mode of vertical transport. The buildings were symbols of oppression, of the vicious dehumanisation of the disenfranchised, raised on high yet denied the opportunity to flower in the light, and reduced to immoral, animalistic behaviour. Rather than the modernist utopia that had been envisioned, tower blocks were the badlands of the British imagination.

The image has persisted. In Joe Cornish's 2011 film *Attack the Block*, the high-rise is the symbol of criminality, immorality and violent behaviour – the anti-social. The people in the block do not know their neighbours, and the fear of the high-rise and the fear of neighbours is intrinsically linked. In the end, the theme of redemption is that of neighbourliness. In a time of conflict (aliens attacking the earth, no less), the neighbours come together as a stronger force, and hate thy neighbour becomes love thy neighbour, but this is in spite of the building.

The British dislike for the high-rise was partly fuelled by the collapse of Ronan Point, a twenty-three-storey building in Newham, east London, on 15 May 1968, just two months after construction was completed. Four people died and seventeen were injured when a domestic gas explosion caused the end of the building to collapse. Poor design and construction, which involved large panel system (LPS) prefabrication, were deemed responsible for the building's inability to withstand the explosion. Many tall buildings constructed using the LPS system were demolished in the succeeding decades, accompanied by an almost wholesale move away from the construction of high-rise social housing.

If we felt more secure as construction techniques advanced, films like *The Towering Inferno* (1974) and then the reality of the collapse of the World Trade Center towers on 11 September 2001 – which occurred while the Shard's planning application was being assessed – questioned our ability to ensure safety up in the sky.

The terrorist attacks appeared to mark a cataclysmic shift in the world order and the West – and especially its symbols of corporate excess – seemed in direct peril. For a while, the events of 9 September 2001 threatened to signal the death of the skyscraper as there was considerable fear that major firms were going to quit high-rises, and such projects would never receive funding again.

Irvine Sellar recalls, 'It didn't exactly help that it was in the minds of everybody that two planes had crashed into the twin towers and destroyed 4,000 lives while we were in the middle of the planning process at Southwark.' He remained ostensibly calm and, in the *Evening Standard* on 17 September 2001, rebuffed the idea that the tragedy marked the end of the high-rise: 'Anyone who tries to take advantage of this by saying tall towers will be in trouble is wide of the mark. Life goes on.'

He was right – there was barely a blip in the worldwide momentum to build tall, and the top six tallest buildings in the world were all built after 9/11 – but the fear, at least momentarily, did seem all-encompassing.

As the tallest prospective tower in Western Europe, Sellar knew that the safety of his scheme would come under immense scrutiny, and he wanted to ensure that his building could not collapse to the ground in the manner of the North and South Towers, whatever future event might unfold. He reacted immediately and ordered a review of the London Bridge Tower's design to examine evacuation procedures, staircase widths, the strength of the steel with a view to high impact on the building, and the idea of having independent staircases and super-strength floors every fifteen storeys.

The tower's concrete core would be built to withstand extreme heat, unlike the steel frame of the World Trade Center, and the core would be surrounded by supporting 'outrigger' columns. Fireproof lifts would be situated inside the core, and other lifts would give onto specially ventilated corridors to reduce the deadly threat of smoke inhalation. Sellar, says, 'To give you an analogy, the safety of a 1960s car and a 2016 car are light years from each other – no air bags, no seat belts, and so on. Safety technology moves on for buildings too.'

As well as playing on our fear of heights, *The Towering Inferno* also pointed to the skyscraper as an object of vanity, where the egos of the architect and developer push upwards at the cost of the humane. Increasingly, in London, the skyscraper has been cast as villainous weaponry in the rise of careless corporatism. The tall buildings of the City are the vertical feeding troughs of the bankers, the heedless pariahs who could destroy our security and cost us billions with a few clicks of a mouse intended to fill their already bulging pockets. Connection is made between the buildings' loftiness and the inhumanity of their inhabitants: they are so high – so remote, so superior – they see us as little worker ants on the ground, no longer worthy of consideration. So they click the mouse and let chaos reign. It is no accident that, in Bret Easton Ellis's *American Psycho* (1991), the superficial, cold-blooded killer Patrick Bateman is a Wall Street banker living on the eleventh floor of a high-rise tower.

Canary Wharf in the Docklands can be portrayed as even worse than the numb City: it is an alien island of silver towers, representing an international class of wealthy Superlondoners, while all around it there is an Underlondon of the disenfranchised of Tower Hamlets, a borough with extremely high rates of long-term illness, premature death and unemployment. In James Scudamore's novel *Heliopolis* (2009), meanwhile, the corporate magnate Zé Fischer Carnicelli 'hasn't been down to street level in the city for fifteen years . . . During the day, he might hop to another high-rise to meet somebody for lunch, or to attend an afternoon meeting, but he never touches the pavement.'[49]

The high-rise, according to our folklore, is removed from humanity in its role of servicing those at both ends of the financial spectrum.

The result of this is that when a scheme for a new skyscraper in London is announced, it is always – without fail – met with some level of fear. It is not only a case of 'not in my backyard' – although the NIMBY does have a role to play – it's a case of 'not in my city'.

The skyscraper changes our world and alters our history, and once it is in place the change is likely to be permanent. The only hope is to stop the threat at source: to prevent the building emerging out of the ground in the first place; once the building is constructed, we are powerless.

Consequently, antagonists must don their battledress early and try to win the media war, often making the most extraordinary claims of cultural Armageddon and the ruination of our history and society if the particular scheme becomes reality. When it comes to describing architects and developers, there is no form of building that draws out the labels 'aggressive' and 'egomaniac' with such regularity, and the usual dull references to the phallic are often thrown in for good measure.

Peter Murray believes that, because of the rise of the Gherkin and the Shard, which have both become beloved buildings at a faster rate than previously imaginable, today such critics may no longer be giving voice to a consensus in their readership; good architecture has reduced the fear factor. 'Whereas those people who are against tall buildings think they have God – and the majority of the population – on their side, I don't think that is the case. The antagonism to tall buildings per se is relatively limited, and I think there is a much larger group who think that tall buildings are fine, but let's make them good when we do them. And the cheesy answer to that is: hire a good architect.'

'It's common sense,' Sellar says. 'You're building tall, and a lot of tall buildings are unattractive, and a permanent scar on the skyline, whereas if you build low density, the visibility is not as blatant. Therefore, if you build tall, in my view, you have got to build exceptionally well. It's got to

Empire State Building (© ONiONA Studio) and
Chrysler Building, New York (© andyparker 72)

International Financial Centre, Hong Kong (© Ashwin)

be a work of art on the skyline. There are some very ugly tall buildings, typically a fridge, straight up and down and maximising the space, and the other one, which is more than maximising by leaning outwards, is taking the piss. It's not clever.'

His own taste veers towards the International Finance Centre towers (2003) in Hong Kong, which are among César Pelli's more interesting buildings. 'They are beautifully elegant, impressive, the space is good. I do like a building to be elegant.' He is also an admirer of the Golden Age of the skyscraper: 'New York, I think, has got a certain something. The Empire State is a powerful building. The Chrysler Building is a great-looking building – an art deco masterpiece.'

The full antidote for fear of the skyscraper is to make sure that the building gives back to the city in terms of good design, its relationship

ne and Elizabeth Sellar on their wedding day, 1964.

e of Irvine Sellar's stores on Carnaby Street in the late 1960s. (*© Michael Putland/Getty Images*)

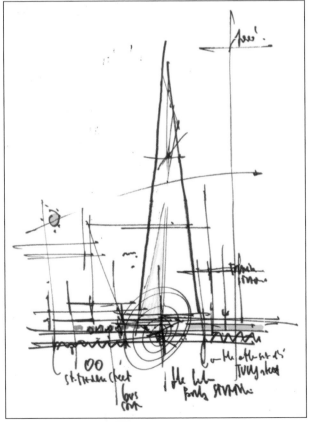

(above) Detail of *The River Thames wit*
St Paul's Cathedral on Lord Mayor's Da
(1747–8) by Canaletto. *(Lobkowicz Palace*
Prague Castle, Czech Republic/Bridgeman Images

(left) Early Renzo Piano sketch of the
Shard. *(© RPBW)*

ws of Shard construction. *(top left, top right: © Rob Telford; above: © Michael Murphy/Getty Images)*

Irvine Sellar in front of a visualisation of the Shard in its Thames-side setting, January 2010.
(© Bloomberg/Getty Images)

Stills from *The Tallest Tower: Build the Shard*. (© DCD Publishing)

(above) Construction workers raising a glazing unit. *(photo by View Pictures/Getty Images)*

(right) Cleaning the Shard's façade during construction, c. 2011. *(© Rob Telford)*

(left) Renzo Piano and Irvine Sellar shaking hands at the top of the Shard, with Joost Moolhuijzen and William Matthews, April 2012. *(© Renée Smith)*

(below) Shard inauguration: HE Sheikh Abdulla bin Saoud Al Thani, Boris Johnson, HE Ali Shareef Al-Emadi, HRH The Duke of York, HE Sheikh Hamad bin Jassim bin Jaber Al Thani, Irvine Sellar and Renzo Piano. *(© Colin Baldwin)*

(above) The laser show marking the opening of the Shard, with spectators lining both Southwark Bridge and Millennium Bridge. *(top: © Eachat; above: © Rob Telford)*

(below) Shard and News Building looking east. *(© Cultura RM Exclusive/Richard Seymour/Getty Images)*

(above) Shard spire looking east to Canary Wharf. *(© Jason Hawkes)*

(left) View up Shard elevation. *(© Shangri-La International Hotel Management Ltd)*

(top) Shard and the almost completed News Building looking west. *(© Cultura Exclusive/Leon Sosra)*

(above) Panorama looking south. *(© joegolby)*

(below) London Bridge and Shard. *(© Ray Wise)*

e Red Arrows fly past the Shard to celebrate the 75th anniversary of VE Day, 2015.
rlie Crowhurst/Getty Images)

Shard and City outline at dusk.
(© Shomos Uddin)

Shard and News Building, day and night. *(© Jason Hawkes)*

(above) View up fracture of the Shard.
(© Bora Tosun Stone/EyeEm/Getty Images)

(left) Shard spire and moon.
(Jeremy O'Donnell/Getty Images)

(top) South across river with Shard on right. *(© Zoltan Gabor/Shutterstock)*

(bottom) Panorama looking north. *(© Greg Fonne)*

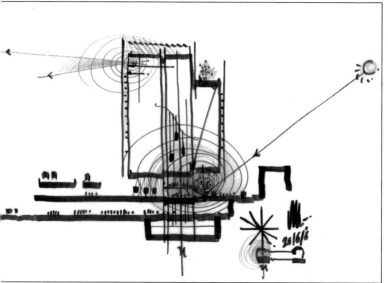

Renzo Piano's sketch of the News Building. *(© RPBW)*

(above and left) The News Building. *(© Michel Denancé)*

(right) The roof terrce of the News Building with a view of the Shard. *(© Michel Denancé)*

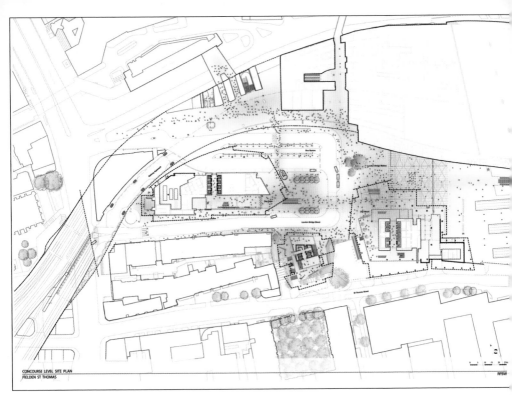

(above) Plan of the London Bridge Quarter. *(© RPBW)*
(below) Visualisations of Shard Place. *(Miller Hare, © RPBW)*

sualisation of Shard Place. *(© RPBW)*

(left) Premier City View room. *(© Shangri-La International Hotel Management Ltd)*

(below) Ground-floor lobby at the Shangri-La. *(© Shangri-La International Hotel Management Ltd)*

Irvine Sellar with a model of the Shard and News Building. *(Chris Ratcliffe / Bloomberg via Getty Images)*

with the public realm and the possibility of a feeling of city ownership through permeability, such as a publicly accessible viewing gallery. Architecturally, there is a responsibility to ensure that skyscrapers are not disassociated from society, that they are not vertical ghettoes for rich or poor; there needs to be porousness, accessibility and integration into the public realm, both physically and more philosophically. They must be part of the city and offer a true sense of it: skylines define cities so they should mean 'home'; they should mean 'place' with specificity and not just 'another place'.

This was part and parcel of the vision of the developer and the architect of the Shard from the outset when they sat down together in Berlin. And this was fully understood by the London Borough of Southwark, even after their own visionary, Fred Manson, had moved on in 2001 to work as an advisor and then to join Thomas Heatherwick's design practice in 2004.

On 11 March 2002, after a whole year of to-ing and fro-ing between architect, developer and the borough council in order to finesse the scheme, the London Borough of Southwark resolved to grant planning permission to the London Bridge Tower. Ken Livingstone, the Mayor of London, declared that he fully supported the council's decision.

Irvine Sellar, it seemed, had won the argument that the Shard would be a positive new landmark for London. The scheme for the tallest tower in Western Europe had finally been given the green light.

Or had it?

The growing hysteria surrounding the threat that London would become an unregulated skyscraper city led the Greater London Assembly's seven-strong planning committee to publish 'Behind Closed Doors'. In the report, Mayor Livingstone was accused of having 'secret garden' meetings with major property developers including Irvine Sellar, making him 'vulnerable to accusations of improper influence'. Livingstone retorted that he had offered to have an independent observer at all planning meetings, but the Assembly had declined. The idea that a Mayor of London should have his meetings in public is bizarre. (After all, how could the rule only be applied to planning? Every single one of his meetings on all subjects would have to be conducted in public.) Sellar said about his own talk with Livingstone: 'It was just a routine meeting to discuss an application. There was nothing secret about it. Forcing the mayor to have all his meetings in public would just slow down the process. Ken Livingstone is very hands-on, and you can't run everything by committee.'[50] Nevertheless, the *Evening Standard* dedicated a full page to the story under the headline 'The 10 schemes Mayor Ken backed behind closed doors' on 10 June 2002. The Shard figured prominently.

Some heavyweight commentators also feared that machinations were under way to allow the supposedly unfettered rise of the skyscraper, a form at odds with London's architectural culture.

Robert Adam, a leading traditional architect whose ideas bear far more relation to the neo-classical work of his eighteenth-century namesake than anything that has emerged in the last century, wrote of the Shard and the Gherkin, 'The Modernism is so ideologically bankrupt that it has nothing left to say and subsists on a lumpen confidence in its own future. All it can advance is abstract shape making. These buildings are architectural one-liners.'[51]

Adam may be conservative in outlook, and he may give intellectual muscle to what can be deemed a matter of taste, but he was far from alone in his disquiet. Jonathan Glancey in the *Guardian* on 29 March 2002 asked of the Shard, 'Do we need another air-conditioned totem pole raised in homage to London's god, Mammon? . . . Might the tower end up as a hubristic folly rather than a real contribution to the economy and culture of the city?'[52]

Piano was forced to counter in the same article: 'We want it to be a democratic project. We will only do it if we can achieve the right quality of design and construction. And, with Irvine, who is a clever man with a very good sense of humour, we have signed binding legal documents that mean that neither the design nor the construction will be skimped on.' The architect explained, 'We need to make a building that doesn't shut people out, one that responds to local as well as city-wide needs. A building of this scale, this ambition, cannot be just for private gain; it becomes a public project privately financed . . . Can I ask you to trust me?'

Glancey was willing to take the gamble but the recent images of the London Bridge Tower that had some critics talking of elegance and

Robert Adam's Sackler Library, Oxford, completed in 2001 (© Doctor Jools)

delicateness still left Deyan Sudjic cold: 'They are meant to represent the scheme in its best light,' he wrote in the *Observer* on 17 March 2002, 'but succeed only in showing a stubbornly stiff cliff-like structure swaggering across the skyline.' The general mood was so against tall buildings that he confidently predicted that 'the fad is likely to turn out to be just as short-lived as Irvine Sellar's loon pants were 30 years ago'.[53]

It was not the critics or jocular references to his past that were the developer's real concern; by now, Adam and Sudjic were among very few commentators that were criticising the design of the building. His problem was that English Heritage and the Commission for Architecture and the Built Environment (CABE) still felt the fear.

As public bodies whose raison d'être is to protect the United Kingdom's architectural heritage and the current built environment, it was of course right and proper that they should consider whether the

London Bridge Tower scheme would damage the existing fabric of London. If they were unhappy with the scheme, their opinion could carry enough weight to ensure that the Deputy Prime Minister would call in the planning application for review. An extremely expensive and time-consuming public inquiry would then ensue, after which the Deputy Prime Minister could overturn the London Borough of Southwark's decision to grant planning permission. Even if consent was seconded by the Deputy Prime Minister, the process could take eighteen months. The threat of having to go to public inquiry had been enough to stop several high-profile projects dead in their tracks and withdraw their planning application.

Somewhat surprisingly, Simon Thurley of English Heritage used sensational language that would not be out of place in a cheap tabloid when he weighed into the argument, claiming that the building would 'put a spike into the heart of historic London . . . If built, it would be Europe's tallest building and London's greatest folly'.[54] The pejorative use of the name 'spike' for the tower caught on for a while, before 'shard' became standard. Perhaps Thurley felt he had to counter in such extreme terms because Ken Livingstone, in November 2001, had referred to English Heritage as 'the Taliban of British architecture' and 'the greatest threat to the economy of London since Adolf Hitler'.[55]

The organisation was particularly worried about the damage the tall tower would do to views of St Paul's Cathedral and the Tower of London, which were protected. English Heritage had supported the planning application of 30 St Mary Axe – Norman Foster's Gherkin – making their approach to building tall erratic in some people's eyes, but here they were interested in protecting particular sightlines of the cathedral from the Hampstead area.

English Heritage claimed that the Shard was 'a structure that would destroy forever some of the most famous views of London and create an inhuman environment around its already congested base'.[56] It was hard to perceive exactly how the site around the base of Southwark Towers could become more inhuman than it already was, but an authoritative assessment would lie in the hands of CABE, not the heritage body, in any case.

CABE itself had reservations about the public realm around the base of the site. As it was an extremely complicated, split-level site, surrounded by pedestrian routeways and transport infrastructure with very high usage, CABE wanted to seek the best possible solution for the area. The age-old problem with urban planning in a built-up area is attempting to create synthesis between a range of different commercial developments, the public realm that comes under the council's purview and transport infrastructure.

As Peter Murray says about the ongoing and much criticised developments near Vauxhall Bridge, 'One area that we don't discuss enough is how buildings hit the ground and what that creates. Nine Elms is going to be one of those areas where the way the buildings hit the ground doesn't join up to create a coherent piece of city. Each site is designed by a different architect with a different developer and they all want to do a different thing.'

Sellar and Piano had first presented their scheme to CABE, headed by Sir Stuart Lipton, on 20 December 2000. At that point, CABE believed that there was little justification for the tower. As *Property Week* reported in January 2001, 'Its objection will severely damage Sellar's chances of winning planning permission from Southwark Council for the project. When CABE raised concerns about Frogmore's plans for an office scheme at Westminster Bridge Road last year, Lambeth council refused permission, sending the developer back to the drawing board.'

CABE claimed that the Shard could be much shorter than the planned 1,016 feet and still accommodate the same amount of floor space (although that would likely mean straightening the façade from the incline; this would make the building perpendicular and it would therefore loom above ground level and appear more aggressively imposing from a distance). They also believed that the building would have inadequate access at ground-floor level and were concerned about the impact of the tower on the London Bridge area.

Over the course of the next eighteen months, with Southwark lauding the effect the building would have on the regeneration of London Bridge, CABE praised Renzo Piano's superior architectural design of the building, and offered no further criticism about its proposed height or placement – it appeared to be in no agreement with English Heritage and Historic London Palaces that the London Bridge Tower would interfere with the Tower of London. CABE commissioners visited the Tower of London on reconnaissance and joked: 'We spoke to a senior beefeater who said he could not see what all the fuss was about. We regarded a beefeater as a significant stakeholder.'[57] CABE's reservations therefore boiled down to the building's relationship with the public realm.

In an attempt to provide some coordination, Paul Evans of the London Borough of Southwark set up a Strategic Development Management Group consisting of all parties involved in the development of London Bridge station and the surrounding area: the borough, the Greater London Authority, Transport for London, Network Rail, the Strategic Rail Authority, the Sellar Property Group and all other landowners and potential developers, as well as CABE. It was impossible belatedly to create a masterplan, as the parcels of land were in the hands of so many different entities, but the group began to originate a looser framework plan for the London Bridge area.

Some of CABE's problems with the public realm related to aspects outside the red-line boundary of the London Bridge Tower development, so they were beyond Irvine Sellar's control. Sellar was willing to improve the tower's relationship to its environment but he could only do so by working with all concerned parties, and the strategic group would help advance this. He was already making considerable progress in his discussions with Network Rail about improving London Bridge station through its structural relationship with the development scheme. He also proposed to create a public piazza outside his red-line boundary at the front of the station and the foot of the tower.

Despite Sellar's manoeuvres and Southwark's resolution to grant planning permission to the tower, CABE's deputy chairman Paul Finch stated that permission should still be denied: 'CABE's view is that the building holds out promise, but has not succeeded in providing adequate settings or surroundings. Until this improves we think the planning application should be refused. The urban setting of the tallest building in Europe is of great importance.' Therefore, CABE was joining forces with English Heritage and Historic Royal Palaces in calling for a public inquiry into the London Bridge Tower's planning application.

While Sellar was not surprised by the call from English Heritage and Historic Royal Palaces for an inquiry, he was shocked that CABE had joined the call on the grounds that permission should be withheld until there was a masterplan for the London Bridge area – a masterplan that no commercial property developer had any power to create or enforce themselves. If permission were denied on these grounds, Sellar felt he would have been effectively prosecuted for what amounted to a failure of state governance. As he says, 'I only owned what I owned.'

Richard Rogers was unhappy with CABE's assessment, writing to Stuart Lipton, 'Only very occasionally are we confronted with a design of integrity and vision. This is such a design and now is the time to back it fully and unambiguously.'[58]

The argument against tall buildings was increasingly heated. There was great animosity towards the pro-skyscraper London Plan that Livingstone was in the course of originating, and around this time the London Borough of Westminster refused to share the mayor's, Southwark's and the City's enthusiasm for well-designed tall buildings, no matter the credentials of the architects: it dismissed both Lord Rogers' designs for the developer Chelsfield's forty-two-storey tower for Paddington Basin and Nicholas Grimshaw's forty-seven-storey one at nearby Paddington station, with both parties being advised to reduce the size of the buildings.

The government, meanwhile, had forced the City development of Heron Tower (now officially named 110 Bishopsgate) to undergo a public inquiry from 22 October 2001, but the scheme was finally granted planning permission on 22 July 2002. Sellar responded in *The Times* the next day, 'This is a breakthrough for London. You know I am a fan of tall buildings. There are similarities and differences between Heron's scheme [and the London Bridge Tower]. As to the decision's effect we will just have to wait and see.'[59]

The response from Peter Rees, chief planner for the City of London, did not help matters. Rees was reported to be advising Ronson to sue if the much taller Shard was allowed to progress without a similar public inquiry: the Heron inquiry was believed to have cost the developer £4 million in legal fees.

Just two days later, on 24 July 2002, the worst thing that could happen to a developer happened: the London Bridge Tower scheme was called to public inquiry by the Deputy Prime Minister of the Labour government, who had the power to kill the project stone dead.

The Deputy Prime Minister, who also held the honorific cabinet post of First Secretary of State, was John Prescott, a man more famous for hitting a protesting farm worker with a left jab than for his familiarity with the aesthetic, social and historical consequences of contemporary architecture. He was a working-class northerner, a self-styled 'man of the people', whose role in the New Labour government was to make sure it still appeared to have at least a nominal connection to the party's traditional trade union supporters who were less enamoured by the cosmopolitan Blairites. (In 2015, Prescott joked about the punching incident: 'Tony Blair rang me and he said "Are you OK?" and I said "Yes. I was just carrying out your orders. You told us to connect with the electorate, so I did."'[60])

Prescott said the scheme 'may conflict with national policies on important matters; could have significant effects beyond their immediate locality; give rise to substantial regional or national controversy; and raise significant architectural and urban design issues'. There was an implication that Prescott would assess the proposal for 'good design', which was interesting, not only because he would be an unusual choice as the arbiter of architectural taste, but also because aesthetics do not have an objective measure. The best that scientific research can do when it comes to objectifying beauty are tests that show that symmetry is a factor in attraction between humans, but people nonetheless differ wildly in what they find attractive. In any case, symmetry is not the greatest of architectural ambitions.

John Prescott would be led by the findings of John Gray, a trained architect he appointed as inspector to lead the inquiry, which would not even begin for another nine months, on 15 April 2003. It was expected to last for a couple of months, and then there would likely be a wait of several more months before Prescott made his final decision – the process for the Heron Tower application was regarded as 'speedy' in taking sixteen months from being called in to receiving clearance.

Meanwhile, Sellar and his partners would spend millions in legal representation, no one would invest in their project, construction would be delayed possibly for years, and it was impossible to predict what the economy or market for office space would be like so far in the future.

Every building needs strong foundations, and the London Bridge Tower was being projected onto quicksand.

I asked Renzo Piano whether he thought the inquiry was the death knell for the Shard. 'You have to fight for it,' he answered. 'Making a project is about optimism. You can be stupidly optimistic, but optimism is not a stupid thing. Irvine and I were born around the same time. We were too young really to suffer the Second World War, but when the war was over, every day that passed, things are getting better: the food on the table, the state of the street, the smile of your mother – time makes things better. So, this is not stupid optimism – you grow with this idea that things will get better. So with the Shard, in those bad moments I thought – this is a personal, irrational interpretation – it will be okay, something will happen.'

Sellar may have rued the day when he had stood at the top of Southwark Towers and decided to build the tallest tower in Western Europe rather than sitting on his safe investment, collecting the rent, and selling it on for a substantial profit.

Yet Sellar was sanguine and, as Piano indicates, optimistic – although his optimism is far from blind. The developer is fond of generating maxims, and one of his favourites is 'Analyse the deal upfront and think of every single reason why you should or shouldn't do it, and what could go wrong. Have the post-mortem before the death.' He had expected the planning application to be called in: politically the government needed to show that it was not simply giving the green light to major, skyline-changing developments without due consideration, and it could not ignore the fears of its own advisory bodies. The government was far less likely to heed the advice of Ken Livingstone, whose relationship with the Labour Party of Tony Blair was so bad that he had been forced to stand as an Independent in the mayoral election.

One would assume that the development was put into effective stasis until the inquiry concluded. Sellar and stasis, however, are not compatible words, and he was still looking at all the angles, ready to seize any opportunity to make his vision real.

Chapter 6

The Inquiry

I'm a genius at picking geniuses.

Irvine Sellar

'$\mathbf{A}$nd then a rather difficult chapter began,' Renzo Piano recalled. 'Our project was effectively put on trial.'[61] It took eighteen months from planning permission being provisionally granted by the London Borough of Southwark until the Deputy Prime Minister made his final decision. In particular, in the ten months between 24 July 2002, when the Shard application was called in by John Prescott, and the public inquiry that began on 15 April 2003, Sellar, his team and the Renzo Piano Building Workshop worked hard on the design. In the renderings revealed in March 2003, the top of the London Bridge Tower more obviously looked like a splintered shard than a point. The analogy 'shard of glass' had begun to take hold and capture the public imagination, and the design made more obvious the connection to Piano's initial conception of masts and rigging. The sculptural fracturing feathered the form into the sky in a manner slightly reminiscent of a wigwam.

The design was acquiring more admirers due to its multi-faceted façade, as well as its impression of transparency rather than solidity despite its great size. Piano had wanted the building to express humility in its relationship with London, but the design was never intended to be timid. When Piano refers to contextual design, he is not seeking anonymity for a building. As Richard Morrison said in *The Times* on

17 March 2003, 'you don't hire the grand Piano unless you want to make a statement'. Richard Rogers, meanwhile, was warming up for the inquiry by calling the existing London skyline 'unbelievably boring'.[62]

To improve the financial viability of the scheme, a sixteen-storey 'backpack' of offices, projecting east along St Thomas Street, was added to the design, increasing the floor plate at the lower levels to make up for the reduction caused by the taper.

Sellar told the *Architects' Journal* on 13 March 2003, 'We're committed to the quality of our scheme and to taking it forward. We think great design and regeneration is a good and proper thing for Southwark – and good design cannot do any harm. If you saw a picture of Sydney without the Sydney Opera House, you wouldn't know where it was.'

On behalf of Teighmore, the company that owned Southwark Towers for the shareholders, Sellar worked closely with the Strategic Development Management Group for London Bridge, convened by Dr Evans of the London Borough of Southwark, and, by the time the inquiry began, had finalised the principles of a Section 106 agreement with the council, Network Rail and other interested parties.

Section 106 of the Town and Country Planning Act 1990 covers 'developers' contributions', through which a proposal is made acceptable in planning terms by mitigating the impact of a development with actions or payments designed to improve an area.[63] S106 agreements have often been used effectively to attempt to counteract the withdrawal of the state as a builder of social housing by pushing the responsibility for funding affordable housing onto a commercial developer: a residential development may, therefore, include a percentage of affordable housing, or the developer will make a payment towards affordable or social housing elsewhere. As Joost Moolhuijzen has written: 'London is a peculiar place when it comes to urban planning, interesting but still peculiar. It is a city of merchants where almost everything is negotiable; no grand masterplans have been executed or exist as they do in cities like Paris.'[64] Mercantile London, which has been historically responsible for the capital's unregulated growth, is caught in an unusual and sometimes complex relationship with the city's authorities because of social need.

Despite the fact that S106 agreements are enforceable by injunction, developers have been known to abuse them on the grounds that, due to a change in circumstances, fulfilment of all the provisions is no longer financially tenable. Faced with the threat that the development will cease altogether, councils have sometimes had to concede.

The agreement relating to the building of the Shard was complicated by the way that the site was entangled with both the local transport infrastructure and a complex public realm, both of which were in dire need of improvement. This took into account, as far as possible, the reservations of the Commission for Architecture and the Built Environment.

Sellar's wish to create a piazza had been put on hold as a result of the Network Rail masterplan for the redevelopment of London Bridge station being at least temporarily shelved (Network Rail had taken over Railtrack in 2002), but he pledged £2 million for improvements to the Underground, £3 million for bus facilities, a roof for the rail station concourse which would connect to the tower, and a further £3.45 million on other entities with a view to improving the public realm of the site. He also made commitments for funds towards affordable housing and job creation in Southwark. Piano designed canopies for the lower levels of the Shard in order greatly to reduce the impact that downdraughts – which had always been a problem within the London Bridge mini-cluster – would have on pedestrians in the surrounding streets.

Sellar explained: 'We will also be contributing to major improvements in the surrounding area which will not only benefit commuters but the nurses, doctors and surgeons at Guy's Hospital who have to walk to work through streets of graffiti.'[65] The split-level nature of the area would be resolved by external public escalators running alongside the building, removing the need for the graceless, utilitarian pedestrian footbridge that led from the station over St Thomas Street to Guy's Hospital.

As the inquiry approached, the revised plan not only had the full support of Mayor Livingstone, but that of his rival Steven Norris, the former Conservative MP who was lined up to oppose him at the 2004 mayoral election. Norris called the Shard 'a masterpiece of creativity', adding, 'The area around St Thomas Street and Joiner Street may be

Southwark Towers and the pedestrian bridge over St Thomas Street in 2003–4. The two buildings opposite the towers were purchased to enable the full London Bridge Quarter development (Sellar Property Group Archive)

rich in history but it is short on contemporary inspiration. London Bridge Tower will define the south bank of the River Thames like no other new building and improve the look of the city enormously.' He was particularly enamoured by the changes to the proposed relationship to the public realm: 'The first rule of tall buildings is that they must avoid suffocating surrounding roads. The Piano tower manages this by transforming the concourse of London's most awkward mainline station, London Bridge. There will be a new bus station, better enhanced facilities and even improved cycling.'[66]

In the jostling for position as the inquiry got under way, Simon Jenkins represented the counter-argument in the *Evening Standard* under the headline 'Save our skyline from the Spike'. He claimed that the building was 'in truth a try-on, an arrogant alien from architectural outer space . . . to overtop Wren's masterpiece [St Paul's] in this contemptuous way is an outrage'.[67]

Royal London Asset Management, meanwhile, announced that it was drawing up plans for a skyscraper right next to the Shard on the site of New London Bridge House. This would only help the arguments of those at the inquiry who wanted to protect the strategic views of St Paul's: planning permission for the Shard could herald a view-blocking, supertall cluster at London Bridge. Piano himself was against supertall clustering at London Bridge, saying of the Shard, 'It's made to be lonely.'[68]

As the inquiry that would decide the Shard's fate approached, Sellar was calibrating his plans for leasing the prospective building. As an internationally renowned assurance, auditing and tax services company, PricewaterhouseCoopers, still resident in Southwark Towers, were an extremely good, stable tenant: they are exactly the sort of single-occupancy tenant that most high-rise developers wish to attract. Paying off their long lease agreement would be expensive, too, so the obvious way forward was to move them into the new building, where they would occupy the majority of the office space. Sellar, being Sellar, was looking beyond the obvious and thought that, if his landmark became a reality, he would take a more radical approach.

Further thoughts on that were meaningless, though, as he approached the daunting hurdle of the public inquiry, the outcome of which would decide whether his new building would ever exist.

'The design of the building was the easy bit that we could control,' William Matthews says. 'Planning, financing and leasing were the biggest mountains, but the good thing is that you only need ten good mountaineers working together to get over them.' One of those mountaineers was Christopher Katkowski.

Irvine Sellar said to me in 2016, 'I'm a genius at picking geniuses: the best architect in the world in Renzo Piano, and the best QC in Christopher Katkowski.' Sellar had a good relationship with the Queen's Counsel, who was soon known as Kit Kat throughout the developer's Mayfair office.

Katkowski had just successfully steered Heron Tower through its planning inquiry to gain consent from the Deputy Prime Minister. The fact that the Shard was 400 feet (123 metres) taller than the proposed Heron Tower and in the 'wrong place' in not being in the City cluster meant that its chances of success were more marginal. Sellar, however, was confident that if anyone could unpick the arguments of English Heritage, Historic Royal Palaces and CABE, along with those of the serried ranks of other detractors who did not want to see his building built, Katkowski could.

For the Shard inquiry, Katkowski was assisted by a junior barrister, Russell Harris, who, today, is also widely regarded as one of the top planning QCs in the country.

Sellar sought to have the best legal team behind Katkowski. The lawyers Berwin Leighton Paisner were appointed to act on behalf of Sellar and his partners. As *Legal Business* reported in September 2002, Sellar had used Nabarro in the original development negotiations with Railtrack, but as the law firm's partner John Samson revealed, 'There were differences of opinion with the client as to how this should be carried forward. In the light of this, Sellar decided to use a different firm.' Sellar commented simply, 'We went to the firm which we thought was most appropriate to the task in hand.' Sellar, it must be said, never buffers with sentimentalism his desire to do what he perceives to be the right thing.

Between December 2002 until the beginning of the inquiry five months later, Sellar conducted weekly 8.15 a.m. meetings with the lawyers, the architects and his own team. He needed to ensure that there was a robust defence for every single objection raised on the grounds of the positioning of the building, its relationship to St Paul's, the Tower of London and other listed buildings of historic interest, and its height, bulk and design.

City Hall – the Greater London Authority's London Bridge home, designed by Norman Foster – had opened in July 2002 and was expected to be the fitting location for the public inquiry. On 16 December 2002, however, at one of the first of those weekly meetings, Sellar informed the assembled company that City Hall would not be available: Ken Livingstone's London Plan would be undergoing its own public examination there at the same time as the Shard inquiry opened on 15 April 2003.

The inquiry took place at Bankside House, Sumner Street, Southwark, situated behind Tate Modern and just half a mile from the site of the prospective London Bridge Tower.

It was not a glamorous location. As William Matthews recalls, 'It was student accommodation, with a top-floor function room with a smelly carpet and two-colour gloss on the walls. We had to do something. Any poor sod would go mad after two weeks in that room. We said to the people running the inquiry, "This is a bit tired. We'll paint it white, change the carpet that smells of beer and chips, and we'll put up some images of the project. We'll get some tables and chairs" – we didn't say they would be Vitra Eames chairs – and we covered the walls with our images and placed a great model of the Shard in the middle. We went for broke.' All the furniture was specially selected and charged to Sellar – much of it remains in use in his Mayfair offices.

By the time the Renzo Piano Building Workshop had finished 'freshening' up the room, it was adorned with 150 images of Renzo Piano's work including computer-generated images of the Shard from every angle, as well as a selection of models. Katkowski says, 'It was rather like working in an art gallery . . . Everything was exactly how Renzo's team wanted it to be. All the sightlines were done in such a way that wherever the inspector presiding looked there were images of Renzo's work.'

'Richard Rogers came to the public inquiry,' Irvine Sellar says proudly, 'and when he saw how we'd laid out the room like a studio he said to his own guys there that this is how you should organise a public inquiry room. It was beautifully set out.'

The 'opposition' were disadvantaged before the opening arguments even began. They were effectively stepping into Piano's own carefully composed exhibition room to try and argue that his building would be a blot on the landscape.

Katkowski remembers that there was a disjuncture between aesthetics and practicality, a conflict almost always at the heart of an architect's work. 'The plan almost came to a terrible end when, on the evening before the first day of the inquiry, I turned up at Bankside House with Russell Harris. Between us we had about a dozen big banker's boxes of papers. We started to put them where we normally would put things for an inquiry: on the desks. Renzo's assistants were horrified. "You can't possibly do that – it spoils the look of the room."'

The barristers were forced to keep their boxes under the desks.

The public inquiry room at Bankside House (© Michel Denancé)

Katkowski had first met Renzo Piano in person only a few weeks before the beginning of the inquiry.

'Irvine treated us all to a visit to Paris, to Renzo's studio there. The barrister Ian Trehearne [who coordinated much of the legal work] and Irvine led a small party. We went on Eurostar. In true Renzo style, the great man kept us waiting for two hours, but I was like a kid in a sweet shop in that studio – we were surrounded by all these wonderful models of buildings and images. Eventually Renzo saw us.'

Piano was going to be called before the inquiry and Katkowski wanted to prepare him. He set out to explain in detail exactly how the planning inquiry would work, and to prime him on the likely questions and the best possible way of answering.

Piano quickly interrupted him: 'I've done something like this in Chicago. The attorney on the other side started asking me a question. I said, "You sonofabitch!" Can I say that in London?'

It took Katkowski a moment to realise that the architect was winding him up.

· · ·

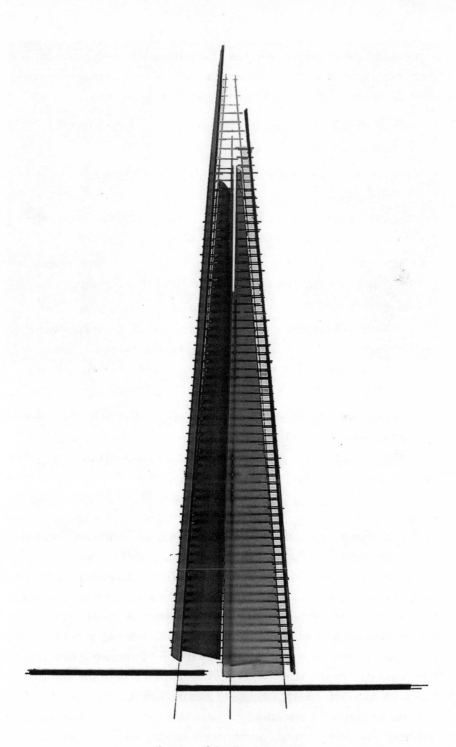

Elevation of the Shard (© RPBW)

As the inspector of the inquiry, John Gray needed to weigh the specific matters that John Prescott had raised in his call-in letter so that he could make an informed decision about the planning application:

- the appropriateness and impact on both the local and wider area of a very tall building in this location;

- the impact of the proposals on Strategic Views of St Paul's Cathedral;

- the extent to which the proposals comply with Government policy advice on the need for good design;

- the impact of the proposals on the Tower of London World Heritage Site and the setting of nearby listed buildings and conservation areas;

- the ability of the transport system to deal with the increase in demand and intensity of use created by this proposal, taking account of both the current and planned capacity of the public transport system;

- the extent to which the proposals comply with other national and regional planning policies;

- the relationship of the proposals to the London Borough of Southwark's Unitary Development; and

- any other relevant matters.[69]

Teams representing the London Borough of Southwark and the Mayor of London lined up alongside the developers in arguing in favour of the planning application. The planner Michael Crook of Cushman & Wakefield Healey & Baker, the architectural historian Nicholas Bridges of Ettwein Bridges, and Professor John Worthington, urban architect and founder of spatial planners DEGW, were all part of Sellar's team. Lord Rogers was called on behalf of the Mayor, and both he and Worthington argued that London Bridge Tower would provide an important and emblematic symbol of twenty-first-century London in a strategically important location.

Those against planning consent were headed by QCs representing English Heritage, Historic Royal Palaces and the Commission of

Architecture and the Built Environment, as well as Martin Stancliffe, an architect who held the rather antiquated title 'Surveyor to the Fabric of St Paul's Cathedral'.

It was assumed by many in the media that those against planning consent would have the upper hand; after all, they were representatives of the state and of national interests, ranged against the ambition of a commercial, self-serving developer. If John Prescott gave consent, he would be in conflict with his own advisors; even if planning permission was given by the Deputy Prime Minister, the assumption was that it would be done so with such stringent restrictions that the Shard scheme would have to be radically altered and scaled down.

Those against, however, may have been disconcerted not only by the Piano-themed inquiry room, but by how quickly the opposition warmed to Gray's personality, thought processes and open-mindedness.

Piano recalls, 'John Gray, the judge, he was a nice guy: impartial, intelligent, interesting', while Katkowski says, 'He is a remarkable inspector. He likes thinking out aloud: "This is what is troubling me; this is something on which I need your help." It is very unusual for inspectors to be so open – they don't like speaking aloud before they've written their reports, revealing what they're thinking.'

Gray has a thorough, investigative mind, and he was willing to step outside the inquiry room to see for himself exactly how the prospective building – still nominally referred to as London Bridge Tower – would affect the views of St Paul's, the setting of the Tower of London and the public realm. In the course of the inquiry, he conducted accompanied visits to Southwark Towers, London Bridge station and the streets around the development.

The claims of English Heritage and Historic Royal Palaces – the latter of which was established by Royal Charter in 1998 as a charitable trust charged 'for the benefit of the nation, with caring for, conserving and presenting to the public the unoccupied royal palaces, including the Tower of London' – appeared to be well grounded in a variety of pre-existing government papers (for those looking for some light summer reading, they included *Regional Planning Guidance 3: Strategic Planning Guidance for London Planning Authorities* [1996], *Supplementary Planning Guidance for London on the Protection of Strategic Views* [1991, amended 2000] and the

St Paul's from Millennium Bridge (© retroimages)

The Tower of London (© tupungato)

London Planning Advisory Committee's *Strategic Planning Advice on High Buildings and Strategic Views in London* [1999]). English Heritage's own *Guidance on Tall Buildings*, which it had created in tandem with CABE, was published in the month before the public inquiry began. The leading purpose of these guidance notes was to protect 'strategic views' of notable historic buildings from obstruction by new tall buildings.

In Sellar's defence there was, among other guidance notes, *Planning Policy Guidance 1*, the very paper that had initiated his desire to build tall on a transport hub when he had stood atop Southwark Towers over three years earlier.

English Heritage contended that London Bridge Tower would damage the protected views of St Paul's from the north in particular, so Gray travelled to Kenwood, Parliament Hill and Primrose Hill. Static computer renderings and models only give a fixed view of a proposed building's effect on the city, so he felt that the consequences would be better understood through a three-dimensional and a moving viewpoint, i.e. seeing the city as it is lived.

Gray also visited the City and assessed the viewpoints from other historic locations of note – the Tower of London and Tower Bridge, in particular, which both English Heritage and Historic London Palaces claimed would be affected by London Bridge Tower. Then, after the public sitting of the inquiry concluded on 9 May, the inspector visited Millbank, Centre Point and the BT Tower in London to perceive these tall buildings' relationships with the public realm, and made trips to the Beyeler Foundation in Basel and Potsdamer Platz in Berlin to examine how Renzo Piano's designs sat within their localities.

It became clear as the inquiry progressed that Gray's assessment would not be just whether any building of the height of the London Bridge Tower would have a negative impact, but whether Renzo Piano's particular design, in its proposed setting, would damage the fabric of London. As indicated by John Prescott's call-in letter, this would be to some extent – and somewhat innovatively in the historical context of local planning officers removing aesthetics from the equation when assessing planning applications – a trial by design.

Consequently, Renzo Piano was called to give evidence right at the beginning of the inquiry. Originally, it was hoped that the Italian would be available for a couple of days, but, as one of the most in-demand architects in the world, Piano would only grace Bankside House with his presence for a couple of hours.

'It was basically a two-hour *tour de force*, a masterclass,' says Katkowski. 'My only role was to introduce him. And after he had spoken for two hours, it came to cross-examination by Neil King, QC. Neil is a lovely chap, a very experienced advocate – he has often acted for English Heritage – I suppose you'd say, part of the Establishment, through and through. But with Renzo, I don't think he knew what hit him. He found the cross-examination ran away with him in the very first minutes. At these inquiries, there is written evidence, presented as something called "Proof of Evidence", a witness statement; but in Renzo's case we decided he wouldn't read any of that at all, he would just talk – which he did for the two hours.'

Having interviewed Piano, Neil King has my sympathy. Piano is charming, witty and poetical, but he has a subtly forceful personality. Whatever the question, Piano turns it to a theme of his own choosing, which he interrogates in a self-questioning, part pictorial, part philosophical manner, spiralling away with related thought processes before returning briefly to the theme and setting off again. He inveigles you into the filigree of his world and his way of thinking, and after an hour you feel you have been given privileged access to the workings of his mind and gleaned something new, but he has wrong-footed you from the beginning. Many of your carefully prepared questions have not even been asked, never mind answered. He is the architect of his own conversation.

Katkowski recalls, 'Neil decided to cross-examine him, as one would expect to do, by taking him through passages in the written evidence. He began: "Signor Piano, can I take you to page so-and-so, paragraph such-and-such?" . . . The book slid across the table, open at the page in question. Renzo looked down at this document and looked up again. Then he said, in his beautiful Italian accent: "What is this?" Neil said: "Signor Piano, this is your evidence." Renzo looked down again, looked up again – very theatrically – and said: "It's not true!" I was sitting opposite Neil and doing my very best not to laugh out loud. I thought, if I were Neil, what would I do now? How would I cross-examine a witness who, in the first few minutes, denied the evidence?'

Those two hours of evidence are clearly fixed in Katkowski's mind, including 'another Renzo-ism'. When King raised the issue of the 'back-pack' on the lower floors, he suggested to Piano that Sellar had 'dictated' that the building should be expanded in this allegedly ugly way.

Renzo answered: 'The clients dictate' – pause for dramatic effect – 'but I no listen!'

Piano, though, revealing the pragmatism learned from his builder father, went on to explain that the backpack would make it 'much easier to connect new volumes to this shape'. This was an important point, revealing that the design was sympathetic to the aims of Southwark's framework plan for the area, and that the Shard could be knitted together with the rail masterplan if and when plans for the development of the station infrastructure alongside St Thomas Street were given the green light.

Piano himself recalls a long discussion about modernity: 'The phrase that every classic has been modern in its own time came up several times, including, of course, about St Paul's,' he tells me. 'St Paul's is classic, but it was contemporary at a certain moment. I remember I came up with the true story of Brunelleschi and the Santa Maria del Fiore dome [in Florence]. It is classic now but he had to spend twenty years persuading people who said, "This is too modern. It's unfeasible, you can't do that."' Similarly, as Piano points out, the building of St Paul's was opposed at the time of its construction and considered by some to be too large, too modern, and too ugly.

He says, 'The thing with St Paul's is not whether it's classic or not classic, but whether it's good or bad. English Heritage said that the Shard was not bad design but it was dangerous because it was taking away attention from St Paul's as an icon. St Paul's is a great building – it's well done, it's not done by an Italian architect but it's well done! – but I kept on saying, no, it will not take away from St Paul's. Then the judge said, "I don't think it is intentional that it will take away from St Paul's, but if it is good enough to take away from it, what is wrong?"'

Part of the reason why Sellar had chosen to commission Piano was because the design would benefit from the knowledge of London the architect had gained as a young man living in the city. Piano drew on that in the inquiry, saying plaintively, 'I lived in Hampstead in the 1960s and used to take my children to Parliament Hill. It is a place I love. I will never do something that harms that view.'

Katkowski says that Piano is the only person he has encountered in his long legal career who is impossible to cross-examine: 'Neil King kept going and kept going. He got nowhere. Then Renzo was cross-examined by Christopher Whybrow QC, who was representing the Historic Royal Palaces. He got nowhere either.'

As part of the evidence, boxsets of books on Renzo Piano Building Workshop projects had been distributed to the inspector and the QCs. After the conclusion of Piano's testimony, all the QCs, even the one for English Heritage, asked the Italian to sign their copies. The inspector himself came over and was heard to say: 'May I shake the hand of the world's greatest living architect?'

Katkowski reveals that he thought at that moment: 'We've got a good chance of winning this one!' He felt that John Gray 'fell in love with the architect and the scheme – rightly so, in my view. Because I think Renzo is the only person I have met who can be described as a genius.'

Sellar was not called to give evidence, but he was a constant presence in the inquiry room: 'I was there every single day. I was motivating Kit Kat, I was motivating Renzo, I was motivating the team, I was kicking the lawyers' arses. I was there continuously throughout the whole period, and then I made sure that when the inspector was taking his trips, to Basel and so on, he had the right people with him. I was in the frontline. I wasn't a spectator: I was running our side of it.'

Christopher Katkowski lauds the performance of Renzo Piano, but it was a cameo in the lengthy inquiry in which the Queen's Counsel himself, as directed by Sellar, was the pivotal figure in carrying the arguments in favour of the London Bridge Tower scheme. The transcripts reveal Katkowski's point-by-point dismantling of the counter-arguments and several masterstrokes. He consistently argued that there was already a cluster in Southwark, and that even though London Bridge Tower would be taller, it would be replacing an 'utterly mediocre' building with a 'world-class' tower that, far from detracting from the views, would enhance them. At the same time, the new building would improve the public realm, be a focal point for the regeneration of Southwark and provide employment.

Fear over the effect that the London Bridge Tower would have on the prized national symbol of St Paul's had been an ever-present since renderings of the original Broadway Malyan scheme were released in early 2000. Renzo Piano had said: 'The two buildings will kiss each other', but the great disparity in size – 1,017 feet to 365 feet – would make it an unusual romantic pairing.

On behalf of English Heritage, Neil King claimed that, in reality, 'London Bridge Tower will represent a step-change in the process by which, in recent decades, the dominance of St Paul's Cathedral has been challenged and undermined by high buildings. The relationship between the two buildings will be that of master and servant.'

King called as a witness Nicholas Antram, a conservationist who was an assistant director of the London Region of English Heritage and had drawn up the national consultation paper, *Guidance on Tall Buildings*. Antram, even though he did admit 'We do feel a bit conflicted opposing something so wonderful' as Piano's design,[70] maintained that the tower would have an adverse impact and cause material harm in consideration of the protected views of St Paul's Cathedral from Parliament Hill and Kenwood House in Hampstead.

As William Matthews says about the defence of the new scheme, 'The three towers of Southwark Towers, London Bridge House and Guy's Hospital have always compromised the view. We had to argue that we were not making the view any worse.'

The Shard site was a mile behind St Paul's in the views, which were seen from five miles to the north, so the problem was one of altering the backdrop rather than causing obstruction. The Shard had been meticulously designed with an incline of six degrees from the vertical so that, in the foreshortening of the distance between the buildings, the Shard would only appear to surround the perimeter dome of the cathedral to the same extent as Southwark Towers. In Sellar's view, the fact that the Shard would continue to a much greater height was immaterial as the interference with the outline of St Paul's would be no greater.

King also called Paul Calvocoressi, a historic buildings inspector for English Heritage, whom Katkowski calls 'by far our most dangerous opponent at the inquiry. He was a very erudite man, who spoke quietly but with dignified expertise. Beware the softly spoken man who really knows his subject.'

Like Antram, Calvocoressi did not seek to demean the design of London Bridge Tower, but he was adamant that the position of the building would cause cultural damage:

> It is my submission that London Bridge Tower, notwithstanding such intrinsic architectural merits as it may have, is an inappropriate location for a very tall building and would have a severe adverse impact on the setting of important listed buildings and landmarks. London Bridge Tower would become the most prominent landmark in London, and in doing so it would create a new symbolic focus for the capital in a location – North Southwark – which is not a site of historical or functional pre-eminence for the capital. For a thousand years St Paul's Cathedral has identified the heart of the metropolis and it is for this reason that its prominence has been singled out in regional policy as worthy of protection.

In the latter stages of the inquiry, Neil King and Christopher Whybrow claimed that the regeneration of an area could not be accomplished by the development of just one building.

They had done well to be deaf to the phrase 'the Bilbao effect', which had particularly strong currency at the time. In 1995, the industrial city in northern Spain had 25,000 visitors a year, but its profile and fortunes were soon to change radically, principally due to the erection of a single building: Frank Gehry's Guggenheim Museum, which opened in 1997. By 2001, annual visitor numbers to the museum stood at 930,000, and 83 per cent of the visitors were tourists.[71] By 2010, tourism was generating 300 million euros a year for the city. Irvine Sellar hoped that the Shard, with its viewing platform, would bring hundreds of thousands of tourists to Southwark, and in time he was proved right, with visitor figures rivalling those of the Guggenheim. English Heritage had form in resisting new cultural attractions: it had opposed the London Eye.

Defending the siting of the scheme, Christopher Katkowski told the inspector that London Bridge is 'a fitting locality to put into practice the principles of sustainable development': 'The area around the station is gloomy and in desperate need of regeneration. The thousands who arrive here each morning, including me, can only despair and hurry to get away as quickly as they can. But now there is a rare opportunity to bring about change for the better.'

In a masterstroke. Katkowski also drew on his experience of the Heron Tower inquiry. In arguing against the siting of that skyscraper in the City, English Heritage had stated that it was unnecessary because there was 'massive potential in areas [including] London Bridge'. Thus, English Heritage had effectively already intimated to the government that the site of the Shard was perfect for a tall building – and even better than the City.

While much attention had been paid to the effect the Shard would have on St Paul's Cathedral, Christopher Katkowski perceived that the principal issue of the public inquiry would be whether the building impacted negatively on the views and the setting of the Tower of London: 'The Tower of London was make or break. If we won on that, the Shard could go ahead. If we lost on that, it didn't matter what else we won on, the Shard would not go ahead.'

The World Heritage Site partly dates from the eleventh century and attracts nearly three million visitors per year. As a royal castle that had been used to imprison figures from Anne Boleyn to Guy Fawkes to the Krays, the Tower is synonymous with English history.

'Of the various impacts of the Shard on the Tower of London,' Katkowski explains, 'the single main problem which emerged, as raised by our most formidable opponents, English Heritage – supported by Historic Royal Palaces – was views from the old Royal Mint, which is just across a very busy traffic junction by the Tower of London. There you had magnificent views of the Tower of London without anything interfering in the immediate backdrop of the Tower. One turn of phrase from English Heritage was that the Shard would be "a dagger through the heart of the Tower of London".'

Ken Livingstone had little sympathy: 'What can you expect? If you live in a great world city, you can't expect that all development should be put on hold just so that nothing can be seen from old buildings.

You either sterilise an area, or you bring in jobs. You have to get a balance.'

In countering the arguments, Sellar's team knew that 'flat' photography and renderings would not give a proper reflection of the relationship between the proposed scheme and the Tower: the Shard would appear to be sprouting from the top of the historic building. In an attempt to show the depth of field, they turned to innovative technology used by Hayes Davidson, a firm that specialises in the 'visualisation' of architecture and the built environment.

Katkowski: 'It was rather like when you go to the optician, you rest your chin on a ledge. In the inquiry, you looked into this box, and it did give you the idea of the distance, that there was a gap – the Thames – between the Tower of London and the Shard.'

Historic Royal Palaces also complained that the views of the Tower of London from the north-east would be harmed. Katkowski countered by referencing Historic Royal Palaces' own 'Management Plan', in which its committee had carefully assessed the relative importance of different views of the Tower of London:

> Time and again, and for good reason, the Management Plan emphasises that the important historical associations are between the Tower of London and the River Thames. The relationship between the World Heritage Site and the City of London is also described, although (as the Management Plan itself states) the historical domination of the City by the Tower of London has been replaced by London dominating the Tower. The historical significance of the relationship between the Tower of London and Southwark is not mentioned once – because there is none.

While English Heritage and Historic Royal Palaces stated that being able to see the top of the Shard from within the Tower of London would ruin the sense of history that a visitor would feel, Katkowski deftly turned the argument on its head. He claimed that the sense of history and uniqueness of the Tower of London would be magnified by the juxtaposition with the visible modern:

The special qualities of the World Heritage Site do not depend in any way upon pretending that the world city outside does not exist . . . The ability to see the evolving world city around the Tower of London, and on the other side of the Thames from it, only adds to the perception that the World Heritage site is different and special . . . the peerless quality of the architecture [of the London Bridge Tower], and its distance from the World Heritage Site, would add to the experience that the Tower of London is a low-lying fortress embedded within an ever-evolving world city.

There is a structure with far more threatening proximity to the Tower of London that survived extreme controversy to become a much-loved building: Tower Bridge. The late Victorian crossing can be seen as the grandmother of Disneyfication and Las Vegas-style inauthenticity, and brought the vituperative best out of Henry Heathcote Statham, the architect and editor of the *Builder*: 'It represents the vice of tawdriness and pretentiousness, and of falsification of the actual facts of the structure.'[72] It is now Grade I listed and very much part of the setting that Historic Royal Palaces wished to protect.

Despite all the commitments the developer had made to improve the public realm, Sellar's team had to deal with the fact that, surprisingly, CABE was still aligned with the opposition against the scheme.

Katkowski points out: 'In that era, you'd expect the conservation and heritage lobbies to be against you. But to have CABE against us, too, was unexpected because usually they would side with the promoters of modern architecture, particularly if it was by a distinguished architect, as was the case with the Shard.'

All Sellar's team could do was lay out the details of the improvements that the building would bring to a public realm that was currently in a terrible state, and hope that Inspector Gray was sympathetic to a commercial developer who could not personally control the master-planning of an entire area.

CABE did, however, give evidence that was a clear contradistinction to that of the heritage bodies, saying that 'a tower of the height proposed, on this site, could be successful, and that the design held out promise of a world-class building, worthy of its promise in views of London'. The organisation described the prospect of the appearance of the building in some views as 'exciting' and believed that 'London Bridge Tower will do no harm to London's historic environment'.

Both Tim Mould, the barrister acting on behalf of Southwark, and John Hobson QC, on behalf of the Mayor of London, emphasised their full support for the London Bridge Tower scheme, and called further witnesses in support. Hobson argued, 'Objectors wish to see the redevelopment of this site deferred until a Master Plan identifying the full range of public realm improvements needed for the area is put in place. That is however a recipe for achieving nothing. A preferable approach is to work incrementally within a flexible framework.'

He added, 'The greatest benefit that the scheme will provide will be the addition to London's skyline of a world-class building of great and singular beauty. Far from causing any harm to St Paul's Cathedral or the Tower of London, it will positively enhance their setting.'

One specific point that Prescott had raised – 'the ability of the transport system to deal with the increase in demand and intensity of use created by this proposal' – was far easier to address than either CABE's or the heritage bodies' concerns. Katkowski called Malcolm Simpson, a chartered engineer and consultant to Arup who had several decades of experience managing transport studies across the world.

Simpson told the inquiry:

> The proposed development is totally in line with current transport policy in the UK and London. All the responsible transport authorities [Network Rail, Transport for London, London Underground and the London Borough of Southwark] have approved all transport aspects of the development. The development will have no perceptible impact on the operation of London Bridge station, the London Underground station, the bus station and the highway network. It will upgrade transport facilities, including the station and bus station.

Another point that was relatively simple to dismiss was Historic Royal Palaces' claim of 'prematurity' – that the planning application should be refused as the decision-making process was not yet fit and able to make a decision – which could be read as an insult to the central government's planning policy and the effectiveness of its instruments. Katkowski said, 'it was raised in a muddled and shifting way – and by only one party, Historic Royal Palaces. English Heritage, having raised and lost on the issue at the Heron Tower inquiry, properly chose not to raise it here.'

Various critics who are negative about tall buildings have said, as a standard weapon in their armoury, that such buildings are beyond the 'human scale' – there is an implication that tall buildings are unnatural – and this accusation had been thrown at the London Bridge Tower from the outset. Indeed, Tom Ball, a member of the public who had published letters in the press expressing his opposition to the Shard, wrote to the inquiry that 'If approved, it would set a precedent for a flood of huge and tall buildings and spell an end for London's much admired human scale.'

While Tom Ball was making a valid point that tall buildings can alter the urban grain, the phrase 'human scale' cannot be appropriate. The human scale relates to the proportions of the body and dimensions within standard limits of human usability, and so should only be applied to the interior of buildings when talking of the heights of ceilings, work surfaces, chairs, tables, banisters, steps and so forth. In reference to the exterior of tall buildings, as long as the mechanics of going from floor to floor are usable within the limits of the human scale, it makes little sense to talk of a transgression. Proper application of the human scale to exterior height per se would mean that no building should be much taller than about 10 feet (3 metres). We would be living in Bungalow-world.

Inspector Gray addressed the matter directly in his report (although his idea of building height in terms of the human scale is more generous than a single storey):

Some of the criticisms of the proposed design refer to its height and scale as being inappropriate. I believe they are wrong in referring to scale – they should refer solely to height, or perhaps to mass or bulk. Despite the floor-to-floor glazing units and the absence of horizontal structural members expressed externally, the proposed building would clearly be sub-divided into floors occupied for work, or residentially, by human beings. The building would thus have a human scale. If one looks at St Paul's Cathedral, the façades are expressed architecturally as having two storeys – yet those two storeys are the equivalent of about six storeys of the buildings around it. St Paul's is built at about three times human scale. Churches and public buildings achieve their prominence or dominance by being built at larger than human scale.

As far as William Matthews is concerned, the person who spoke at the public inquiry whose point was particularly pertinent was a member of the public, Ms Jo Dubiel, a local resident who expressed neither support for nor objection to the proposal. She posed the question: 'Regeneration is invariably proposed as a benefit – but whom does it benefit?'

While she conceded that much-needed improvements to the public realm would be welcome, she said that as a result of the development house prices and rents would increase so local people would no longer be able to live in their own area, while some local shops and other small businesses would close. She was making a salient point relevant to areas of regeneration and gentrification across London. Matthews asks what the alternative is – to deny the opportunity to make London Bridge a better place? – but believes that the social cost of regeneration always should be weighed alongside its benefits.

As a tough and critical man with extraordinarily high expectations of others, Sellar rarely hands out compliments, but his view of Christopher Katkowski remains undimmed by time: he describes the QC's closing comments, summarised here by Inspector Gray, as 'poetry'.

> This is a once-in-a-lifetime opportunity. The realisation of Renzo Piano's definitive masterwork is in the hands of the Secretary of State. The world city of London stands to gain so much from this superb building. London Bridge Tower would rank as one of the very finest modern buildings in the world. It would be a breathtaking symbol of regeneration. It would be a tragedy to refuse permission for such a wonderful scheme.
>
> There can be no doubt at all that, if London Bridge Tower is permitted,

in future years, nothing but pride and a sense of achievement will be felt by all those responsible.

The public inquiry ended on 9 May 2003, and on 23 July Inspector John Gray delivered his 153-page report to John Prescott's office.

Despite CABE's reservations about the lack of a masterplan, Gray commended the proposed improvements to the public realm:

The existing public realm is deplorable. The London Bridge Tower proposal would bring a clear enhancement. It is an obvious first step in the process. It would not prejudice further enhancement through other developments. Indeed, it ought to stimulate further improvements. A masterplan would likely be counter-productive in that its production would delay rather than encourage development and regeneration. And there is much more than a grain of truth in Renzo Piano's view that it is better to work incrementally, 'otherwise you are paralysed by perfection and never start'.

He added, 'I, personally, am very impressed with the quality of the design.'

Gray made it clear that it was not the duty of the developer to improve the strategic views of historic buildings, but rather to ensure that the views and settings were not reduced or undermined: 'On my reading [of '*Supplementary Planning Guidance for London on the Protection of Strategic Views*'] its purpose is to protect the Strategic Views – not to enhance them. In other words, the intention is not to return St Paul's Cathedral to its former pre-eminence in the views', i.e. the views prior to the publication of the guidance note in 1991, by which time many buildings, including Southwark Towers and Guy's Tower, were already impinging on views of the cathedral. While Southwark Towers could not claim any architectural quality, the qualities of the London Bridge Tower, including its spire-like form, would, according to Gray, enhance the view in any case and make a suitable signpost for the cathedral.

Regarding the effect the building would have on the setting of the Tower of London, Gray wrote, 'the evolution of the modern city cannot be ignored. I find that the juxtaposition adds to rather than diminishes the historic character of the Tower.'

He was supportive of the mixed-use concept and the regeneration the building would bring to Southwark. Overall, he believed that 'It would be difficult to find a site that could better exemplify Government policy on sustainability.'

Gray then addressed each of the points raised in the Deputy Prime Minister's letter calling in the planning application for review:

- there can be no doubt that what is proposed is of the very highest architectural quality and that those details as yet unresolved can be satisfactorily designed;

- in the Strategic Views of St Paul's Cathedral, the proposed building would reduce neither the visibility nor the setting of the Cathedral and would be an enhancement of the present background;

- the distance of the proposed building from the Tower of London would cause no harm either to its architectural character or to its historic setting;

- I found nothing so sensitive about the settings of other listed buildings and conservation areas as to be noticeably undermined by the proposed building;

- the travel demand generated by the proposed building would have no serious implications for the transport system; the location is highly sustainable;

- in light of these five conclusions, the proposed very tall building must be considered appropriate in this location;

- there is no conflict with national, regional or local policy that could undermine this conclusion.

He signed off with his conclusion: 'I recommend that planning permission be granted subject to conditions.'

Irvine Sellar, his development partners and Renzo Piano knew none of this. They were not given access to the report and could do nothing other than await the verdict of the Deputy Prime Minister. Gray had managed to undertake further research, write, edit and submit his lengthy report in just two and a half months since the end of proceedings, but Prescott would take far longer to read the report and give his own, final judgement on the future of the Shard.

Despite Gray's positive recommendation, the verdict was far from assured. Gray had arrived at his conclusions having looked at the weight of evidence about the particular circumstances and siting of the Shard, but Prescott would be making a political decision that could make all the fine detail irrelevant in an instant. If the Labour government was set against building supertall – especially outside the City – and if it was disinclined to agree with the philosophy of the rebel mayor and his vision for London, Irvine Sellar's tower would never be built. Even if Prescott accepted the inspector's recommendation but stipulated a reduced height to comfort the naysayers, all that Sellar would have been left with in terms of the Shard scheme was a pipedream and a rather attractive scale model.

Sellar recalls: 'It was really on a knife edge. I was nervous of what the final decision would be. In life you always have a plan B, and I would probably have gone back to try another design, but that would have been several million and three years thrown down the drain.'

In the meantime, he waited, and waited. On tenterhooks, he would phone Ian Trehearne of the law firm Berwin Leighton Paisner every day to see whether the decision had come through.

Prescott finally made his decision on 19 November 2003, a full six months after the conclusion of the public inquiry, and a letter was despatched to Trehearne.

'Eventually,' Sellar reveals, 'I got a phone call when I was with my son James in the office. Ian's rather laid-back, and after a rather long-winded explanation, I said, "Can we get to the bottom line? Have we got it or not?"'

'Yes, we have,' came the answer, 'but with conditions.'

Sellar was overjoyed and barely able to listen to Trehearne as he spelled out the terms.

The letter was sent by Miss A. Gerry, Decision Officer of the Planning Central Casework Division of the Deputy Prime Minister's Office, and stated:

He agrees that the building would stand comfortably in its immediate urban or townscape context, that it would significantly enhance the existing setting and public realm, that the design detail is appropriate and that the quality of the architecture should be considered secure. The Secretary of State . . . is very impressed with the quality of the design . . . The Secretary of State has carefully considered the impact of the proposal on the strategic views of St Paul's Cathedral. He agrees with the inspector . . . that the proposal would represent an improvement over what exists and would not reduce the visibility or setting of St Paul's, nor would it devalue or diminish its status or significance to any material extent.

The fifth page of the letter contained the prized words:

The Secretary of State accepts the inspector's recommendation. He hereby grants planning permission for the demolition of the existing Southwark Towers and construction of a mixed-use building totalling 124,242 sq. m. gross . . . subject to the following conditions . . .

Eventually, after the first surge of euphoria, Sellar took a close look at the conditions, which had been recommended by Inspector Gray. They included a list of ten design details that had to be submitted and approved by the local planning authority, but these related to matters such as the quality of glass and the type of blinds that were in any case intrinsic to Renzo Piano's design. Piano, in fact, was delighted by these terms and conditions: 'I must say I was quite pleased to see that the list coincided with the conditions we ourselves had proposed. [He] transcribed them in a document, the Decalogue, in order to protect them against future modifications.'[73]

The other conditions, far from jeopardising the scheme by ordering a reduction in height or bulk, were standard. They required the provision of a few further details of minor logistical aspects; that the developer should afford an archaeologist access to the site; and that construction would start within five years.

An archaeological find could set the development back by years, but Sellar had always known that he would be building in an ancient part of London – bringing focus back to Southwark had always been part of the appeal – and he knew the risks.

As for the five-year specification, few developers want a deadline to be placed upon them, but Sellar was confident that, having initiated the project over three and a half years earlier, surely the major hurdles had finally been overcome: he had the right site, he had the right architect, and now he had the right to build. It couldn't possibly take more than another five years for construction to start.

Could it?

The full planning process set back the development considerably, and the public inquiry is believed to have cost in the region of £10 million, with approximately £4 million of that coming out of the pockets of Irvine Sellar and his co-owners to cover professional, legal and architectural fees. Nonetheless, both he and Piano were magnanimous in victory.

The architect said, 'I am grateful for having been challenged for three years to do better . . . now our real work will begin.'[74] Almost a decade later, in 2012, he added: '[Architects] perform a potentially dangerous task for the community, and if we get it wrong our error is around for a long time. Maybe [an inquiry] should be mandatory, as it would prevent many mistakes, provided of course that the process is not excessively long or inconclusive.'[75]

Piano tells me, 'When we went through the long public inquiry, there were very many intelligent people. If you are doing the wrong thing, you can be as obstinate as you like, but you will not get to build. You have to be humble and say that maybe the stars or an asteroid were in the right position to make the miracle – but essentially we were given permission to build the Shard because it was right, because it was not arrogant, because it was not about showing muscles. It was more about bringing attention to Southwark, and making out of a tower a little town that never goes to sleep, so that, unlike most towers – which shut the door at 6 p.m. and everybody goes away, leaving them mysterious – this is a building that is awake and accessible. Those values are values that are right, the value of community.'

Like Piano, Sellar remains sanguine about the planning process despite how much it cost him personally, telling me, 'We are surrounded by history – St Paul's and the Tower of London – and quite rightly it should be protected. London is a great city, a fantastic city, with thousands of years of history, art and culture that should be respected. Whatever you are building, but particularly if you are building tall, you should respect the environment. In the end, it doesn't take much longer to really think about the impact a building has and to think about good design.'

If Sellar and Piano believed that criticism of the Shard scheme would now cease, they were much mistaken. The decision was met with shock amid fears that Prescott's pronouncement, coupled with Ken Livingstone's emerging London Plan, would lead to a rash of tall buildings in London. James Sellar, Irvine's son, was forced to point out: 'This does not open the floodgates for mediocrity; it opens the door for good design.'[76] What the public inquiry had achieved, albeit at great expense, was that the argument about building tall should not simply be about height but about quality.

CABE continued to be critical, upset that Prescott's decision made no mention of the problems it had raised about the public realm. Peter Stewart, the design review director at CABE, said, 'It is a plus and a minus. We support the architecture, but we're disappointed that it didn't go the extra mile to meet our concerns.'[77]

English Heritage also stuck to its guns, saying that 'the tower, if it is ever built, would be an inappropriate addition to the skyline in that area'. Livingstone was soon on the attack again, quoted in *Building Design* of 12 December 2003 as comparing English Heritage to the Taliban once more and saying it was 'opposed to anything taller than a wattle and daub hut'.

As for Prescott, he was due at Prince Charles's conference on 'Traditional Urbanism in Contemporary Practice' on 20 November 2003, just a day after he had given consent. Royalty was still taking it upon itself to interfere with the prospects of building tall in London, with Queen Victoria's great-great-great grandson shouldering the ermine mantle and attempting to mock the Shard: 'At the moment it looks as though London seems to be turning into an absurdist picnic table. We already have a giant gherkin. Now it looks as if we are going to have a giant salt cellar as well. Whatever next?' As an attempt to create a more ridiculing nickname than 'the Shard', it was a failure.

In Prescott's own speech, he alluded to his decision to ignore the complaints of the Royal Historic Palaces and said that he was familiar with the whereabouts of the Tower of London: 'After last week's decision on the Shard of Glass perhaps that's where I'm heading anyway.'[78]

Christopher Katkowski says, 'Of all the clients I have represented, Irvine is the one who has impressed me most. He had a vision. He was always positive, never gave up. Once the thing was called in – given that there was opposition from English Heritage, and even CABE was against it – he was told: "You've got no chance." The idea of siting the tallest building in Western Europe on the wrong side of the river, outside the City cluster and in a grotty part of London! And when we'd got the permission he was told: "You've got no chance of getting the funding you need." The thing that really marks Irvine out is not so much the great battle to get the Shard consented to, but what happened afterwards – winning the funding to get it built.'

Chapter 7

A Frantic Lull

Make an impact. Sometimes, I find myself in meetings with people who have zero personality, zero ideas, zero anything. They are the walking dead and really make me believe in birth control.

Irvine Sellar

The building, by now known almost exclusively as the Shard of Glass or simply the Shard, finally looked like it was going to make it from a sketch on a menu card in Berlin to Western Europe's tallest tower. The letter from the Office of the Deputy Prime Minister, however, was merely a thin sheaf of paper: the factor that was going to hoist the glass sail on the south bank of the Thames was money – at least £350 million of it in construction costs alone.

Irvine Sellar and his partners needed major investment to construct the building. It was still assumed by many that now Sellar had planning permission, and had thereby multiplied the value of the Southwark Towers site by many times, he would sell because he would never raise the money to build in any case. Investment on that scale only comes with confidence, and as the property press had been suggesting since the former market trader stepped to the fore in spring 2000 and said he was going to change the London skyline, why would anyone invest in the dream of a man who had never developed any tall buildings before, never mind the country's tallest?

One person who was not lacking confidence was Sellar himself. Immediately after the scheme was given clearance in November 2003, he announced that construction would begin in 2005 and that, by 2009, London would have a new landmark.

If media coverage is taken to be the meter, after planning permission for a major development has been granted there nearly always seems to be a lull – the period in which the developer reconsiders their options, finds tenants and raises finance, or considers putting the site up for sale. In Irvine Sellar's case, the lull would be frantic.

Sellar's energy fizzes continually and he is not known for his patience. He loves tennis and is a debenture holder at Queen's Club, but it's difficult to imagine him sitting through a long, three-set match; he gives the impression that he's more likely to push one of the players to the side and finish off the game himself.

He had taken the male/female combined retail idea from a little shop in Carnaby Street to almost every major high street in the country in just a decade: if he has a good idea, he likes to explode it, quickly, and push it as far as he can. He took the same characteristic into property development, despite the fact that it's usually a long game.

On 11 September 2003, the Sellar Property Group and its Shard development partner CLS announced that they had bought New London Bridge House, a 131,000-square-foot (12,170 m²) office block. The Richard Seifert-designed, twenty-five-storey building was 308 feet (94 metres) tall. It was a wholly unspectacular modernist building, completed in 1967, and would have been of very little interest if it was not situated a few metres away from the Shard site, just across London Bridge Street.

Sellar and CLS bought the property from Royal London Asset Management Ltd in an off-market deal worth £39.4 million, a couple of million more than Southwark Towers had cost in 1998.

The date of purchase was extremely surprising: it was two months before John Prescott gave consent to the planning application for the Shard. Sellar and CLS were taking what could be seen as a huge gamble, committing their funds before their development was given the go-ahead, and they could have had two large buildings on their hands with little chance of radical upward development if permission had been

New London Bridge House (© RPBW)

denied. Both buildings may have ended up in sustained torpor prior to, at some future point, unspectacular mid-rise development.

The partners, however, had good reason to move early. In the run-up to the public inquiry, Royal London Asset Management had announced that they intended to build their own tall tower right next to the Shard. The proposed building would be a 690-foot (210-metre) skyscraper. While not rivalling the Shard, it would still have been taller than any other existing building in London outside Canary Wharf. As a sign of intent, Royal London Asset Management had hired the highly experienced American skyscraper architects Kohn Pedersen Fox. The news put Sellar on red alert.

If the dealings with CABE and the London Borough of Southwark's Strategic Development Management Group had taught him anything, it was that if he was to resuscitate the London Bridge area, and improve the setting of the Shard and the cohesion of the public realm, he would need to control as much of the ground as possible.

When the possibility of buying New London Bridge House arose, he leaped at it. The timing was essential: if the Deputy Prime Minister's decision turned out to be positive, possibly paving the way for other major developments at London Bridge, the asking price would have risen monumentally. The seemingly premature, off-market deal gave him a good price, control and options.

By this point, Sellar's vision had expanded. He was no longer thinking of only bringing a huge but solitary building to Southwark. He now wanted to build a London Bridge Quarter.

Sellar did not want to create a supertall cluster, and he did not want the work of other architects impinging on the sculptural, standalone design of the Shard. He says, 'The Royal London design was inefficient. It was about fifty-odd storeys, which would not have done the Shard too much good in that location. We made an offer to Royal London and came up with a scheme for a more efficient building, with greater square footage without being so tall. We bought the freehold. It was income producing through about twenty separate tenants. It was not a good building, not a good design, and the lifts and everything were not in good nick, but it produced income, and that is what I like in development: while you are working up your plans, you have an asset that is working for you.'

Sellar says, 'We saw it as a great opportunity to create a sister building, because we were committed to building the bus station, committed to building the train station concourse, which was great design. It made complete sense to have another Renzo Piano building for this tight area.'

He turned to Piano to start drawing up plans for a sympathetic, moderately scaled high-rise development to abut the Shard, thereby terminating the Kohn Pedersen Fox scheme. The original Piano scheme for the second site was for a thirty-storey building. James Sellar said, 'We are working with a number of partners to deliver our commitment to provide public space at ground level', although CABE said it was concerned by the 'lack of absolute commitment', especially to a public piazza. The Sellars countered that the public space issue would be seen to be resolved once plans were finalised.[79]

Irvine Sellar said categorically in *Building Design* on 19 September 2003, 'We don't want to take on the KPF scheme. We won't redevelop the site now but we are very much committed to Renzo Piano as an architect for that area. If we develop the site, it would not be taller than it is now. We don't see a cluster there in the long term.'

There were claims that the Shard plans would have been migrated onto the New London Bridge House site if the Shard did not win planning permission from Prescott, but, as Sellar points out, that was never an option due to the positioning of the Jubilee line tube station and associated tunnels which envelop the site below ground. Adrian Dennis, a planning case officer at the London Borough of Southwark, had a clearer understanding of Sellar's intention, telling *Building Design* on 19 September 2003, 'CABE criticised the scheme because it wanted more public space, and this purchase could allow that to happen . . . Sellar is making things available so his pos-sibilities will increase in preparation for the planning inquiry decision.'

From 2000 onwards – both during the period of the planning application for the Shard and following the Deputy Prime Minister's decision – there had been differences between the shareholders over their respective shareholdings in the development. None of the parties ever formally made any official comment on the consequent dispute. So far as can be gleaned from press reports,[80] the issue involved the Irish Nationwide Building Society, which had been a lender to the Ironzar Trust from 1997 and which appears to have held a stake (associated with that of Ironzar) in the Southwark Towers development when the building was first acquired in 1998. Subsequently, in 2001, there was a 'rectification' of the stakes. This rectification was later challenged by Simon Halabi who claimed that the Ironzar stake had been wrongfully reduced and issued legal proceedings against his joint-venture partners, Sellar and CLS. They, in reply, claimed that Halabi had misrepresented the involvement of his backers, including the Irish Nationwide, and in the process had gained a larger stake in the deal. Halabi rejected that. The consequent trial opened in the Royal Court of Jersey in October 2005 and was adjourned to resume two months later in December. On 8 December, the three parties settled their differences. No statement was ever made as to the terms and the three stakeholders continued as joint-venture parties.

When I ask Sellar about this episode, he says, 'I bear no grudges. It's a waste of energy. This is what happens; we litigate to sort out our disputes but then you just have to move on and get the job done.' He says he did not have a bad relationship with either Halabi or CLS, and that any stories that pointed to major difficulties between the partners were overblown.

This is borne out by the fact that, in a move typical of Sellar's go-ahead approach, in early 2006 the partners made their first planning application for the New London Bridge House site, with the intention of creating a new quarter for London Bridge.

Given the extreme volatility of the construction and property industries, the best way to give major banks and other investors confidence in a development is to pre-let a substantial proportion – if not all – of the building. If Sellar was to fund the construction of two huge buildings, plus all the other major work related to the public realm and the transport infrastructure, he would require lease agreements to be in place. The easiest solution would have been to find a single tenant, for instance a major corporation that would make the Shard its London headquarters. The multi-use nature of the building mitigated against that option: much of the space was supposed to be occupied by the hotel, restaurants, retail, apartments and viewing gallery, leaving under 500,000 square feet for offices – less than the total floor area of the much shorter Gherkin.

The Gherkin itself was a pointer as to why Sellar's Shard was being greeted with praise from the public, but also why he was finding it so difficult to attract major tenants.

Norman Foster's building opened its doors on 27 April 2004, and was widely acknowledged to be the most exciting skyscraper to have been built in London. It altered the landscape in more than purely physical terms. Peter Murray says, 'The Gherkin changed people's attitudes fundamentally towards what tall buildings were like. Up until then, people's only experience of tall buildings was "concrete monstrosities", as Prince Charles called them, where tall buildings were seen as homes for the poor. Now, people were more worried about losing their view of the Gherkin that they were about losing their view of St Paul's.'

In 2007, Simon Thurley of English Heritage was still talking, as a result of the cultural impact of the Gherkin and plans for the Shard, about the skyline being ruined by 'a small number of individuals' extraordinary ambition and desire to create a monument to themselves',

30 St Mary Axe, London (© rgbdigital)

but he conceded that 'we have to accept that building tall is one of the expressions of our age'.[81] The desire to build tall, of course, is not an expression of our particular age, as humans have always wanted to build upwards. The post-millennial change in Britain was the result of a relaxing of rules and a greater perceived need (rather than an increase in desire) combined with the 'fear of neighbours' being decreased by commitment to good design – but Thurley's concession was a sign of how far the ground had shifted.

In the close relationship between form and function, the skyscraper offers authenticity, but there is a deep human hankering for beauty, no matter how subjective that might be. Detractors of the Shard such as Simon Jenkins and Robert Adam may see little beauty or exquisite detail in many contemporary expressions of the tall tower in London, but the general public has a growing aesthetic appreciation of the form.

The Gherkin won the Royal Institute of British Architects' prestigious Stirling Prize later in 2004, and soon became culturally symbolic, with its unusual elongated ovoid shape and triangulated external skin making it instantly recognisable.

Despite this, problems were afoot. The building's owners, Swiss Re, the international reinsurance company, moved 800 employees into the fifteen lower floors of the building when it opened in spring 2004, but by October of that year they had failed to sign up any tenants for the remaining twenty-five storeys, despite the architectural prestige of the building and the views afforded by the upper floors. Swiss Re was thought to be asking too high a rental price, supposedly between £47.50 and £56 per square foot. As a result, Swiss Re needed to switch away from finding an anchor tenant and sign up a range of smaller tenants (it now has over a dozen office tenants). In the meantime, it was reportedly losing around £35,000 a day in rent.

The *Financial Times* on 4 October 2004 cited one anonymous property expert as saying, 'If you look at the history of most towers, most of them are built by owner-occupiers because of the risk associated with construction. The risk–reward ratio is not always sufficient to justify a speculative development.' The same article reported that Irvine Sellar had said that he would not go ahead with the Shard development without pre-lets of about a third of the space.[82]

As a plumber once said to me (rightly, as it turned out): 'If you want to live in an unusual building, you're going to have unusual problems.' The very thing that made the Gherkin distinctive – its unconventional shape – worked against its viability because it had unusual floor plates that obviated modular repetition in open-plan working. It was largely because of this that it took quite a few years for the success of the Gherkin as an office building to match its architectural acclaim. The unusual building required unusual tenants who could think beyond conventional norms.

The Shard design was even more unconventional in tapering so continuously inwards while having eight differently shaped façades separated by recesses or fissures. On top of that, the floor space was eaten into by up to four winter gardens on each floor. Joost Moolhuijzen of the Renzo Piano Building Workshop recalls:

> When we started working the typical floorplates many experts, including
> letting agents, told us we were mad. Looking back, it is a miracle that
> Sellar stood by us, a bunch of foreign architects, and did not let early

third-party opinions influence the design substantially. Now the irregular floorplates are praised as an asset, creating good and interesting workplaces with a sense of scale and place.[83]

'We thought the floor plates worked for us quite well,' Sellar explains. 'If you are building a "fridge" and you have the same floor plate from top to bottom, it's a little boring. The fact that our building tapers is much better from a light point of view than the square or rectangular buildings that are dark in the centre. And that we had different floor plates to suit different tenants in the office element was an advantage.'

Sellar will not follow conventional wisdom if he believes that he can still balance the books through a more original approach that brings other advantages – greater creativity and uniqueness being prime among them. Sellar is not shy of firing off a colourful insult, but his greatest condemnation is that something, or someone, is 'boring'. As he says, 'Sometimes, I find myself in meetings with people who have zero personality, zero ideas, zero anything. They are the walking dead and really make me believe in birth control.'

Sellar was absolutely convinced that the uniqueness of the Shard – both exterior and interior – was its selling point and would eventually draw the sort of tenants he was looking for. Multi use was not enough for him: he also wanted a mixture of tenants within the office space. There is some commercial if uncommon sense in this: the rates per square foot one can command from a range of smaller tenants is always likely to be higher than that for a single or anchor tenant, but there is a much greater risk that the building will not be at full occupancy as tenants come and go, and the work that goes into maintaining the level of occupancy is much greater.

By early summer 2004, Sellar was making initial appointments with the beginning of construction in mind. The most significant appointment was the engineering consultancy WSP to oversee the structural engineering work in what would become a multi-million-pound contract. Arup, which had been connected to the Shard project from the outset, even before engineer Tony Fitzpatrick played matchmaker for the union between Sellar and Piano, was appointed to the development team to look after building services design. Both WSP and Arup would remain involved in the building of the Shard until its completion.

Although engineering firms were now signed up, a deal was yet to be arranged with a construction company. It soon emerged that there was no immediate hurry. The lack of progress in finding pre-let tenants, and therefore investors, took its toll on the schedule: in August 2004, it was revealed that construction of the Shard scheme would be delayed until 2006, and the building would not be ready until 2010.

During the following month, PricewaterhouseCoopers announced that it would not be arranging a pre-let of the office space in the building, and the *Sunday Telegraph* suggested that, consequently, the entire project was once more under threat.

It had been assumed that Sellar would have wanted to pursue the obvious route and keep PricewaterhouseCoopers as the anchor tenant for the new building, but at this point the developer surprisingly revealed: 'The only discussions we've ever entered into with PwC were over them vacating. We have never assumed they would take occupation – that would be a daft proposition.'[84]

Despite the leasing problems that the Gherkin was encountering in the supposedly more desirable location of the City, it seemed that far from trying to cling onto the Southwark Towers tenants, Sellar wanted to remove them in preparation for demolition work and start afresh with new tenancy agreements for his landmark building.

Sellar was quoted in *The Times* of 18 September 2004 as saying: 'We've agreed terms for them to vacate and are looking at serving notice at the end of this year or the beginning of next.' PricewaterhouseCoopers would be given a year to quit. The company said it had enough spare capacity in its other London offices, including Embankment Place, Plumtree Court and the Docklands, for relocation of the 2,000 staff based at Southwark Towers.

There were reports that Sellar and his Teighmore Ltd partners agreed to pay PricewaterhouseCoopers an astonishing figure of £70 million to relinquish its tenancy lease on Southwark Towers, which still had ninety-six years to run. One could be forgiven for assuming that the press had plucked a figure out of the air and doubled it, but Sellar, while refusing to confirm the figure to me in 2016, did reveal that the lease 'was worth

£40 million on a good day, but we had to take them out. When we won planning consent, I got a standing ovation from PwC's partners because they knew they were going to pick up a great deal of money each.'

At the time, Sellar was negotiating with five other companies with a view to pre-letting 35 to 45 per cent of the Shard's office, hotel and retail space. Ever bullish about his building's prospects and desirability, he did not want to pre-let more of the capacity, as he felt he would secure higher rates in post-construction agreements. The market was tough, and few industry commentators thought he would have the luxury of choice: if he had the opportunity to pre-let 100 per cent of the building, he should grab it with both hands and praise providence – any other attitude would surely jeopardise his steel and glass shard ever piercing the clouds.

Southwark Towers may have been a much-abused building in terms of both functionality and aesthetics, but it provided the platform for the Shard in a literal sense. Its roof was the viewfinder to the future: Irvine Sellar had stood on it when he foresaw the possibility of building tall; Renzo Piano had stood on it when he starting putting shape to that vision; and in 2005 Giovanni Angelini stood on it just as the sun was setting and also saw the future. Sellar remembers: 'He looked north to the City, west to Westminster, and said, "We've found our Shangri-La."'

Angelini was referring to the mythical, utopian paradise conjured by James Hilton in his 1933 novel, *Lost Horizon* – an exotic Eastern land where the residents are permanently happy and almost immortal. More prosaically, Angelini was also referring to the site for the latest outpost of a hotel chain.

The chain's owner, Robert Kuok, was not unlike Irvine Sellar in being a largely self-made man who took the kernel of his father's business and turned it into a major company, only rather than fashion retail the commodity was sugar, and the company was major on a global scale. The Malaysian Chinese businessman took over almost all sugar production in Malaysia in the 1960s and became responsible for 10 per cent of world production, leading him to be christened the 'Sugar King of Asia'. In 1971, he built the first Shangri-La hotel in Singapore, and expanded the company into property, oil, bottling plants and media, and today he is, according to *Forbes*, a multi-billionaire and Malaysia's richest man.

By 2005, his nephew Edward Kuok was steering the hotel chain with Giovanni Angelini as chief executive, and it had expanded to forty-six locations across Asia. Sellar says that, by the time Angelini stood alongside him at the top of Southwark Towers, the hotel chain had been searching for a perfect site for an expansion into Europe for about a dozen years. London, they thought, would be a perfect location for their luxury five-star hotel operation, aimed primarily at wealthy Eastern Asian business travellers and tourists.

The view, and Renzo Piano's design, put paid to any ideas of launching in the West End or Mayfair: one of the most luxurious hotel brands in the world was coming to Southwark.

They wouldn't sign up immediately, though. Sellars says, 'Edward is one of the most dynamic charming individuals you could care to meet who can really eff and blind. They wouldn't sign the deal until a lucky date, and when that date arrived I went to Hong Kong with my wife and they put us up at the Aberdeen Marina Club. We spent Christmas with him and his in-laws. Edward took me on a motor boat trip around the islands – he loves to spear fish. I was sitting there with him, and the only other person left on the boat was his chef. Edward said to me, very seriously, "Last night, I dreamt I was dead and all it said on my tombstone was 'At least he wasn't a wanker.'" You have to like a man like that. I think we recognised in each other that we were winners. It was a great relationship.' Sellar is a dominant personality, but he is drawn to other strong personalities. None of his business partners and none of his principal staff are submissive characters.

Shangri-La signed a thirty-year lease, with a further thirty-year option, to operate a hotel in the Shard on floors 34 to 52. Barry Ostle of the Sellar Property Group says, 'The keys to the safe emerged when we got the Shangri-La pre-let, which was bank financeable.' It was a massive step in confounding the detractors who claimed that Sellar would never fill the tallest building in Western Europe, and especially not on the wrong side of the river.

Despite the agreement, on 7 October 2005 the *Evening Standard*, in a round-up of tall-building propositions for London, was still stamping the word 'unlikely' in red over an image of the Shard. An anonymous commentator summed up the building's prospects: 'the Shard is going to be built in SE1, so it's not in the City, which makes it less desirable.

It probably won't get built unless it gets 40 to 50 per cent pre-let, which you won't get without market confidence.'[85]

Around that time, when Sellar was asked if the Shard was Sellar Property Group's most daring project to date, he said, 'This would be anybody's most daring project.'

He knew that the hotel deal alone was not enough to secure all the funding: investors would only start to believe that his scheme was not an expensive folly when office tenants had signed on the dotted line. Try as he might, with his legendary determination and obstinacy in overdrive, he was getting no nearer. To many City corporations at the beginning of the twenty-first century, the Thames was just as much of a barrier as it had been before the Romans built a bridge.

Ken Livingstone, the Mayor of London, became Irvine Sellar's saviour, at least temporarily.

Having struck up an unlikely liaison with the commercial developer in 2000, and having realised that they had a shared vision for architecture and regeneration in London, Livingstone kept in touch with Sellar after the end of the public inquiry.

Livingstone admired Sellar's ability to think beyond the conventional, as well as his determination. He says he wanted 'to maximise Irvine's driving force in the rest of the area' and, in fact, he wanted to utilise it beyond the boundaries of Southwark and into the heart of the City itself.

Thinking back to 2001, he recalls, 'There was this other angle. All the British Rail lands were put up for sale – a semi-private corporation was redeveloping all BR land.' This included Bishopsgate's Goods Yard, which had been derelict since the 1960s but was about to get the London Overground going through it, improving its connectivity to places as far apart as Watford and Croydon.

'So I thought – this was before 9/11 – these could be London's twin towers: the Shard at London Bridge and a twin at Bishopsgate. I phoned this man and said, "You've got the site, nothing on it. You could put what would be the joint tallest building in Europe there. There's huge potential." He said: "It's not part of our immediate programme." If it had been, I would certainly have wanted to involve Irvine in the twin. Then, after 9/11, that didn't seem such a good idea.'

Barry Ostle says, 'Ken Livingstone understood architecture. He said there were three "world cities" – New York, Tokyo and London – that rise and fall in relation to each other, and the criteria that dictated their rise and fall was architecture, what was happening on the skyline, and who has built the biggest, best and most talked-about buildings in the world that everyone wants to see. He was determined to make London number one, and he thought the Shard would be iconic and he wanted it built. Irvine and I were at the Shard stand at Mipim [real estate exhibition] in Cannes, and Ken walked over and said, "Irvine, I want this built, and I might be able to help."'

Livingstone confirms the story: 'Irvine said he needed a tenant, he couldn't start development without a tenant. So I said: "We'll take all the offices for Transport for London" – which was scattered over half a dozen places. I liked the idea of having all my Transport for London staff within a two-minute walk. So I told TfL, "I'm going to sign a deal for all of you to move into this great new building when it's completed."'

On 16 May 2006, Ken Livingstone said that Transport for London would be taking space in the Shard. Geographically it made sense, as the former Mayor points out, as the London Assembly was already based at Tooley Street in London Bridge. It made sense in terms of symbolism, too, with the headquarters of London's transport body perched immediately above one of the capital's busiest hubs for rail, tube and bus.

Livingstone, however, would not see his desire to take up all of the office space in the Shard come to fruition: Irvine Sellar stuck to his unconventional idea of wanting the Shard to be a multi-tenant as well as multi-use building: 'I wanted a variety of tenants that were quality. I'm talking hedge funds, finance, legal, media. Blowing it to TfL would not have given it the character and the class that I wanted.' Less than half of the available office space would be given over to Transport for London.

Sellar recounts that when he met the representative from Transport for London, 'He said, "We'll take 100, 200, 300, 400 or 500,000 square feet, but it has to be at this rate." I said, "I don't want it to be a transport building, because it doesn't suit this building, but you can take 200,000 at the lower level." We agreed the deal and we signed the lease with them.'

On 8 August 2006, Transport for London confirmed it would take a thirty-year lease for 190,000 square feet (17,650 m²) of offices at the Shard, on the lower levels 4 to 10. It would also be taking up 200,000 square feet (18,580 m²) of space at Palestra, another high-profile new building in Southwark. That building was designed by the adventurous and controversial British architect Will Alsop, who coincidentally had been the runner-up to Renzo Piano and Richard Rogers in the Centre Georges Pompidou competition over thirty years earlier, when he was just twenty-three.

As the deal was being finalised, Bårry Ostle of the Sellar Property Group said that, with a major leasing agreement now in place, 'The project is effectively moving into its construction phase . . . We will have this building completed for letting at the peak of the cycle, when there will be most demand and fairly limited supply. So we're very confident that we'll be getting prime rentals.'

It was finally time to start talking about the building again rather than its financing. In the same *Property Week* article, Ostle pointed out that the scheme would be completely compatible with whatever happened regarding the rail masterplan at London Bridge station, and the developers would take it upon themselves to provide the public with a significantly better station concourse.

Hamish McKenzie, Sellar's development manager at the time, said that 'The real challenge is construction next to and around a railway station. On that front, I think we've got a relationship with Network Rail's technical people that's unique.' He was now free to turn his attention to the practicalities of constructing a multi-use building. 'Being mixed use creates two challenges,' McKenzie explained, 'one in terms of design and the other in terms of management. But it doesn't create a construction challenge.'[86]

Initially there were mutterings that Livingstone had led Transport for London into a glamour deal that it couldn't afford. When the terms of the deal were revealed – apparently an index-linked £37.50 per square foot rather than an expected £45 per square foot – astute observers realised that Livingstone and the transport organisation had secured an impressive rate. Public knowledge of the deal could even upset Sellar's attempts to secure a higher rate on the upper office floors.

Despite the securing of two major tenants in Shangri-La and Transport for London, the *Evening Standard* was still putting a question mark over the entire enterprise: 'Erecting a 1000ft glass tower next to a busy railway station to budget is seen by rivals as possibly a challenge too far.'[87]

Finally, the Shard and London Bridge Quarter development was moving at pace. On top of the positive news regarding leasing, the Mayor of London confirmed on 10 August 2006, just two days later, that he would not be calling in the London Borough of Southwark's decision to grant planning permission for the redevelopment of the New London Bridge House site. The First Secretary of State John Prescott announced, likewise, that he would not be calling in the scheme for review.

The proposed second building was called the Place, although it was generally referred to as the 'Baby Shard', a name that infuriated Sellar almost as much as the description of Mates as a 'unisex boutique'. The Sellar Property Group's preferred name was originally 'The Gem', which more accurately reflected the faceted design of the un-spired building, but the London public have never warmed to developers or architects christening their buildings with overtly positive names. The design featured a sloped roof, but this feature was soon amended. Some design changes were enforced, as Sellar explains, because 'Network Rail moved the viaduct closer than we envisaged, which meant we had to redesign it and cost us a year.'

Model of the London Bridge Quarter with an early version of the Place
(which was renamed the News Building) (© RPBW)

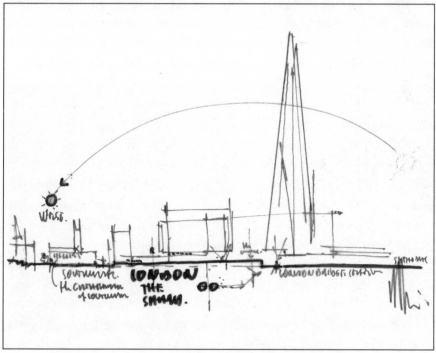

South elevation of the Place (the News Building) in relation to the Shard and
Southwark Cathedral (© RPBW)

Unusually for a development that had already been given planning permission, the height was reduced from 289 feet (88 metres) down to 243 feet (74 metres). The seventeen-storey office building shared some of the design features of its big sister, with much of the steel and glass building cantilevered so the ground-floor reception was set back from the perimeter to give the impression of space – Renzo Piano said that the building would 'float like the rock of Magritte above the ground'.

Like the Shard, the design featured floor-to-ceiling glazing and interior winter gardens, and the glass façades overshot fissures in the body to create wing walls. The roof would now have a pair of terraces. The building, despite being 600,000 square feet (56,000 m²) gross, was designed to complement rather than compete with the principal structure.

Sellar, as he had promised, took the opportunity to create public space in the area connecting the station concourse, the Shard and the Place. Sellar and Piano's teams convinced the authorities that the existing fifteen-stand bus station, located in front of the entrance to the Shard, should be moved to the north and rotated: aesthetically, this would align the bus station with the tracks and, more importantly, it would allow clear sight lines into the train station, diminishing the number of people who would wander around London Bridge, wild-eyed and disorientated.

William Matthews said of the existing chaos: 'When I get off the bus I don't know where the station is. When I get to the station I don't know where the platform is. Irvine wanted people to see where the trains were and enabled that. It was like doing your neighbour's home improvements for them in order to create a better environment. The impact on the public environment is huge, without the public paying for it.'

The resultant space enabled Sellar to create a small piazza between the Shard and the Place, helping to create a focal point for the envisaged London Bridge Quarter while vastly improving the public realm.

The amended design for the Place was approved by the London Borough of Southwark in July 2007. Work was not due to begin until 2009, when the leases of the tenants of the existing twenty-five-storey building were to expire.

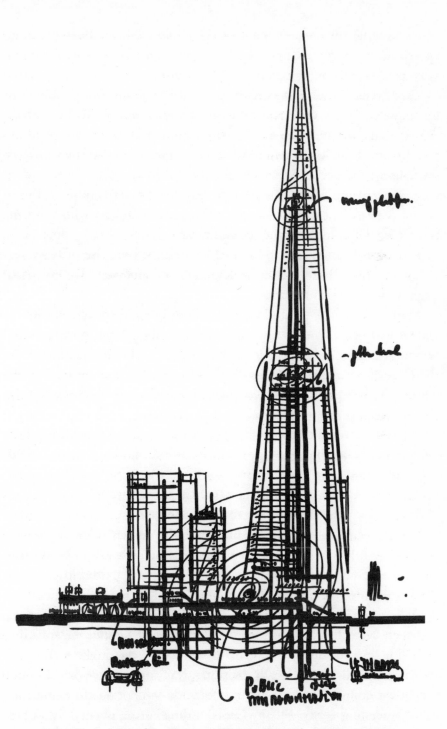

Renzo Piano sketch of the Shard and the Place (the News Building) (© RPBW)

Meanwhile, on 1 September 2006, Teighmore Ltd and Network Rail agreed the extension of the lease of the Southwark Towers site from 150 years to 250 years on completion of the Shard.

Two weeks later, as a consequence of the Transport for London tenancy deal, the prospects for the Shard were dramatically improved. A two-year interim finance package of £196 million was arranged by a multi-firm team led by Ashurst, the leading international law firm that specialises in structured finance. The debt facility would be provided by a combination of the Nationwide Building Society and Kaupthing Singer & Friedlander, the corporate investment bankers who were, at that time, riding high on the Icelandic wave.

Part of the money was to be used to fund the purchase of PricewaterhouseCoopers' lease so that the demolition of Southwark Towers could begin towards the end of 2007.

Sellar reveals, 'We found another building for them to relocate to and we had a plan where we would take them out of Southwark Towers, temporarily house them for four or five years and then put them into the Place as permanent tenants. We had agreed heads of terms, but we couldn't agree a price with the owners of the building we wanted to put them in temporarily, which screwed up that plan. PwC couldn't wait and they had to make other plans, so we were left without a pre-let.' Sellar would have liked to have kept PricewaterhouseCoopers housed in what became the London Bridge Quarter in some way, but, as he told *Property Week*, 'we can do better than the rent we negotiated with PwC and that's the silver lining to the outcome'.[88]

The expected date for the opening of the Shard was altered to a more realistic 2011. Having secured their interim debt facility, the consortium of owners was now talking to banks to raise about £1.35 billion to fund the development of both buildings.

As so often in the story of the Shard, the good news that a challenge had been overcome was soon accompanied by bad. Despite the securing of major tenants and the interim financing, *Property Week* was still wearing its Halloween 'Death' costume, claiming that the Shard's new scheduled completion date would coincide with a flood of available office space in the city. Meanwhile, building costs had risen by 14 per cent in the two years up to 2007, and were set to rise by the same percentage over the next two years. Significantly ominous for the construction of the Shard, the price of steel alone had risen by 25 per cent in a single year due to heightened demand from Asia, especially China and India.

Nonetheless, the 'over-ambitious folly' was in danger of becoming a reality.

Chapter 8

The Crash

You succeed in spite of people, not because of them. When you do something like build the Shard, it's against the odds. Everybody wants you to fail. Your confidence has to be absolute.

Irvine Sellar

There are two types of entrepreneur: one with good ideas who is not a good manager; and the other with good ideas who *is* a good manager. The latter is much rarer.

Irvine Sellar

Marketing the Shard was still a problem. For a start, there was the name: Irvine Sellar and his team continued to refer to the skyscraper as the London Bridge Tower, a name that may have had the benefit of absolute clarity as a geographical and structural label, but was too bland to be accepted into contemporary parlance.

Originally, Irvine Sellar disliked the nickname but, strong-minded though he is, he was not intractable on the subject, especially when he realised that the nickname was of a stronger currency and had a higher recognition factor than London Bridge Tower.

William Murray of Wordsearch, who contributed to the marketing of the tower in the early days of the development, reveals: 'Irvine was keeping to London Bridge Tower, and there was a lot of discussion about "the Shard" as a nickname. Irvine was always saying that "shard" is a nasty word, it's broken glass, it's not a good image to have in one's mind. We and other people involved argued very strongly for the fact that he should take that name, and Irvine listened to that advice and said, "Okay, you're the experts." He very generously in an article a few years ago said, "I was against it and my marketing team advised me what to do. I went with them and they were right."'

Sellar later joked, 'We did consider calling it the Rockersellar Centre but the Shard of Glass – which started as a description of the scheme in a presentation Renzo made – has become more than just a nickname.'[89]

Murray was involved in creating marketing material for the project at a critical time: although Shangri-La Hotels and Transport for London had committed to leasing a combined total of twenty-six floors, Sellar and his team were still having difficulty in attracting other tenants.

He says of Sellar: 'He's bloody difficult, but with reason: in order to achieve things that other people don't achieve.'

He recalls one meeting in particular: 'I'm sitting at one end of the big table in the boardroom at Sellar's offices, and all the agents are sitting around – Knight Franks and all the other guys doing the Place and the Shard – and Irvine comes in and decides, "This is the day I'm going to give them a bollocking." He lets off effing and blinding. "What about fucking this . . . Why haven't you done this?" Rant, rant, rant. "I did all the deals that have been done so far, I did the TfL deal; what have you done?" Rant, rant, rant. A lot of office agents are public schoolboys and they don't quite get Irvine's way, so they don't know what to do. I've known him a long time by then and I'm just looking at him. Then at the end of the rant, he just looks down the table and gives me a wink.'

Murray says that Sellar knows how to motivate people and that he skilfully manipulates and capitalises on aspects of the caricature of himself as a larger-than-life and sometimes aggressive figure. 'He knows when to turn it on and what it takes. He knows he's seen as a character. It's like with the Mates thing. He was an innovator in the 1960s, he was willing to do things that hadn't been done before, and he knows you need a bit of character to deliver those things, that people buy into character. He's very skilful in doing that but in a completely genuine way. What he wants from long-term relationships is the same belief.'

The architect William Matthews agrees. 'Irvine is very challenging, but he's a loyal person. The people who work for him are loyal to him and he is loyal to them. He oozes character, oozes determination, but he is not the type of person who takes on more than he can handle: he knows how to work with other people. He is a man who knows his own weaknesses even though he probably won't admit to any of them.'

Sellar revealed his approach to leadership when I interviewed him shortly after the Tate Modern extension opened in 2016: 'I was at a dinner at the Tate Modern extension last night, and I was sitting next to Michael Burke, the chief exec of AECOM, one of the world's largest integrated civil engineering practices, and he was sitting next to a guy that builds power stations and another top guy – all leaders of major government and transport infrastructure projects. The power station guy asked me how I started out, and told him it was through the markets, through fashion, through property, and I said I have no professional qualifications, but I've got my lawyers and my architects and my engineers and surveyors and my team. My excuse for being able to lead a whole lot of professionals is using the analogy that you can't conduct an orchestra if you're in the pits playing an instrument. If I was qualified, I'd be in the pits playing the cello or the clarinet and I wouldn't be able to oversee anything. I don't know how to play every instrument, but I know exactly what the orchestra should sound like.'

Sellar has long been surrounded by a loyal team within the Sellar Property Group. These include family members James Sellar (who was heavily involved in the Shard project from the beginning and now runs the sister company Sellar Developments) and commercial director Caroline Sellar, the semi-retired head of finance Paul Turpin, investment director John Davies, development director Barry Ostle, group solicitor George Josselyn and construction director Flan McNamara. All of them – with the exception of McNamara who is a comparatively 'late starter' having joined the company in 2009 – have been working with Sellar since construction of the Shard began, and many for considerably longer. Even Sellar's press representative, Baron Phillips, the former property correspondent for *The Times*, has stuck by the developer for decades despite the regular barrage of slings and arrows thrown at him by the press, critics and Sellar himself.

McNamara joined Sellar as project director for what became the News Building (originally the Place), but eventually took over as the construction director for the whole London Bridge Quarter development, including the Shard itself. He was used to large-scale, challenging schemes, having been the construction director at Westfield, the shopping centre that is effectively an enormous groundscraper in Shepherd's Bush. He stayed with Sellar following the completed construction of the Shard and the News Building, and his main priority is now Shard Place, the third of the buildings in the quarter, which will be ready in 2018. He explains that part of the reason why he has stayed, despite offers to move onto other high-profile construction projects, lies in the character of Sellar himself: 'I would never work for someone I don't respect. He immediately made me feel that we are a team. There isn't a day when he doesn't phone. Nothing is too small for him to be annoyed or excited about.'

He continues, 'Irvine inspires loyalty, not because he is easy to work with or pays well, but because he believes in getting it right – it has to be the best. And that means you can be proud of what you have achieved.'

In examining the events of 2007, it is a surprise that Flan McNamara ever had cause to join the Sellar Property Group. In fact, it is a surprise that Sellar's existing staff did not desert his Mayfair office, leaving him alone to brood on the cruelty of fate.

In 2007, Irvine Sellar was facing a series of deadlines, each of which could easily have brought the Shard project to another shuddering halt. The partners had assigned the rumoured £70 million to PricewaterhouseCoopers so that they would vacate the building as agreed in the autumn – this emptied much of the remaining interim pot provided by Nationwide and Kaupthing Singer & Friedlander; and the deadline was approaching to pay back that £196 million loan itself. He was facing a deadline on the agreement he had made with Network Rail to begin redevelopment. And he needed to begin demolition of Southwark Towers as soon as possible because of a deadline that was potentially even more threatening to the future of the Shard.

It stated clearly in the terms of John Prescott's letter when he granted planning permission in 2003 that construction had to begin within five years. If work did not begin in 2008, consent to build the Shard would be voided, and the planning process, which had taken almost three years the first time around, would have to begin again. In the meantime, Teighmore had already paid out approximately £60 million in costs relating to the development, never mind over £70 million in purchase costs plus the money to terminate the PricewaterhouseCoopers lease, and it would be bleeding more money, with no rent revenue coming from Southwark Towers and no end in sight.

Teighmore needed to secure its huge £1.35 billion financing for the development of both the Shard and the Place, and it needed it fast.

With the pressure now immense, Sellar finally found his backer in the spring of 2007. Credit Suisse, the investment bank, had been in existence since 1856 when it was set up to fund the development of the railway network in Switzerland; it then played a key role in helping establish the country as a global financial centre and had a grand tradition in investing in large-scale building projects; and it now owned First Boston, so experienced American bankers were leading its investment arm. Sellar, it seemed, could not have found a more secure partner to finance the development.

To Sellar's relief, contracts were soon being finalised for Credit Suisse to provide the full £1.35 billion finance package: 'They wanted to fund the entire development, and they would only do it provided I stayed and didn't cash in, but they weren't interested in the other partners. They would earn millions in fees, so it was a good deal for them. It was very, very advanced, and they had credit approval, so they told us.'

On Sunday 19 August 2007, two articles in the 'Business' section of the *Sunday Telegraph* gave an inkling of the global storm that was to come: 'Business fears over "Big Chill"' was the heading of one, and the other was 'Market wipes £200m off British Land's shop sale'.[90]

In the first, Dan Roberts opened his article with 'Business leaders are bracing themselves for a "big chill" to spread throughout the British economy as a result of recent turmoil in financial markets.'

The turbulence was caused by the US economy slowing down and tighter lending conditions, and £2,000 billion had been wiped off share prices globally. Even though the underlying economy in the UK was thought to be in decent shape and the London Stock Exchange appeared to be rallying from the dive, the director-general of the CBI, Richard Lambert, warned, 'We just don't know what's lurking out there. We are in for a period of uncertainty as the scale of investment losses becomes clear.'

The second article, by Jonathan Russell, about British Land having to wipe £200 million off the book value of a major shopping centre, carried a specific reference to Sellar: 'Large development schemes requiring huge amounts of debt, such as Sellar Property's Shard of Glass building on London's South Bank, are also rumoured to be struggling to find backing. But despite the gloom, deals are still being done.'

Sellar may have still enjoyed his Sunday breakfast. Russell was right: deals were still being done. The £1.35 million deal with Credit Suisse was in its very final stages: heads of terms had been signed back in May and it was only the minutiae that was being agreed between legal representatives. The deal was heading towards signatures and further progress was due to be made in the week of 20 August. Demolition work was going to start in September. Finally, after seven years, all planning, legal and financial hurdles seemed to have been surmounted: the Shard was going to become a reality.

Perhaps, though, Sellar might have caught a whiff of something other than burnt toast during his breakfast. It would become clear over the next couple of weeks exactly what the smell was: the Credit Suisse agreement had just gone up in smoke.

Not that Sellar was directly informed. As George Josselyn says, 'The bankers were starting to be slow at returning calls and then disappeared altogether. It was like the Cheshire cat. The cat faded away and we were just left with the grin. And then the grin disappeared too.'

Sellar says about typical dealings with American bankers, 'They say yes, yes, yes, all the way down the line, then the last word you hear sounds a bit vague. After a while, you realise that it meant no.' At some point during the rapidly blooming financial crisis, Barry Ostle recalls, one of the American bankers did finally call Sellar, but only to exclaim, 'There's blood on the streets, blood on the streets!'

There were waves of tremors shaking corporate America, tremors frightening enough to put any major new building project in the City at risk. During this time, Sellar had to steel himself against another raft of negative comments concerning the Shard. 'I never thought it was going to be built and I'm not changing my mind', reported a 'senior market source' in the *Business* newspaper on 1 September 2007. This was yet another naysayer, and there had been plenty of those since the Shard project was first mooted back in 2000, but this time even Sellar's closest allies, who had seen him clear hurdle after hurdle in his career, may have agreed.

Transport for London, meanwhile, appeared to be making contingency plans for a new home if the Shard was never built, which, while prudent, was hardly a vote of confidence. On 11 September, the *Evening Standard* reported that the number of people in the property world who thought that the Shard would ever be built was 'dwindling'. Even if Sellar could raise the money to finance the construction, who would attempt such an endeavour during the credit crunch? Property and yields on rent were bound to slide as the full scale of the crisis was becoming evident.

During those weeks, the tremors became an earthquake in the States, and the resultant tsunami ripped across the Atlantic. The Northern Rock bank had to accept an emergency loan facility from the Bank of England on 13 September, and a day later its depositors withdrew £1 billion, the biggest run on a British bank for over a century. Then, on 19 September, the Bank of England offered £10 billion in loans in a desperate attempt to shore up other British banks and building societies.

A day later, Credit Suisse became terminally silent in its dealings with the Sellar Property Group. On 1 October 2007, the reason became clearer. The bank was in crisis itself due to the US subprime credit woes and warned that it was about to report very low third-quarter results.

Sellar joked to me in 2016, nine years later, 'We're still waiting to hear whether they are going to sign the deal.'

In the meantime, PricewaterhouseCoopers were about to evacuate Southwark Towers and the demolition crews were at the ready finally to start the process of developing the Shard.

On 7 September 2007, despite the rapid shift into financial crisis, *Building* magazine had ploughed ahead with its front-page story, 'Works starts on Renzo Piano's monumental London Bridge tower', and a series of inside spreads. The front cover carried a graphic of the words

'The Shard is rising' being craned into the air. Below, the project's remarkable statistics – 310 metres tall, 11,500 tonnes of steel, 120,000 m² of glass and so on – were stacked in the shape of the tapered building.

The magazine reported that Kamran Moazami, WSP's lead structural engineer, was so fed up with being asked when the work was going to begin that he was considering wearing a T-shirt that said 'It's happening'. If he had gone to the effort of having the T-shirt printed, he would have had to put it back in the drawer. Demolition was put on hold.

Almost simultaneously, CLS was effectively publicly announcing that the Shard project was, at best, now in a cryogenic state: 'It is hoped that the funding can be finalised in the near future in conjunction with a restructuring of the shareholding structure. We will not commence any major development work until the loan finance has been secured.'

What the statement did not say was that this meant the entire project was about to reach the ultimate point of jeopardy in relation to its planning consent, and therefore it was very unlikely to see the light of day, ever.

The Shard quickly became an oft-repeated example in the newspapers of a high-profile victim of the credit crisis. As far as the press was concerned, the Shard was no more and Sellar was dead and buried.

Despite the horror of the situation, the developer might have smiled. He had been buried before, six feet under and with no hope of return.

Irvine Sellar says, 'I was in retail, but once you have got a few shops, you are also in branding, logistics, property and finance.'

In the early 1980s, as the recession in the United Kingdom started to bite, he says, 'Retail got tough. I had so many shops that I had been in property for years anyway, and I knew how to make money from it, so I sold Mates and focused on property.'

Mates was sold to a South African consortium in 1981, but difficulties with their financial structuring, and the absence of Sellar's steerage and relentless drive, meant that Mates soon slipped from being a household name into non-existence. 'I thought they would accelerate the business,' Sellar says with a shrug, 'but in two years they managed to screw it up.'

One of Irvine Sellar's final significant acts before his move into property was to open a new Oxford Street store called Jonas, rather than Mates, in memory of his father Joe who died in 1978. In another mark of respect for the man who was partly responsible for both his drive and his passion for fashion retail, Sellar commissioned a large mural for the Liberal Jewish Synagogue near his home in St John's Wood.

Sellar would have a long association with the synagogue after he left the area and moved back to Mayfair.

'We've always been the more open, welcoming, understanding branch of Judaism,' says Rabbi David Goldberg. 'It gives me great personal pleasure that since first meeting Irvine to conducting the funeral of his father Jonas, I have been involved in every family occasion, from births to weddings to deaths. He and people such as Richard Desmond [the media mogul] are generous. They all back each other's charities. It'll be: "Irvine, I've got this charity dinner – take a couple of tables at £15,000." Whenever I have gone to Irvine with a charitable request, he has always responded positively.'

After he sold Mates, in 1982 Sellar teamed up with Mel Morris, his old friend from the judo club in Orange Street, and formed Sellar Morris Properties. Morris also had a background in retail, so they utilised their years of experience to seek out retail development opportunities. Sellar took primary responsibility for the UK operation. In retail, he had shown a theatrical sensibility, attracting both financial interest and customers to his brands, and he took that skill into property, window-dressing his investments to lure a better return. Morris, meanwhile, focused on developments in the United States.

Sellar says, 'Mel would be the first to recognise that I was doing 95 per cent of the work [at least in the UK]. Partnerships can be difficult – joint ventures are a different thing altogether. I've had partnerships where I seem to be doing all the work. I sometimes say, "If partners were a good idea, God would have had one."' There was a good reason why Sellar had to lead the UK operations. 'I knew every paving stone on every high street in the country,' he says, 'and I also knew the retailers already. We would split large stores up, pre-lease to Superdrug or Harris Carpets, and it was a very simple thing.'

They purchased Binns department store in Liverpool and rearranged it into five distinct units for major retailers. Sellar says, 'We carved it up, made use of the upper floors, created a very valuable investment and forward-sold it.' They repeated the formula with the Callers furniture store in Newcastle and House of Fraser department stores.

Sellar says that Morris, by contrast, was developing brownfield sites in cities in Florida. 'We would either build industrial distribution centres or in some cases residential: so it was multi-use development in that country.' It was partly this success in spreading both risk and opportunity through these developments that laid the foundation for the Shard to be the first multi-use skyscraper in Europe.

During this period, Sellar met a resourceful entrepreneur, Tony Leyland, whom he still refers to as his 'right-hand man' and 'foil' even though they have not been in business together for a long time. Leyland was a director of the Rush & Tompkins construction company, and wanted to sell a site to Sellar Morris. Sellar tells me, 'A mutual friend said I should meet him because when he's in a room, the room listens.'

Sellar was impressed by Leyland, and appointed him managing director at Sellar Morris in 1986. 'I knew Mel Morris didn't have the management skills – he's a deal finder and very clever, but he's not a manager. Entrepreneurs are creators, but they are not good managers. There are exceptions, including Richard Desmond. I'm a reasonable manager but a good entrepreneur will recognise where their weaknesses are, and I saw in Tony someone who could work with me, who would be difficult for me to persuade if we were at the opposite ends of a discussion, and it worked very well. It's a bit like Renzo. Renzo put on paper in thirty seconds what I had in my mind. Tony understands my mind. Not only can he articulate what I want, he can make it happen in an organised fashion.'

Leyland remembers, 'When I joined, I was struck and impressed by Irvine's ability and confidence at one minute to convince a landowner that he could pay £10 million for a site and, at the next, deal with a cash-flow crisis over the rental of the coffee machine.' It's a fine line between attention to detail and control-freakery.

Part of Sellar's faith in Leyland comes from their similar can-do attitudes. When Leyland was a young man working for ICI Pension Funds, concentrating on property and construction, a senior partner of the chartered surveyors Weatherall Green & Smith asked him, 'Do you speak French?'

He replied, 'No, but I could learn.' As a result, he spent six years working in Paris as the firm's investment partner.

In 1987, Sellar Morris worked with the fashion retailers Wallis to buy a stake in the discount retailer Amber Day, which was sold on to Philip Green, the future chairman of Arcadia, but the focus was on other ambitions. Sellar and Leyland wanted to push forward as a major commercial developer and launch as a public company.

In order to sidestep the long, complicated process of becoming a public company, they decided to undertake a reverse takeover, by which a private company takes over a public company and adopts its legal status. The target was Martin Ford, a fashion-retail company in which Sellar already had shares.

The takeover was completed in October 1987, and the company became Ford Sellar Morris. It now had forty-seven Martin Ford shops, a stock exchange listing, and the correct market positioning through which it could expand as a major property developer.

'That was an interesting exercise in itself,' Leyland says, 'taking a private business and re-stating it in accounting terms to make a public business. It took a lot of work, skill and perseverance – all helped by the well-respected accountants Coopers & Lybrand.'

By the time of the reverse takeover in 1987, Sellar Morris had undertaken £75 million-worth of business in its four-and-a-half-year history, raising an income of just over £3 million from its property activities. Its ongoing development programme comprised seventeen projects, including a nineteen-acre retail park in Manchester, with an aggregate estimated value of £138 million, and it also owned the Take 6 retail chain in the West End.

On the day that Martin Ford became Ford Sellar Morris, one might have assumed that Sellar, Morris and Leyland sauntered off to Sellar's favoured haunt of Claridge's to celebrate with a few bottles of champagne. Leyland recalls, however: 'There was no celebration. We just went back to work.' As far as they were concerned, it was just a stepping-stone on the road to becoming a major force in UK property development.

Sellar, of course, was soon inspecting the shops he and Morris had now acquired. He recalls that they were not up to the standard he had pursued relentlessly at Mates: 'The merchandise was not good – cheap. Martin Ford came from the same dynasty, the same period, as Chelsea

Girl. Their window displays were shocking – the dressers were told off if they left a space in the window.'

When he visited the Tooting store, the manageress said, 'I'm glad you have taken over the business.'

'Well,' he replied, 'tell me what you think of the merchandise.'

'Let me put it this way,' she said. 'The shoplifters steal the coathangers and leave the clothes behind.'

The step back into retail was a distraction: the aim was to use the status of the new company to buy assets in the property sector. Ford Sellar Morris soon positioned itself to acquire a company twice the size of Martin Ford: Centrovincial, which had been snapped up by Singer & Friedlander. (The merchant bank was later absorbed into Kaupthing Singer & Friedlander, who co-provided the interim £196 million facility for the Shard development.) The bank wanted to sell Centrovincial as soon as possible.

'It was a race,' Sellar remembers. 'We were competing against two or three other companies to buy it. We set up a meeting with Tony Solomon, the chairman of Singer & Friedlander. He said, "Provided you can move fast, you've got yourself a deal."'

Tony Leyland says that they careered around London to raise the finance: 'We got in the back of Irvine's Bentley – the one with the number plate BUY IS – we drove from our offices in Grafton Street, along to Barclays' headquarters in Swan Lane on the river; we had a meeting there; they took us across the road to their sister company BZW [Barclays de Zoete Wedd]; BZW took us up to Bankers Trust in the City – and by the end of the afternoon we'd raised all the debt finance. We raised eighty-odd million pounds from the back of Irvine's Bentley in one afternoon.'

Leyland explains that it was Sellar's drive, rather than the flashy car, that secured the finance: 'Irvine is a charismatic figure, and he had built up some very good relationships over the years with people who were now in senior positions at Barclays; they knew the personality of the man, they knew the drive of the man; and they knew that in a market going in the right direction, he could be relied on to latch on to goodquality opportunities.'

On 22 April 1988, Ford Sellar Morris acquired Centrovincial from Singer & Friedlander for £44.6 million. Ford Sellar Morris's assets were already considerable but they were dwarfed in terms of both value and profile by those of Centrovincial. These assets included numerous central London properties such as Melrose House in Savile Row (valued at £7.1 million); buildings in Grafton Street and Brook Street, W1; and a six-storey property in Fenchurch Street.

As its slightly awkward trading name implies, Centrovincial also had interests further afield, including in Worcester, and it owned a tower block called Leon House in Croydon that was being held for investment and was valued at £10 million. There was a wide portfolio of other properties being held for investment or disposal that were in the meantime earning rental income.

Sellar is usually obsessive when it comes to fine detail, no matter how big the deal, but he overlooked one small matter in the rush to complete the purchase of Centrovincial.

Joe Gold, the founder and chairman of Centrovincial, was in his late eighties, but he still had an ongoing contract that stated, as Sellar recounts: '£50,000 a year; Bentley; chauffeur; office; secretary.'

Sellar telephoned Gold and said: 'Congratulations, Joe, you did a very good deal. I've seen your contract. I would like to know what you're going to do.'

'Nothing,' Gold replied.

'What do you mean, "Nothing"?'

'If you read the contract, I don't have to do anything. By the way, make sure my office has plenty of light – my eyesight isn't too good these days.'

When Sellar met up with Gold, he pushed the matter: 'Look, Joe, you've got this five-year contract. If you're not going to work for the company, then I want to buy you out.'

'What are you offering?' Gold asked.

'Keep the car, and I'll give you £150,000 if you'll call it a day.'

Gold turned down the offer and said to Sellar: 'Let me tell you something: when you buy a company, you buy good assets and you buy bad assets. You've got yourself Melrose House, Fenchurch Street and that property in Croydon – they're your good assets. Well, I'm one of your bad assets.'

Nonetheless, Sellar says that the takeover of Centrovincial was 'one of the best deals I ever did'. 'That property in Worcester town centre was another of the good assets. We hadn't got planning consent, but about six weeks after we acquired the group, we got consent. I think it had a book value of about £2 million in the £45 million that we paid for the group. And a few months later I sold it to the Crown Estates for £21 million – so I made £19 million within eight weeks.'

Centrovincial, though, was not the endgame for Sellar's ambition. Typically, when Sellar sees an opportunity, he throws everything at it. Leyland explains, 'It was another stepping-stone for us to be able to borrow more money and acquire more assets. And those assets increased not only in volume and in value, but in quality.'

The step up from Centrovincial in 1988 was Brookmount in the following year. The company was a joint venture between an entrepreneurial developer and Trafalgar House, which was part of P&O, and the two parties had fallen out.

The offer for Brookmount was £111.4 million, which reflected its large-scale development programme including an office, retail and residential project in Port Hamilton, Edinburgh, the retail and leisure development of Stockton Racecourse, and shopping centres and offices in provincial towns across Great Britain and Northern Ireland.

Within two years, Sellar had gone from being an almost unknown developer to a notable player. Then disaster struck.

The seeds had been sown just two weeks after Sellar Morris reversed into Martin Ford: 19 October 1987 was the folkloric Black Monday, and within a couple of days almost a quarter of the value of the stock market was wiped off. The stock market crash became an extended property market crash.

When Ford Sellar Morris was first listed on the exchange, Tony Leyland explains, 'Our share price was high against the net asset value. We had the paper, but we never had the opportunity to *use* its value for new purchases. Our ability to raise money through the paper that we had was taken away by the drastic change in the stock market that immediately followed the first of the Black Mondays of 1987.'

One day, Sellar was flying to see his sister in Los Angeles. By the time he landed, the value of Ford Sellar Morris had dropped to a third of what it had been when he had boarded the plane.

Sellar says, 'My reaction was obviously, "Oh, fuck. What's going to happen now?" We lost our buying power overnight. The only good thing was, everybody else had, too. It didn't single us out. It was a crash of everybody, it was Black Monday.'

Another flight underlined the scale of the problems. 'At one point,' Sellar recalls, 'I flew to the States on Concorde because I needed to get there quickly – there was so much going on. I was with Tim Eyles, my lawyer, and, during the flight, the pilot came out and said, "Guys, welcome to your private jet – because you're the only two passengers on it." That was what the market was like. You could have fired cannonballs down Bond Street and not hit anybody. Everybody went at the same time, even the Reichmanns, the developers of Canary Wharf, were hurt. Those who were left standing weren't developers. It was a nuclear holocaust in development – the buildings still stood there, but the developers had vanished.'

Ford Sellar Morris's rapid expansion at the end of the 1980s was funded by debt and that proved to be the fissure in the company's stability. 'There was a lot of corporate activity. We were buying companies, buying assets,' Sellar says, 'and selling off chunks of those assets to help finance and fund and re-finance. They were big numbers in today's terms.'

Bankers Trust had provided the debt finance for the purchase of Brookmount, 'We had a good relationship with them,' Leyland says, 'until the whole thing unravelled and we found out that they had sold their interest in the debt to about seventy-two different banks – an unmanageable situation. No one could work it out.'

With the market still in difficulties at the beginning of the 1990s, Ford Sellar Morris may have had a long list of assets, but it did not have enough income.

Mel Morris says: 'You couldn't get money. Up to that time, the company was doing really well. It was riding beautifully. We had deals coming through – we always had a lot of deals, Irvine was voracious in his appetite to get as much as he could, and was very capable. So he was running the business – and the interest rate just shot up to the sky. We couldn't get the money to do what we wanted to do. We'd bought a big portfolio, the company was making a lot of money – it made

£25 million pre-tax, which was a lot in those days; and yet it couldn't be sustained as we couldn't get cash. We tried everything, and we just couldn't do it.'

'We were going from hand to mouth, keeping the business running,' says Leyland. 'The assets had not changed – it wasn't a fault with the assets. It was that the climate in which they were being looked at had completely changed. So people's opinion as to what you could use as security values had changed.'

Ford Sellar Morris needed to keep its major property developments moving forward. Due to the lack of cash, Leyland negotiated with his ex-employer, Rush & Tompkins, to start financing their own building work at Stockton Racecourse so that the developer could buy some time. The construction firm, however, was in trouble itself.

'They didn't make it,' Leyland says. 'They were already stretched on other things – they'd done too many arrangements like that with a number of developers.' In May 1990, Rush & Tompkins called in the receivers.

On 17 July 1990, *The Times* was suggesting that Ford Sellar Morris was on unstable ground despite its portfolio: 'Shorter term, net assets are likely to be flat this year, and profits depend on some big sales, particularly the 750,000 sq. ft. Stockton complex. Investors need faith.'

They did not have any. The market believed that Ford Sellar Morris was running on empty. The company was over-geared, and while estate agents would still give high valuations to its assets, Coopers & Lybrand valued them at two-thirds less.

In August, the company was still trying to push ahead, and made an offer of approximately £40 million for the property development portfolio of Next – the retail company that Sellar has always regarded as the ideological progeny of Mates. 'I got very close to acquiring their property division,' Sellar says. 'If I had acquired that I could have saved the rest of Ford Sellar Morris because it was good, income-producing property. But they couldn't do it. They were in trouble themselves, struggling, and it didn't materialise.'

Ford Sellar Morris was increasingly vulnerable and was subjected to two bear raids – in which the share price was deliberately sold short to make a quick return – in December 1990 and January 1991, beleaguering the company still further.

Amid a fall in profits, it attempted to restructure its debts, but the bell was tolling. On 21 March 1991, 'pending clarification of the group's financial position', trading in the company's shares was frozen.

Two months later, on 30 May 1991, Peat Marwick McLintock was appointed as the administrator for Ford Sellar Morris's operating subsidiaries; on 1 June, the holding company went into administration too.

During this time, Bankers Trust's decision to sell off its interest in the company's debt, which amounted to an excess of £110 million, came home to roost. Sellar recalls a meeting with myriad bankers. 'There were Norwegian bankers, Japanese bankers, they were all totally unconvinced by our arguments – if they listened to them at all. Half of them couldn't speak English. When we were having a meeting, it was very difficult because there was no relationship whatsoever. So I very much blame the American banking system for funding my deals and then selling on the debt.'

The debt could not be restructured. It was the end.

Ford Sellar Morris collapsed with estimated losses of £132 million. Sellar was not declared bankrupt, but he personally lost £28 million.

Sellar is rarely wistful, but he says, 'There's a lot of ifs in life, but that business could have been the size of British Land if we had kept it going.'

Reflecting on that period, Mel Morris tells me: 'People like us don't see a way down. We only see a way back.' Irvine Sellar, meanwhile, reveals that he never lost his optimism: 'I wouldn't say that I was down and out. I would say, "I'm in between fortunes."'

It turns out that he was correct. As always seems to be the case with Sellar, he refused to acknowledge he was beaten, wrapped his knuckles in fresh bandages and came out for another round.

Having saved himself from both the ignominy and legal complications of bankruptcy, he formed his own enterprise, Sellar Property Group, and over the course of the 1990s slowly, and for once warily, worked his way back into property development. He says, 'You either lie there and feel sorry for yourself or you fight back', but he describes his decision to return to the same industry as 'an attack of amnesia'.

He still had an eye for an opportunity: among a range of other deals, he acquired the 200-acre West Wilts Trading Estate and, in

1996–7, bought and sold Lombard House on Curzon Street in Mayfair for a £8.5 million profit in just eight months. He became involved in the redevelopment around the Fratton Park football ground in Portsmouth; struck up a deal to redevelop thirty Civil Service health clubs across the country; and began development schemes in Warrington and Ealing.

By 2000, having bought Southwark Towers with his Teighmore partners, his swagger was back and he was ready to undertake what would turn out to be the most difficult challenge of his life. He told the *Wall Street Journal*, 'After Ford Sellar, I said I wasn't going to get too attached to my work. Well, I've done it again.'[91]

Sellar has a surprising talent for sanguinity when reflecting on the pitfalls of his career. He said to the *Daily Mail*,

> Luck is an evenly dispersed commodity but you have to make the most of your opportunities. Back then, I had the Rolls-Royce, the plane, the big house and it was a long fall. But I had a few loyal friends, I got lucky with a couple of deals and if you have bad news and you're fit and healthy, then you just have to say, 'Tomorrow is the first day of the rest of your life.'[92]

The reputation of the golden boy of Carnaby Street was sullied, though, when it came to announcing plans to build the Shard – to some, the idea that a failed property developer was going to build the tallest building in the country was ridiculous.

In 2000, just as he was revealing Renzo Piano's initial designs for the Shard, he said, 'The memory and lessons of that time are indelibly printed on my mind, but I can't see any clouds on the horizon. I assume they're there though.'[93]

He drew on the lessons of Ford Sellar Morris when he faced the second major crash of his career. As he said when Ford Sellar Morris went under, 'They can take your money but they can't take your brain.' In 2007, with American bankers scuppering his fortunes again, his brain went into overdrive.

• • •

In autumn 2007, Irvine Sellar and his fellow shareholders were left with no investment and a huge debt to repay. In that situation, almost every single developer, especially one that had previously been battered and bruised by a crash, would have conceded that their number was up and that they had taken the project as far as it would go: it was time to sell.

Like him or loathe him, Sellar is like no other developer. As Milan Mandarić once said of Sellar – with respect despite their own time in the courts over the development around Portsmouth Football Club – 'Whatever he says he will do, he does.'[94] And all along, Sellar had said he was going to build the tallest tower in Western Europe.

As soon as it became clear that the Credit Suisse deal was going up in smoke and the Shard project was on the precipice of folding completely under the weight of the £196 million interim loan, Sellar moved with great speed.

He found a solution for all his woes – the lack of funding, the need to begin construction and the need to pay back the loan – in a single masterstroke.

In insecure times, you need a secure partner. With the effects of the credit crunch looking increasingly long term, there was almost nobody in the world more secure than the Qataris.

Quietly, hidden from the eyes of the ever-interested press and prior to the Credit Suisse crisis, Sellar had already begun negotiations with Qatari concerns to fund the buyout of both Ironzar and CLS's interests, effectively to take a majority share of the development. The story of the design of the Shard started with a lunch in Berlin; the project was reborn over coffee, this time at the Berkeley Hotel in Mayfair with Professor Abdul Latif Al Meer of QInvest, the leading Qatari investment bank. Sellar said that the scheme for the London Bridge Quarter 'blew the Qataris away. They shared my vision entirely.'[95]

Qatar at the time, according to its 2004 census, had a population of only 742,883 plus an estimated 400,000 expats, but it was becoming a global player and was taking on Dubai to be the financial capital of the Gulf. The Qataris were not scared of building big – they were funding huge developments in their home country and were expanding abroad – and they wanted profile, especially in London, which they saw as a friendly territory for investment opportunities. Around this time, Qatari parties also became involved in the purchase of the Chelsea Barracks and One Hyde Park, the luxurious residential development designed by Rogers Stirk Harbour + Partners.

These were early manoeuvres in what has become an ongoing trend for Middle Eastern countries to diversify beyond their dwindling natural energy reserves. In 2008, a Kuwaiti fund bought the Norman Foster-designed Willis Building, at 410 feet (125 metres) one of the tallest buildings in the City at the time, and Saudi Arabia was originally funding the Pinnacle, otherwise known as the 'Helter Skelter'.

This was merely a return to the world order – after all, the highly civilised Golden Age of Islam began in the eighth century, making astonishing medical, cultural, economic and legal advances – while at the same time, the forebears of an indigenous City trader thought Bede was a mystical wizard because he could write. The collective Middle East had returned as a significant economic power since the formation of OPEC in 1960, but buying or financing the most significant and high-status contemporary buildings in London – that was new.

When news of the potential deal for the Shard leaked out, Peter Bill of the *Evening Standard* was in favour, writing on 12 October 2007, 'Because this feels very much like the endgame for the 70-storey tapering tower . . . With current sentiment so brittle, a breakdown in talks would shatter Sellar's dream of a Shard of Glass shimmering over London, forever.'

By early October, within weeks of the effective withdrawal of the Credit Suisse offer of investment, the new Shard deal was gaining pace. QInvest, along with fellow Qatari concerns Qatar Islamic Bank, the real-estate developer Barwa and later the Qatar National Bank, were considering joining forces to take over all of Ironzar and CLS's interest.

Barry Ostle says, 'The Qataris had decided fairly early on that they liked the Piano design, they were in love with the building. They had a fine sense of architecture, and London was on their radar. When the Qatari Prime Minister's son arrived at London Bridge, we knew that this thing was moving forward with them.'

This was exactly what Sellar needed at that moment, but he didn't just want to swap partners, he wanted a joint venture with other players able to provide hard cash. This would buy time to recalibrate, time that was never afforded Ford Sellar Morris. With the markets in freefall, Credit Suisse performing a vanishing act and the Shard scheme in peril, the deal evolved. The Qataris were not just going to buy out the partners: they were going to raise the finance.

By January 2008, the arrangements were in place for the Qatar National Bank to put up a deep discount loan of £195 million, and for the Qatari consortium to begin raising investment to fund the development. Sellar had neatly sidestepped both a world and a personal crisis.

In a positive and astute piece of business, the Qataris took advantage of the credit crunch market and secured a knockdown price, rumoured in the press to be less than £100 million, for 80 per cent of the Shard/ London Bridge Quarter development.

When the deal was announced Abdul Latif Al Meer said, 'Our investment in this £2 billion development not only reflects our admiration for what has already been achieved in getting the scheme to its present level, but also underpins our confidence in the London commercial real estate market.' Salah Jaidah, chief executive of Qatar Islamic Bank, pointed to the unusual nature of the deal: 'It is the first time that a consortium of Qatari banks has been formed to invest in an international project of this kind.'

Qatar Islamic Bank had been set up in 1982, with the Qatari royal family member Sheikh Jassim bin Hamad bin Jassim bin Jaber Al Thani – the son of Sheikh Hamad bin Jassim bin Jaber Al Thani, the country's prime minister at the time of the deal – as chairman. The bank was in the course of expanding through offices in the Middle East and Asia, and set up a subsidiary, the European Finance House, in London to undertake sharia-compliant financing, including for the Qatari buyout of Ironzar and CLS's shares of the Shard development. Sharia-compliant financing avoids interest payments, and investors are not allowed to rent assets to organisations involved in pornography, gambling, the arms trade or pork production.

When I asked Sellar if his association with a partly sharia-compliant deal conflicted with his own Jewish faith, he replied that the bank should act according to their own beliefs and that was fine by him. Luckily there were no plans to house any casinos, sex shops or abattoirs in the Shard.

Flan McNamara says about Sellar, 'There is an intrinsic charm needed to get things done – he has that.' He points out that the developer has a strong relationship with Sheikh Abdulla bin Saoud Al Thani, chairman of Qatar Central Bank (which later became involved in the Shard on behalf of the State of Qatar), despite one of them being a Jewish ex-market trader and the other a Muslim member of the Qatari royal family: 'They are both men without airs and graces who get things done.' In reference to the shared Abrahamic roots of Judaism and Islam, he says, 'I remember once that Irvine said to Sheikh Abdulla, "I lost you a few thousand years ago in the desert."'

As William Murray explains, the deal with the Qataris was a perfect match: 'The Shard wouldn't have happened without the Qataris because Sellar Property needed the money, and they also needed someone who wanted a trophy, globally, and who would take a really long-term view rather than immediately needing to make money.'

Sellar tells me that he enjoys working with the Qatari interests: 'I have great respect for their thought processes and the way they want to do business – more respect than I do for most English company directors. They appreciated our vision when everyone else was looking the other way.'

With the major American, British and European banks still manically bailing just to keep afloat, and unlikely to invest heavily in the unpredictable property world for a long time to come, Sellar's feet were finally on terra firma. In 2013, the specialist property news service *CoStar News* was still referring to the agreement as 'one of the most significant property deals of the last decade'.[96]

In return Sellar would reduce his share of the Shard to 20 per cent. He took a considerable hit in giving up 13.33 per cent of a project that was predicted to be worth over £2 billion. He said at the time, 'I would much rather have 20 per cent of something good than 100 per cent of something that isn't.' He revealed that there were operational benefits: the Qataris had great experience and technical knowledge gained from building towers in Doha, and brought that to the table in the fortnightly meetings of the steering group.[97]

Eighteen months later, the State of Qatar bought out the original four Qatari investors and injected its own additional capital. At the same time, finance was arranged for the balance of the development cost for both the Shard and the Place by way of a loan from Qatar National Bank. Sellar's percentage was further reduced but he held onto what would be an extremely valuable stake. The arrangement meant that he had defied the odds and, what's more, he would still be the developer of the scheme. Sellar said to me, 'There are now only two shareholders and the other is a country – the State of Qatar – and that is unique.' He is hugely proud of his family's relationship with his Qatari partner; and this relationship has proved to be so good that in subsequent years their shared interests have extended into other joint ventures.

In the meantime, almost a decade after Sellar had stood on top of Southwark Towers, the building was finally going to be torn down to make way for his vision.

Chapter 9

Breaking Ground

> Prepare a to-do list every day. When you wake up in the morning, say, 'This is what I want to achieve.' Make the list so tough that it will be almost impossible to achieve everything. As Benjamin Franklin is supposed to have said, 'If you fail to plan, you are planning to fail.'
>
> Irvine Sellar

> Build a good team around you because any bad member of the team can spell disaster. The chain is only as strong as its weakest link.
>
> Irvine Sellar

———————————

There had been a skyscraper boom in the UK after plans for the tower at London Bridge were first announced at the beginning of the twenty-first century. In 2008, nine of the thirteen buildings in the UK over 150 metres (492 feet) in height had been completed since 2002.[98] Yet *Property Week* was right to be pessimistic. While construction prices were due to rise, the whole UK economy was entering crisis mode and beginning to slump desperately. The construction industry is built on confidence, and its house can be blown down before the Big Bad Wolf has even taken a deep breath.

Lehman Brothers had been floored in 2007 by the subprime mortgage crisis in the United States. It jettisoned its subprime lender, BNC Mortgage, in August 2007, but it kept spiralling downwards and, in September 2008, it crashed into bankruptcy. It was the fourth-largest investment bank in the United States, but it was merely the most noticeable victim amid the global carnage. The years 2007 to 2009 became known as the 'Great Recession' (at least in the United States, land of the biggest, best, most and greatest; in Britain, the period is usually known as simply the recession – lower case 'r', nothing great about it).

Skyscraper development came to a virtual halt across the United Kingdom: the Cheesegrater, the Walkie-Talkie and the Helter Skelter were all put on hold. Three Sisters, 100 Bishopsgate, Cosmos, Bishop's Place, 1 Puddle Dock, St Alphage House and almost every other development of over 400,000 square feet (37,161 m²) were rightly assumed to be in at least temporary jeopardy.

The message was obvious: do not build big in this climate. On 1 November 2008, Edwin Heathcote, the *Financial Times*'s architecture critic, pointed out that multiple plans for skyscrapers often portend doom, as they did in New York's Golden Age before the depression. Jonathan Russell in the *Telegraph* was saying that 'it will take a very brave developer with very deep pockets to press ahead'.[99]

Meanwhile, on 15 May 2008, Yousef Hussain Kamal, Qatar's Minister of Economy and Finance and Qatar National Bank's chairman, launched the development of the London Bridge Quarter and the only supertall building (i.e. over 984 feet or 300 metres) in Western Europe at a glamorous party.[100]

The only developers who constructed a very tall building – over 150 metres – in London at that time were Irvine Sellar and Gerald Ronson. Some deemed Sellar's determination to pursue construction in the current climate as simply crazy, despite the security of Arabian investment. 'There were many times when I thought we might not make it,' Sellar concedes, a grand admission from a man who thrives on forward drive and optimism. 'If it wasn't for my sense of humour, I wouldn't have got through it. It's a great defuser of pressure to be able to see the funny side of anything. You need a release valve.'

In more bolshie mode at the time, he performed his usual trick of turning what everybody else sees as a negative into a positive. He said that he was not building at the wrong time: he was building at exactly the right time. With little work around, construction firms and suppliers needed to contest keenly for his business, and when his spanking new offices would be ready, there would be little competition.

He told *Property Week* in July 2008: 'There is no quick fix to what we are in but in a few years' time there will be far less development taking place and far fewer competitive schemes, and construction prices are going to come down.' He took the opportunity to stress that the Shard would be an exceptional building: 'There aren't many buildings in this country like it and I think that it is a top 20 building within the world.'[101]

In the same article, his son James said, 'I have been on this project for a decade and that has taken me through engagement, marriage and two kids and it has been a fantastic experience.' James is his own man, but he shares his father's mix of optimism and stonewall determination. The Sellar family, it seemed, was not going to be stopped by the greatest global economic crisis since the 1930s.

Speed was of the essence. With the Qatari funds guaranteed, Sellar, not one to miss a marketing opportunity ever since his early retail days, wanted to build the Shard in time for the opening of the Olympics in July 2012 when the world's focus would be on London.

Demolition of Southwark Towers began in May 2008, enabling Sellar to meet the five-year deadline stipulated by the Deputy Prime Minister back in 2003. The amount of abuse to which T. P. Bennett's building had been subjected by the developer's team, the press and even the inspector at the public inquiry suggests that there may have been a large and happy gathering if the building had been dynamited to smithereens. Blowing up a building requires complex arithmetic, physics, chemistry and much hands-on experience, but that option would have been far too straightforward for the story of the Shard.

The demolition of Southwark Towers and the construction of its huge, sky-scraping replacement would have to take place while, on the corner of the site, London Bridge remained one of the most commuter-heavy stations in London, with 54 million customers a year. Guy's Hospital, just a few metres across St Thomas Street, treats 750,000 patients per annum and there could be no interruption in its normal services, including operations – major vibrations caused by the building work could have had a life-threatening impact. The hospital had already encountered trouble with large construction works: the drilling of the Jubilee line extension, running underneath St Thomas Street, led to the fracturing of a water main, resulting in the flooding of the hospital.

The Jubilee line tunnels themselves, which were completed in 1999, almost touch the corner of the Shard site so were another huge consideration. As well as the possibility of a calamitous accident, damage to the tunnels would threaten to bring long-term, daily strife to hundreds of thousands of passengers. The Jubilee is the third busiest line of the Underground network, servicing 213 million passengers every year.

On top of that, the London Bridge bus station, also bordering the site, had to remain fully functioning, and the site was surrounded by narrow access roads, so traffic around the site could easily come to a standstill.

The result: uniquely, the old building and its huge replacement would have to be demolished and constructed almost completely within their own footprints, and without disturbing vital medical and infrastructural services. If the Shard had not been built and Sellar and his co-owners had sold on the site to another party, there is no doubt that the replacement building would have had a smaller footprint, thereby making the construction of the building much easier, much cheaper and far less impressive.

The demolition was conducted by the specialists Keltbray. To minimise dust and noise, the removal of Southwark Towers had to be gradual rather than explosive. It was taken down floor by floor at the rate of up to one floor per week, with large structural chunks lowered down by crane into waiting lorries. The material totalled 1,100 lorry-loads, but only 30 were allowed to be taken away per day in order to prevent congestion.

The demolition took place behind white acoustic screens, and water sprays were used to dampen dust, which could have caused a serious problem within the hospital, while London Bridge would have become dirty and hazardous for commuters.

Around 95 per cent of Southwark Towers was recycled, including the metal, glass and wood. The 14,000 cubic metres of concrete were

Start of the demolition of Southwark Towers, 2008 (Sellar Property Group Archive)

taken away to be crushed and reused in other building projects, particularly under road surfaces.

The removal of the great weight of the building, no matter how gradual, would inevitably destabilise the soil below, and therefore threaten the stability of the surrounding buildings as far as 260 feet (80 metres) away. As Hamish McKenzie, development director of Sellar Property Group at the time, explained, 'Just like when you remove your foot from the sand on the seashore, all the sand moves in to fill the gap, immediately – that's what happens with buildings as well.'[102]

Sol Data, which had been involved in the huge redevelopment of King's Cross, was appointed to look after the structural monitoring of the site. The overland and Underground stations, tunnels and tracks and the Victorian brickwork vaults underneath the rail station along St Thomas Street, as well as Guy's Hospital, would all need extremely careful monitoring for any movement caused by the building works on the exceptionally tight site.

The monitoring scheme involved Cyclops robotic theodolites, which operated in groups via wi-fi networks, together with traditional instruments such as tilt sensors, tilt meters, electrolevel beams and crack gauges. Nine Cyclops were used to monitor the Network Rail tracks, with six monitoring the station building façades and those of Guy's Hospital. Four further Cyclops were placed within the Underground to monitor the Jubilee line platforms and tunnels. Every day, 100,000 readings were imported into a database, and an automated alarm was triggered if pre-determined levels of movement were exceeded.

There was trepidation among the engineers when, during the process of excavation, they detected that a Jubilee line tunnel had shifted by fifteen millimetres. Although significant, the level of movement was within the prescribed limit and did not affect the tube trains. If the tunnel had moved much further, though, the work on the Shard would have been immediately terminated and the entire design would have been compromised. When construction work was completed, the tunnel gradually settled back again by four millimetres, and the Jubilee line remained unaffected.

The Keltbray demolition crew removed the above-ground building during a ten-month period, leaving the 2-metre-thick reinforced concrete foundations. The simple use of pneumatic drills to break up the slab inevitably was not an option due to the level of disturbance this would have caused to the patients and staff at Guy's. Large amounts of explosives were also out of the question, so explosives expert Mick Williams and his team resorted to using very small, controlled explosions. Up to a maximum of 700-grams worth of nitroglycerine sticks were inserted into a series of drilled holes, which were covered by blast mats to dampen the noise. The results were visually unspectacular, with the blast mats just kicking up like an unwanted duvet, but effective.

During 2008, Sellar brought in Bernard Ainsworth as the managing director of the London Bridge Quarter company. Described by *Building* magazine as the 'ultimate project manager' due to his delivery of the Millennium Dome and the venues for the 2002 Commonwealth Games in Manchester, Ainsworth had been considering slipping into retirement before Sellar diverted him to London Bridge. [103]

By the close of 2008, demolition of Southwark Towers was approaching completion and everything was more or less in place for Ainsworth to oversee the beginning of construction work, working with Turner & Townsend, a leading construction project management consultancy appointed by Sellar.

There was only one problem: Sellar had yet to agree terms with a construction company.

The engineering company was, by contrast, securely in place. Having been linked to the Shard project since 2001, WSP was ready finally to begin work in earnest. Originally called the William Sale Partnership, WSP was founded in Surrey in the early 1970s as a small building services consultancy.

Co-founder Chris Cole recalls, 'Three people – I was the youngest – began to build a young new consultancy. A colleague who had been left some money by his mother thought it might be a good idea to start a business. I was working for a large consultancy as a young guy who was pretty disillusioned. He said, "Come and join me."'

By the time construction started on the Shard, WSP had a turnover of £600 million, worldwide offices and a staff of 9,000. In 2012, the number of staff would multiply to 33,000 following a friendly merger with the Canadian firm Geniver.

Back in 2001, when Chris Cole first heard that Irvine Sellar was working with Renzo Piano on a skyscraper, WSP was still finding its feet as a global player willing and able to undertake large projects. Cole vividly remembers that first meeting, in which he was 'hoping to get some traction – hoping that one day I would work with Irvine'.

The meeting was not as formal as he had feared: 'Irvine was larger than life. In those days he smoked a cigar. He was sitting there, putting the world to rights, talking about vision and throwing his arms about; and he knocked the end of his cigar off. It went right through his shirt and burned him. He was jumping round the room, shouting: "That was a bloody good shirt!"'

Sellar liked Cole and was willing to offer him a chance, eventually saying, 'OK, present yourselves. Tell me how you could do the job.' WSP had just bought a US engineering practice, Cantor Seinuk, which had great experience of building high-rise, so he brought over from New York a team of engineers and presented his plans to Sellar and Renzo Piano at Southwark Towers one Saturday morning. A long-term relationship was born, and Cole says they 'went through hell and high water together'. WSP continues to have a relationship with Sellar through the latter stages of the London Bridge Quarter development and other ventures.

Cole says: 'I'm a great promoter of Irvine. One of the characteristics in people that I really like is their being driven. He is an absolutely driven man. Every obstacle that could possibly be put up against him, he dealt with: it was partly sport for him, partly people earning his respect. It's in Irvine's DNA that he doesn't bear a grudge. You can disagree with him – and you will disagree because he is pretty dogmatic about certain things – but he won't respect you if you don't stand up to him. If the Shard project had been in the hands of a corporation it would never have happened: there would have been every reason not to go ahead with it . . . The Shard is one man, which is pretty rare. None of us would have been party to the Shard if he hadn't driven it.'

The other key appointment was the construction company, but this was a far more drawn-out process that, with the site now prepared, threatened the prospect of the Shard being completed before the 2012 Olympic Games. Many of the contracts for particular aspects of the design and construction were already in place with other companies before the developer and the construction company finally came to an agreement in 2009. In June 2008, Stent was appointed as piling contractor, with Severfield-Rowen supplying the steel, Dutch company Scheldebouw the glass, and KONE the lifts. Oakwood Engineering was appointed in July 2008 to design 17,000 pieces of steelwork, but there was a delay until 2009, when the construction terms were agreed, before Byrne Bros were awarded the £50 million contract for the concrete.

Arup, meanwhile, had already been given the responsibility of designing the building services, which required an innovative approach to the mechanical, electrical, public health (including specialist IT and lighting systems) and fire engineering systems. The Shard, in fact, is such an unusual building, and on such a difficult site, that almost every aspect of its construction required design, methodological or material innovation, even right down to the way that concrete, that most unglamorous and rudimentary of materials, was used.

The construction company, to the initial surprise of many in the industry, was Mace.

Ever since he dealt with both suppliers and customers face to face when he was running market stalls in the 1950s, Sellar has liked to have a direct relationship with individual people, not faceless companies. No matter how large the project and how massive the corporations involved, he sees personal relationships as vital to ensuring a successful outcome. Sellar had a good relationship with John Roberts, the Australian founder of Multiplex, which was in the course of completing Wembley Stadium and had built the thousand-foot Emirates Towers in Dubai. The firm was involved in pre-construction consultation work for the Shard, and Sellar says that had Roberts not passed away in June 2006, Multiplex might have constructed the building. Instead, two major firms, Laing O'Rourke and McAlpine, were initially in the running for the contract, while a smaller firm, Mace, was considered an outsider.

Barry Ostle says: 'There was no chemistry between Laing O'Rourke and Irvine. It would never have worked. There was fabulous chemistry between John Roberts of Multiplex and Irvine, but he sadly passed away. Skanska had just taken on the Heron Tower, and all their resources in London were on that. McAlpine made it clear that they couldn't do it: there wasn't an appetite there. If you looked at it long and hard, there wasn't really a major contractor out there who was prepared to do it. Mace were effectively just a construction manager, running the demolition contract. In a construction management contract, the client takes all the risks in the design and construction, and the contractor is nothing more than a package manager.'

Sellar's decision to turn to Mace was partly based on costs and the company's commitment to complete construction in time for the London Olympics in 2012, but it was also fuelled by his faith in the company's chairman, Stephen Pycroft: 'He is a can-do man and he's got leadership qualities. He's a good negotiator and he's also a man who's proud of what he wants to achieve. I can relate to people who are winners. He's one, and Chris Cole is in the same bracket, as are many of the other team leaders or professionals we employed at Turner & Townsend and Arup, although there were too many changes of staff at Arup.'

When they were young, Sellar was a hands-on retailer and Piano was a hands-on builder working for his father. They may both be called visionaries in their own way – but there was nothing abstract about the way they learned their trades. Stephen Pycroft shared that trait. He started in construction at the age of eighteen, working as a labourer on building sites in his home town of Bradford, West Yorkshire. His father, though, gave him an all-important pointer for his future: 'It's not the guys digging the holes that make the money: it's the people managing them.' The younger Pycroft wanted to stay in construction, but he took his father's advice, gained a degree in quantity surveying, and donned a suit.

He joined Bovis in London, where he made an impression on the construction director, Ian Macpherson: 'I spent a year in that office arriving fifteen minutes before Ian. Every day I said good morning but he never said it back. Eventually he came over to me and said, "Who are you, then?" I told him and mentioned that I did not like the project manager on my job. Macpherson said: "Do it yourself."'

Macpherson and four colleagues left Bovis and founded Mace in 1990, and Pycroft joined the company three years later. His ascent there was rapid: he soon established himself as a major figure in the nascent company, led a management buyout in 2001, and became the majority shareholder.

Pycroft was aware that Sellar, with little experience of major construction, would need to form a new relationship with a contractor to deliver his massive tower. Mace was seeking a new relationship, too. Prior to that meeting in summer 2004, Mace had constructed the Department of Trade and Industry building on Victoria Street, and worked on British Airways' headquarters in Heathrow and the London Eye, but it had little experience of building very tall or of a project on the scale of the Shard.

Consequently, the tallest building in Western Europe was to be built by a developer, an architect and a constructor who were surprisingly inexperienced when it came to working on a supertall structure.

Mace had originally been approached on a standard construction management contract deal but this was changed to a fixed-price deal – which was far more attractive to the new Qatari partners as costs would be guaranteed rather than spiralling out of control. This delayed the signing of the contract as Mace needed all aspects of the design, including belated alterations to the angle of the backpack and changes to the canopies, to be finalised and approved by Southwark before it could stipulate its fee.

Mace put together what it considered to be a tightly costed offer, but Irvine Sellar is a famously tough negotiator. He explains, 'I always say, "You don't agree a deal until their eyes water." I don't want them to cry – that's too emotional – and I don't want it to be bad enough for them to run away, but I need to see a little moisture in their eyes.'

He made the highly unconventional move of calling in McAlpine, one of Mace's competitors, and EC Harris, the long-standing real estate asset consultancy firm, to assess Mace's bid. The fixed fee was battered down and the construction contract was finally agreed in 26 February 2009, after piling work on the Shard site had already begun.

The £425 million deal was the first fixed-fee contract in Mace's history, and it was a set-up some other major construction companies attempted to avoid at all costs, as the burden of overrunning expenditure can rest with the constructor. Mace chose not to walk away from the project, with good reason.

Pycroft says: 'Before the Shard, Mace was, in footballing terms, in the Championship. The Shard put us right at the top of the Premier League. Before the Shard, some people thought Mace would not take risks. The Shard proved, beyond doubt, that we would.'

The punt paid off. By 2014, Mace had become a significant player in the construction industry, with a staff of over 4,000, revenue of almost £1.5 billion, and offices worldwide.

Pycroft had a close working relationship with Sellar throughout the three-year construction of the Shard: 'If it wasn't a daily phone call between him and me, it was every other day; and at least every two weeks – and then going to every month – there were formal meetings of all the principals of each of the organisations involved – Mace, Arup, WSP, Renzo's team – so that no one was in any doubt about their contractual obligations to deliver. Sometimes Irvine would read us the riot act.'

Sellar says, 'It doesn't matter how big a company it is. It matters what team they put together who are devoted to a particular project. It's a matter of quality and leadership. And they respected me because they saw me at the coalface when I needed to be. The ups and downs – the politics – that went on pre-construction and during construction needed to be managed, and needed to be directed. There are always issues – some people call them problems – and it's a matter of how you resolve them. That's what development is about. And that's what life is about.'

The force of Sellar's personality was always evident. Chris Cole remembers one meeting at which someone ingratiatingly commented: 'That's a very good point, Irvine.'

The response: 'I wouldn't have fucking made it if it wasn't!'

As friction is part and parcel of the relationship between developer and construction company, Sellar and Pycroft would often be at loggerheads. 'We had some pretty vociferous discussions,' Pycroft recalls. 'But the great thing about Irvine is that you can have those barneys – rows, if you like – but then a decision is reached, sometimes in favour of what you've been saying, more often in the direction of what he's said. You have a glass of wine and life goes on. The obverse side is that, one evening, Irvine will be the life and soul of the dinner table with his anecdotes and jokes; at eight the next morning, he'll be bawling some complaint down the telephone at you as if the night before never happened.'

Sellar keeps his focus and motivation by making a to-do list – one that is usually impossible to complete – every day. If I arrived to interview him early in the morning before his working day theoretically started, he would already be on the phone, a glint in his eyes, firing off a rocket in the direction of someone who still had sleep in theirs. If his day is not filled with meetings and telephone calls through which he can push a project forward, preferably at pace, he is best avoided.

Whatever disagreements he had with Sellar, Pycroft emphasises a point made over and over again by those who know the developer: 'It is impossible to overestimate the loyalty and confidence that Irvine inspired. Most of his team would have jumped off a cliff for him, and most of my team, too.'

With the fixed fee finally agreed in February 2009, Salah Mohammad Jaidah, the chairman of London Bridge Quarter Ltd, the company consisting of Sellar and the Qatari interests, said, 'The investors have great confidence that the Shard will be completed on schedule in what are very difficult economic conditions.' Pycroft added, 'This is a fantastic milestone for our company and an encouraging sign for our industry in difficult times . . . we are all delighted to conclude the negotiations so that we can get on with the challenge of building what will be a highly prestigious project for London.'

When construction of the Shard started on 16 March 2009, Chris Cole said, rather less formally, 'This is one of the few shows left in town.'[104] All eyes would be trained on the changing Southwark skyline for the next three years.

But what would they be seeing emerge from the ground? The numbers game: 1,016 feet (309.6 metres) high, 1.2 million square feet (110,000 m²) of floor space, 602,800 square feet (56,000 m²) of glass façade, 95 floors (72 of which are habitable) including, from bottom to top, 25 office floors, 3 restaurant floors, 19 hotel floors, 13 residential floors and a 6-storey viewing gallery, 49 lifts and escalators, 306 flights of stairs, 8,500-person office/residential capacity, plus around 1 million annual visitors to the viewing gallery.

The similarity between Renzo Piano's sketch drawn at the restaurant table in May 2000 and the finished Shard is striking but, as William Matthews explains, the design of the building, except for its elemental shape, had been so refined since its origination that the shell had been effectively 'gutted and gutted again'.

Structurally, the most obvious changes since the very early concepts were the faceting of the façades into different planes separated by fractures, partly in response to the unusual geometry of the site; the fact that those façades did not meet at the apex, which was fourteen storeys shorter than in the initial concept; and the addition of the backpack.

Less obviously, there was a multitude of details that were either originated or altered during years of research, development and redesign before Southwark Towers was finally removed from the map. It was those decisions that took the building from being just a new hulk on the skyline, worth an initial look but then perhaps forgotten as part of the fabric of the city, to a building that people look at again and again as they go about their London lives. There was also much focus on making the Shard a functionally successful building that would be just as rewarding on the inside as it was to admire from the exterior.

Model of the spire of the Shard, 2009 (© Michel Denancé)

The Shard from four sides (© RPBW)

Much of the focus was on the environmental sensibility of the building, both in ecological terms and through the building's aesthetic relationship with its setting, the city and the sky.

The form of the skyscraper can provide ecological benefits (which need to be offset against the energy expended in vertical transport) beyond consuming less acreage at ground level: the large surface areas can be used to reap solar energy, the height means that high winds can be harnessed and used for energy or part of a natural cooling system, and the depth of the foundations into the ground can make it possible to collect geothermal energy.

There is sometimes, however, a fracture between such good intentions and the end result. The seventy-one-storey Pearl River Tower (2011) in Guangzhou, China, was designed by Skidmore, Owings & Merrill to be a clean, futurist building incorporating micro wind turbines, radiant heating/cooling, solar thermal collectors and photovoltaic cells. It is the same height as the Shard and should have been a net zero building as it could produce as much energy as it siphons off the grid. The local power company, however, refused to allow the owners to sell energy back to the grid, so the micro turbines were scrapped.

One of the notable features of the Shard's design was to be a giant radiator held within the spire above the viewing gallery. It was designed to be an open lattice structure of twenty-four horizontal decks of piping, which would be open to the elements and cooled naturally by the high winds. Excess heat in the building would be captured by heat-pumps and used to heat the residential and hotel levels, with the remaining heat naturally dissipated through the radiator. This would hugely reduce the energy expended for heat reduction through air conditioning.

The giant radiator concept was abandoned, however, after calculations revealed that more energy would be expended in pumping the heat towards the top of the thousand-foot building than would be saved. As Sellar Property Group project manager Michael Donnelly also points out, the water pressure on the way down would have been approximately 25 bar – fifteen times the water pressure in an average household. 'To be honest, the radiator wasn't great looking, either,' says Donnelly.

Consequently, the open upper levels of the Shard's spire above the viewing platform are more aesthetic than functional (although they do house building maintenance units [BMUs], the permanently installed suspended access equipment used for cleaning and maintenance of the exterior). Prime space in the backpack had to be given over to a more conventional cooling system.

Nonetheless, buildings such as the Shard and the Gherkin pushed forward the idea that not only can tall buildings be accepted as a notable, aesthetic benefit to the London skyline, but they can be environmentally responsible. In the Gherkin, for example, the multiple mini-atria provide natural ventilation, reducing the carbon footprint.

The floor-to-ceiling glazing of the Shard creates the exterior aesthetic, offers the unique views and allows the greatest amount of natural light to enter the building, thereby improving the work environment in the broad floor plates of the large office floors. But, as William Matthews pointed out to *Building Design* in June 2010, 'What we are building here is a great big greenhouse.' Greenhouses are, of course, designed to capture heat and, in the case of the Shard, 11,000 panels covering 600,000 square feet (56,000 m²) would optimise solar gain and cook the innards – and the inhabitants – of the building.

There is also a cautionary tale relating to the 787-foot (240-metre) John Hancock Tower in Boston, with which the architects, engineers and constructors of any tall building, but particularly the Shard of Glass, should be familiar. In 1968, as the Henry N. Cobb-designed building finished going up, some of it was coming down.

The façade was constructed of mirrored, blue-tinted glass in large panes each weighing 230 kg. When the wind reached speeds of 70 km/h, glass started to fall hundreds of feet to smash onto the buildings and pavements below. Meanwhile, people in the upper reaches of the building could feel it swaying so much that they suffered motion sickness.

Belated wind-testing of a model revealed that the building was twisting in the wind. Retrofitted crossbeams and a large mass-damper added to the fifty-eighth level cured the problem of twisting and swaying, but not the problem with the glass. Testing of the glazing, which consisted of an outer layer, a mirrored layer and an inner layer, revealed that thermal stressing from a heated to a wind-cooled state meant that the outer layer of glass was pinging off and plummeting

John Hancock Tower, Boston (© ntzolov)

towards the ground. Every single one of the 10,344 panes of glass had to be replaced, at a total cost of more than $5 million.

In 2005, closer to home, a glass panel fell from the newly opened Gherkin about a hundred metres onto the pedestrian plaza below. A covered walkway had to be temporarily erected on the plaza so that visitors could reach the building's entrance while engineers checked all of the building's other glazed panels.

As well as trying to avoid a repetition of such horror stories, the architects at the Renzo Piano Building Workshop – and Irvine Sellar himself – were also concerned by the look of the glass for the Shard. Standard-issue glass, due to its iron content, can look dark green *en masse* in a tall or broad building, and even the Gherkin can look slightly green. Joost Moolhuijzen has written that 'there are a lot of bottle-green buildings around! We could not accept this for a tower which is so prominent on the London skyline.' Instead, they wanted an 'immaterial crystalline effect that would play with the light and the mood of the weather'.[105]

The sophisticated façade system was such a crucial part of the design that Sellar allowed the architects to explore variants of glazing design on a pre-contract service agreement with a specialist contractor, Scheldebouw, rather than simply putting the curtain walls out to commercial tender in a more usual manner.

The result was a low-iron, laminated glass in 4.3 × 1.5 metre panes, incorporated into a naturally ventilated double-skin façade. Air is allowed into the glazed units through a series of gaskets set between the mullions, which cools the inner skin and reduces heat gain, with hot air escaping through the top of the frame. The outer skin was turned into a significant design feature, over-sailing the edges of the fractures between the façades for between 1.5 and 4.2 metres to create 'wing walls'.

This outer skin is extra-white glass, which gives the building a crystalline effect, with a 20 per cent reflective coating. Float glass, rather than toughened glass which has a roller wave that distorts reflections, was used for flatness and crispness. The inner panes are also extra-white glass with a low-emissivity, high-performance coating, which helps reduce heat gain through reflection. Using white glass allows 55 per cent of heat (G-value .55 for those of a technical disposition) to be transmitted into the building, but the blinds reduce this to just 12 per cent (G-value .12).

The motorised roller blinds are incorporated within the façade between the outer, single-glazed panes of glass and the hermetically sealed double-glazed interior skin of the building. The blinds are woven in almost translucent fibre so, although they cut down solar radiation drastically, they allow the curtain wall to still seem somewhat transparent while they are in the down position.

The blinds are controlled by the building management system, which is informed by light sensors on the individual façades. They are automatically raised to provide the utmost natural light when there is no direct sunlight, thereby reducing energy expended on artificial lighting, and at night to enable cooling through maximum heat loss. They are lowered during direct sunlight to reduce solar gain and therefore reduce energy expended on air conditioning.

Renzo Piano wanted the scheme to have a small element of colour and the blinds' orange-red housing boxes provide this, breaking up the translucency. The boxes are not noticeable until a pedestrian is close to the building, but when the low winter sun hits them, the Shard takes on a warm glow.

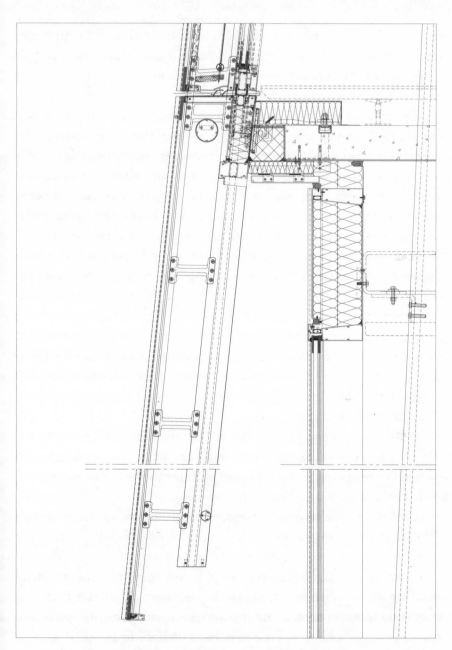

Side view of the Shard's façade system (detail) (© RPBW)

During their joint research, Piano's team and Scheldebouw made a mock-up of a section of façade and hoisted it 30 metres into the air to witness the effect of the double skin and the glass treatment, including its 20 per cent reflectivity. It worked. For the actual build, no existing glass created exactly the right effect so Interpane developed Ipasol Bright specifically for the Shard, working through forty variations until the final effect was achieved.

The resulting façade, according to Piano, is 'not like a mirror, because it's not made of reflective glass, but even extra-white glass takes on the colour of the sky and the clouds, and assumes a warmer tone in the evening at sunset . . . given the multitude of surfaces of which it is comprised, one face becomes reflective as the sun turns, while the others do not.'[106] The research and innovation, crucially as far as Piano and Sellar were concerned, prevented the Shard from looking like a domineering, hulking mass, and made it more like a sensor for the weather of London, changing from hour to hour and from façade to façade according to the weather and the position relative to the sun.

For all the eco-sensibilities of its double skin, optimised blinds and building management system, the most important aspect of the Shard in ecological terms is simply its location on a transport hub. Piano had said back in 2003,

> This building is not designed to bring more traffic into the city. It is situated on one of London's main transport hubs. If you consider that London, or any city, is a living, breathing thing then the railways are the arteries and the bus routes and underground are the veins. There is no need for a car park as we have everything there . . . This building is about gentleness.[107]

Piano and Sellar stayed true to the eco-friendly concept of the building that they pushed at the public inquiry. The finished building houses up to 8,500 people, but it has precisely forty-eight car-parking spaces in an efficient stacking system. It is hard to imagine another construction, be it campus, building complex, town or village, that has such a high footfall without contributing to traffic congestion and pollution.

Those few parking spaces still caused a headache for project architect William Matthews: 'I remember one meeting where we were talking about getting rid of the car park and having the car-stacker instead. I knew Irvine would ask me about it so I had already checked the measurements of his Bentley and, sure enough, Irvine asked, "Will my car fit in it?" When I told him it would fit he said, "No, my new car." It was a Rolls-Royce and, no, it wouldn't fit. He looked delighted.'

In the years following the public inquiry, the architects continued to improve the prospects for the public realm around the Shard. As Moolhuijzen says,

> You cannot construct a tall building in the middle of London if it does not have a profoundly positive impact on the immediate surroundings. I cannot think of any tall building that touches the ground more lightly than the Shard. We have taken away volumes at the lower levels of the building and given them over to public open space: 35% of the site at concourse level is given over and 15% at St Thomas Street level.

As construction progressed, though, he noted, 'It is fortunate that we did not know in advance how formidable the challenge would be to improve the public realm, especially in relation to the adjacent train station. For us it has always been an integral part of the project to make improvements to the existing nodus roof and concourse.'[108] The new station roof and concourse had to be put in place without interfering with hundreds of thousands of passengers a day.

There was also great concern about the effect of high winds on the building's occupants and of the downdraught on passing pedestrians.

Many towers deserve their bad reputation, not only for what they can do to the skyline, but because of the effect they have at street level. Clusters, and even just one or two tall buildings, can force high winds down façades and channel them along streets. The Renzo Piano Building Workshop teamed up from the outset with RWDI in Canada to create a good pedestrian environment.

Initially, wind-tunnel tests implied that St Thomas Street would need to be almost entirely protected by canopies so the practice kept remodelling and retesting until they found a graceful solution. This involved the erection of glazed canopies at different heights, which in their placement responded to the local roof heights and the arched brick wall of the station viaduct. This brought a sympathetic alignment to the surrounding structures. The Shard's taper away from the right angle also helped to protect pedestrians without lowering light quality. (Gordon Ingram Associates had already done an analysis of every window within half a kilometre of the site of the Shard to see the effect the building would have on 'right to light'.)

In terms of the movement of the building – and protection from a terrorist event – that was the responsibility of Kamran Moazami, head of structures at the WSP Group. He explained to *Ars Technica* on 5 December 2011 that 'Every building is a cantilever.' The high winds can exert a tremendous lateral force greater than the vertical load of a building's own weight, so the Shard was built around a concrete core that would stop the building from torqueing. Highly detailed computer models and physical models were tested in simulations of high winds and extreme events. The ambition of the Shard was to withstand a one-in-500-year event.[109] That all-important concrete spine would also include the lifts, stairs, water mains and electric cables.

The lift system – a rather necessary alternative to the 306 flights of stairs – had to be carefully considered, as an inability to cater for high volumes at design stage can lead to an unhappy and irresolvable legacy; in extant earlier-generation skyscrapers, there is often frustrating lift congestion leading to half-hour waiting times at the end of the working day.

The mixed-use nature of the Shard, with residential, hotel, offices, restaurants and bars and viewing platform, necessitated a complex lift and other vertical transport management strategy. The building has forty-nine lifts, fire lifts, goods lifts, hydraulic lifts and escalators, all supplied by KONE. To save space, thirteen passenger lifts are double-deckers, serving two floors simultaneously.

The main lifts do not have call buttons, but are directed by an intelligent hall-call system, which uses information attained by proximity sensors and informs the user which lift will be fastest for their destination. As Michael Donnelly explains, 'Lift speeds are between 4.5 and 6 metres per second, and the duplex lifts help with loads. The delivery from the foyer to the desired floor should take less than two minutes including waiting time.'

Sellar referred to the lifts as 'champagne bubbles' providing effervescence to the flute of the Shard. The celebratory mood brought about by construction finally getting under way may have spurred this foray into the poetical.

Chapter 10

The Impossible Made Possible

All hopes of progress lie with the unreasonable man. That's my adaptation of a line from George Bernard Shaw's *Man and Superman*. The reasonable man thinks it can't be done, and therefore doesn't try. The unreasonable man tries and often succeeds.

Irvine Sellar

Renzo Piano once said, 'I like to fight against gravity.'[110] He may have been talking about his desire to make his buildings appear 'light on their feet', despite their volume and mass, but the engineers and construction crew of 1,500 attempting to raise the Shard from the ground had a more literal fight against the forces of nature.

The Shard was never going to be fitted out and ready for service in time for the 2012 Olympics, but Irvine Sellar wanted the building to be topped out and physically complete by the time the Games were under way. Following the long series of issues and delays – from the extended, gruelling campaign to win planning permission through to the protracted process of agreeing a fixed-price contract with Mace – that ambition looked impossible to achieve. There simply was not enough time to construct the Shard, at least using traditional construction methods.

Sellar, the 'unreasonable man' with his alpha-male drive and strong character, strives to make the impossible possible, and he loads that expectation onto the team around him. As Michael Donnelly, who works with construction director Flan McNamara, says: 'Irvine Sellar is an extremely brave man. He is extremely focused, and he is unrealistic in his targets and demands. Flan will tell me that Irvine wants this and that to be in place by the weekend, and to start with I'll be thinking, "How am I going to get Harry Potter to magic this up by then?" But you end up striving to make the unrealistic realistic. Irvine drives you to do things better.'

Sellar's deadline, alongside the need to interfere with the hospital and transport hub for as short a time as possible, meant that the building had to go up with great speed. Ian Eggers, the project director at Mace, was the master of cool understatement when he said, 'The programme is sporting at best.'

The engineers' and constructors' response was to turn towards bold, radical and time-saving techniques never before used in the construction of a supertall building.

Buildings are built from the ground up (or rather, in the case of a building bigger than a shed, from below ground up). This is so elemental, so logical, that any eighteen-month-old baby will try to stack their building blocks from the bottom up without any explanation required. The Shard, however, would defy gravity. It would be built from the top down.

That does not mean that its spire was somehow suspended in mid-air while the rest of the building was constructed downwards beneath it. Rather, in almost as daring a logistical feat, both the core of the building and its three basement levels were built from the ground floor down; at the same time – well before work on the foundations was complete – a large part of the building above ground was erected, so the Shard simultaneously sprouted upwards into the sky and downwards into the earth. It was a world first for a skyscraper.

As Roma Agrawal, a senior structural engineer with Mace, revealed: 'Top-down construction for a core has not been used in the world – it's the first time we're trying this new approach. We are obviously slightly apprehensive because there is no precedent for us.'[111]

Sellar was willing to take the risk: 'Effectively, it's doing two jobs simultaneously. There's a huge cost involved in this project, and every second, every minute, every hour is valuable to us.'[112]

The technique, which involved specialist engineering designers from the Robert Bird Group working with Mace, WSP and the concrete contractor Byrne Bros, saved three months of construction time, allowing the building of the Shard to be kept to the extraordinarily tight schedule without affecting the running of the rail and underground stations. Throughout the construction period, the relationship with the hospital and the transport companies was key. Two people were assigned full-time by Mace to liaise with London Underground and Network Rail. Every time the work transgressed onto the rail station concourse, the contractors would need a permit for access, a statement of method, and surveys of the ground and drains.

With thousands of people swarming to and from the stations, hospital and other buildings, and narrow, traffic-laden roads around the site, the logistics of moving materials on and off site were a major factor. Initially there was a desire to try to use the railway lines to bring materials to the site but that proved too expensive and too difficult, so the contractors were reliant on lorries, which would need to be kept in the very small, on-site holding area in order not to jam surrounding roads. Due to the vast quantity of lorries, this meant creating a buffer zone a few miles from the site, where they would be held and despatched to the site at regular intervals. There would be detailed liaison with suppliers to ensure that each type of material was despatched at the right time to reach the buffer zone at the appropriate point in the schedule.

The ground floor of the building was cast in concrete first; the earth beneath that floor was then excavated down to the second basement level, and another concrete slab was cast; then excavation continued downwards to what would become the very bottom of the structure, the third basement level. The three basement levels, reaching down 42 feet (13.34 metres) below ground, are now used for plant, services and the limited parking. The building is supported by 120 piles, 900 mm in diameter, driven down to 177 feet (54 metres) deep.

Kamran Moazami of WSP believes that the Shard is 'probably one of the most efficient buildings ever designed'. To enable Sellar and his Qatari partners to tease the greatest value out of their development, the engineers had to make sure that the structural system – primarily the central core, which incorporated services, communications and lifts

– took up as little of the floor plate, and therefore leasable space, as possible. The core was built upwards from the ground floor to level 21 while the construction of the basement and a section of the subterranean core continued underneath.

There was some complexity in the geology of the site. The high water table was on top of a permeable layer of gravel, and while the top layer of clay was relatively level, its thickness varied according to a pre-glacial fault running from north to south of the site, adding to the subterranean problems.

As the building is positioned so close to the River Thames, and the foundations would need to be deep enough to support a thousand-foot building, an extraordinarily strong secant or retaining basement wall had to be built around the underground perimeter, securing the building from the threat of water and earth movement.

In the Channel 4 documentary, *The Tallest Tower: Building the Shard* (produced in consultation with Maurice Sellar), Mace's lead construction supervisor was being interviewed on site when a voice from behind the camera said, 'What's that happening there?' Ian Henderson looked over his shoulder in surprise before replying, 'That's a fuck-up. That's what shouldn't be happening. That is a disaster.'

Water was pouring through the perimeter: just a light stream, but requiring immediate emergency action before more water burst through and flooded the entire site. Fast-setting grout was quickly injected into the hole – a surprisingly rudimentary solution for the most technically advanced build that the UK had ever known.

While the creation of the basement levels was under way, the building of the core was jump-started. Twenty-four steel plunge columns that support the core were fed down the top of the pile shafts to sit on top of the piles, and were additionally strengthened by a concrete casing. It was crucial to the stability of the building that the enormous weight of the concrete core as it advanced towards the sky did not buckle the steel plunge columns.

At the end of February 2010, the Shard was heading towards the heavens at a rate of one and a half storeys per week, and Irvine Sellar reported that, despite the credit crunch and the global recession, the Shard was on track to be completed in May 2012. Meanwhile, the Heron

Tower had become the tallest building in the City, surpassing Tower 42 at the end of 2009 prior to its topping out in April 2010. The Shard, though, was catching up. Fast.

By April 2010, the core, which is 82 × 73 feet (25 × 22 metres), had already reached twenty-one storeys but the steel plunge columns supporting the core could not take any further weight and the foundations were still not complete. The reinforced concrete raft slab at the bottom of the basement had to be put in place to transfer the weight of the building evenly onto the bearing piles so the upward trajectory could continue.

The creation of the huge, 13-foot (4-metre) thick slab involved the largest single pour of concrete ever conducted for a commercial building in the UK, and it remains one of the biggest such operations undertaken anywhere in the world. Time was of the essence for the pour of 194,000 cubic feet (5,500 m³) of concrete.

In the process of thirty-six hours, 700 truckloads of concrete were brought onto the site in a finely choreographed ballet for the huge, continuous pour. The trucks came from four different plants, so that if two of the plants ceased functioning properly, the pour would continue. Blind positivity is of little benefit in the world of construction: it's better to prepare for the apocalypse.

The organisers arranged the ballet for a weekend free from significant public events when there was likely to be less traffic clogging the roads. Tim Goldby of Mace together with Byrne Bros worked out the primary and secondary routes for the trucks, all planned in consultation with the London Borough of Southwark, so that the trucks could have access to the site with as little interruption as possible. The lorries were held in the buffer zone a couple of miles from the site and despatched at regular intervals to prevent clogging.

At the peak of the pour, a concrete-laden truck entered the site every three minutes. During each hour of the operation, what one would normally consider to be a full day's worth of concrete was poured. Three pumps were used to lay down up to 5,300 cubic feet (150 m³) of concrete per hour, with the speed carefully worked out so that the laid concrete could dry and harden at the correct rate. During the setting process, concrete generates heat, which can lead to cracking, so enormous fans were used to regulate the temperature. If there was a single major crack, the entire operation would have been a failure.

The planning paid off: the job was successfully completed in a day and a half without any critical interruptions.

The team was then able to complete the top-down construction of the subterranean element of the core around the plunge columns. The building would now be stable from the bottom up as it progressed ever upwards and started to threaten height records.

The concrete core construction itself was highly innovative. As a tall building rises, work often has to stop while sections are added to the free-standing cranes to adjust to the new height. At the Shard, the engineers' innovative solution was to perch a crane on top of the core, secured into what would become the lift shaft. The crane was connected to hydraulic jacks, using steel rods, so that, as the core continued to grow upwards, the crane would rise too. It was the first time the method had been tried outside North Korea and, as Flan McNamara says, 'In North Korea it hadn't worked because they couldn't stabilise it.'

The concrete that formed the core was poured at a constant speed, gaining 4 mm in height every minute, which was enough time for it to set progressively before too much weight was added. This operation was undertaken twenty-four hours a day for six days a week, with two crews doing shifts on the slipform rig, each working twelve hours on, twelve hours off.

To add to the litany of firsts, the crane sitting on top of the core was eventually used to build a second, 111-metre crane that cantilevered off the building at level 55 – this was the first time the technique had been used in Europe, with the only predecessor being 7 World Trade Center (2006) in New York.

The core crane was effectively aiding its own demise as the cantilevered crane was then used to dismantle the core crane. The cantilevered crane's next role was to enable the construction of the 217-foot (66-metre) spire, and it was 'jumped' higher up the side of the building as the spire grew.

The longest-serving crane operator at the Shard, John Young, aged forty-nine at the time, told *The Times* in April 2012 that being perched

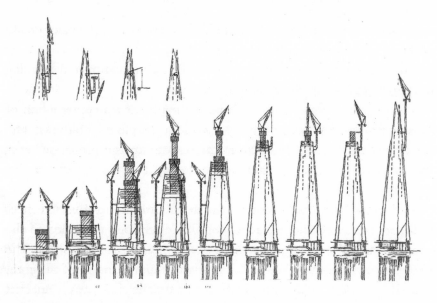

Sketch of crane use as the tower rises (© WSP Ronscade)

at the top of the building, over a thousand feet up, involved its perils: 'There is no margin for error. I dread to think about the consequences.' The wind was his greatest enemy. 'You can work in rain, snow, but wind's the killer. Whatever the weather there are times when the load might slip . . . It keeps you awake.' Never mind the wind, the only thing that our lavatorially obsessed nation was concerned about was how he went to the toilet. He explained that the job required great bladder control as there was no special facility up on the crane, and he would sometimes only come down from the crane once during the day as it took so long.

There was a continual fight against time to keep the construction to Sellar's schedule. With frequent high winds putting cranes and external hoists out of action, the team applied another audacious solution: the jump lift, which had never before been used in the UK. Developed by KONE, this is a self-climbing elevator system, which offers an alternative to exterior hoists. A lift is positioned in one of a building's permanent lift shafts in the core, with a temporary machine room, which powers the lift through winding gear, situated towards the top of the core while it is still being constructed. As the building of the core and its shafts progresses above, the machine room is 'jumped' higher, using its own hydraulic ram system to scale the newly completed section of shaft.

Without this, the Shard construction team would have been reliant on hoist lifts for both people and materials, which would have been too slow and inefficient. Five jump lifts, the largest of which could transport 3,500 kg of materials or forty-five people, were installed in the Shard's shafts and the machine rooms would be jumped three storeys during a weekend so that work would not be interrupted. As Tony Palgrave, Mace's construction director for the Shard, said: 'It represents our ongoing commitment to finding better ways to deliver this landmark project.'[113]

While the lifts enabled smaller materials to be moved when high winds prevented the use of the cranes, the supply of concrete could also continue as it was pumped up from the base using the most powerful concrete pump in the country.[114] The slipform operation of building the core was so fast that the core rose 10 feet (3 metres) every day, requiring 11,300 cubic feet (360 m³) of concrete to be pumped every twenty-four hours. The slipform rig had three levels to cover the upper, working and trailing decks.

A rational person might expect, correctly, that for the sake of stability the weight of a building should be at the bottom: typically, in the construction of a tall building, concrete is used for the lower floors with a much lighter steel frame used for the upper levels. Not so the Shard.

The weight of the building is situated in the top half of the structure because having the mass of the concrete in the upper floors reduces movement in high winds. Rodolfo Giannini of WSP explained, 'It was about defining the maximum height the core could reach before the permanent concrete frame was in position to take the full loading.'[115] The unusual structural division of the primary internal materials – from steel at the bottom to concrete and back to steel at the very top – was an extraordinarily efficient match to the multi-use nature of the Shard.

For the first forty-one levels – incorporating the receptions and all of the office floors – the building has a steel frame linked to the core, using fixings set into the concrete. Once the core had reached level 8 above ground, steel erection commenced and started to catch up with the slipforming. The distinctive tapering shape of the Shard started to emerge. Four tower cranes were used to put the steel structural columns and rafters in place. The floors were constructed from a deck of steel beams, on which a smooth concrete slab was laid. This steel floor allowed services such as parts the of air conditioning system to be placed between the beams, and enabled long spans without columns to suit open-plan working. The white steel columns at ground floor are a visible architectural feature of the lower floors, marking the open perimeter of the building, and are also visible at the corners where the interior winter gardens of the offices are situated.

As the envelope of the building narrows so does the core, stepping inwards at the hotel section, and again at the residential section. A circulatory corridor follows the perimeter of the core in the hotel section, with the rooms fanning off the corridor, so all guestrooms are close to the lifts and services.

There is a switch from steel to concrete for the internal structure of both the hotel-bedroom and residential areas. There, the levels are separated by 200 mm slabs of post-tensioned concrete (whereby the concrete is strengthened by steel tendons made tense by hydraulic jacks). The shallowness of the slabs affords the generous floor-to-ceiling height and views that are a principal draw for the Shangri-La hotel.

The concrete absorbs noise and vibration, which is handy if your neighbour above or below is a fan of thrash metal or, worse, *American Psycho*'s Patrick Bateman, with his doubly anti-social passion for Phil Collins and torture.

On the residential floors, the floor plates are smaller so the apartments have a whole floor (or in three cases, two floors) to themselves, allowing for a substantial and very private living space.

For most of the height of the building, internal perpendicular columns aid the support given by the sloping perimeter columns. The internal columns in the top half of the tower have their footings in the steps of the core. Near the very top, internal columns are not necessary as the core can take the weight with the help of cross beams.

It was essential that there was as little sway as possible in the apartments at the top of the building; otherwise the residents' enjoyment of their hyper-expensive views would be marred by the need to carry a sick bag around with them. Consequently, there is a 'hat truss' of diagonal beams

The Shard during construction (*left* Photo: Nic Lehoux, © RPBW *right* © Rob Telford)

connected to the core at level 67 to bring greater stability to the building without the need for mass-damping.

Another switch in structural material occurs very near the top. The spire, in which residential noise is not a problem, is made of steel and therefore comparatively lightweight.

All this proved to be an interesting challenge for the engineers and construction company. Richard Mawer of WSP said, 'With many tall buildings, you get a lot of repetitive structure. The fascinating thing about this building is that nothing is the same, nothing is typical.'[116]

The engineering innovations of the Shard led to its nomination for an ICE (Institute of Civil Engineers) Civil Engineering Award in 2010, along with the Olympic Park and King's Cross St Pancras Underground station, while the building was still being constructed. The Olympic Park won, but the judges praised the Shard, saying that the techniques revealed a 'great collaboration between specialist and main contractors and a logistical and engineering solution that equals Renzo Piano's iconic vision of the tower itself'.[117]

Construction abseiler working on the Shard (Photo: Nic Lehoux, © RPBW)

The lower sections of the façade were added as the structure pro-gressed skywards, with the first glass panel installed on 25 May 2010. The glazing was assembled in units, incorporating the blinds and blind motors, prefabricated by Scheldebouw in the Netherlands and lowered from a spider crane. Each panel is 3.5 metres high and 1.5 metres wide, and weighs 300 kg. Six specialist industrial abseilers would instal the panels by hand while hanging perilously in the air. As an example of their workload, by the time they reached level 35, their schedule was to instal 143 glazing panels over a seventy-hour period while suspended 132 metres up in the air.

The media and members of the public had long been transfixed by the stump of the core growing up from the ground and the addition of the floors, but it was not until this huge new neighbour began to be dressed in its façades of glass that they had a true sense of its rather graceful presence on the skyline. The intricate detail of the design started to become apparent, with the wing walls of the outer skin cantilevering away from the main volume and over the structural fissures.

By November 2010, with the core passing 770 feet (235 metres) at the fifty-fifth storey, the Shard was already the tallest building in Britain, overtaking César Pelli's One Canada Square in Canary Wharf, which may have brought a smile to Sellar's face.

Irvine Sellar told the *Estates Gazette*, 'It's just what we expected from the designs, and thank God for that. It is a beautiful design and now from different parts of London you are beginning to see it pop up.'[118]

By then, the ordination of the Shard as a successful and 'generous' building was already under way. In September 2009, Paul Finch, the new chair of CABE, which had resisted planning consent back in 2003, highlighted a change of attitude towards the building. When discussing the 'reversal test' to assess whether a building should or should not have received planning permission, he stated: 'If Renzo Piano's Shard, currently under construction in London Bridge, existed, would we really want to demolish it (and the brilliant below-ground reconciliation of conflicting transport infrastructure)? Certainly not.'[119]

With the Shard already making an impact on the horizon at the end of 2009, Boris Johnson, Livingstone's replacement as Mayor of London, stridently claimed, 'If you want a symbol of how London is powering its way out of the global recession, let me direct you to a building site a couple of hundred yards from my office in City Hall. They said it couldn't be done. They said the credit crunch would kill it off. And yet up it goes . . .'[120] This was a man who, during his mayoral campaign, had been cynical about the benefits of building tall in London.

At the same time, Simon Jenkins was once again showing his talent for an imaginative insult by calling the Shard 'a phallus from capitalist outer space', but the *Commercial Property Register* was more prosaically in favour: 'If there is one building that will symbolise the return to a stronger commercial property market then it has to be the Shard of Glass, Irvine Sellar and Renzo Piano's ode to London.'[121]

With the 586,509 square feet (54,488 m²) of office space becoming a reality, Irvine Sellar could gauge just how unique the offices would be and therefore how appealing to prospective tenants. The floors ranged from 31,379 square feet (2,915 m²) to 14,456 square feet (1,343 m²), which would suit the variety of different tenants he had envisaged. Each floor contained two or three naturally ventilated and naturally lit winter gardens, which could be used as meeting areas or for functions and would make use of the unrivalled views from the building. The offices would be reached from the station concourse level, where workers and visitors would enter a double-height reception lobby clad in grooved, hand-riven white Calacatta Apuano marble from Italy – the entire wall is from a single section of marble cut from the quarry, having been chosen there by Piano himself. The intention was to ensure that the reception would be bright while giving a suggestion of restrained luxury. Architect William Matthews says, 'we aimed to reflect the solidity of the core itself' while dressing the core appropriately for high-end office use.

In June 2010, Sellar, confident in his product, did something unthinkable. He paid off his only confirmed office tenant.

Transport for London was given in the region of £15 million to surrender its thirty-year pre-let agreement of 190,000 square feet (17,650 m²). The Qataris had given Sellar both the time and the licence to make the Shard – inside and out – the building he wanted it to be.

'We had a board meeting in Doha,' Sellar recalls, 'and the Qataris said, "Could you take them out, Irvine?" And I said that I might be able to, because we hadn't leased the other building, the Place, yet. I saw Steve Allen of TfL and said, "Look, it doesn't work, does it? You would feel uncomfortable for your staff to be in one of the best-known landmarks on the globe. It would be like your team driving around in a Rolls-Royce Phantom. It's not the right image for public transport." They were interested in the Place, but I was negotiating with News Corp, and I went for them because TfL weren't offering the right rent anyway.'

Having lost the mayoral election to Boris Johnson in 2008, Ken Livingstone says, 'If I'd still been Mayor, I'd have said to Irvine: "Look, give it a year or two, and if you still want to sell the space then . . ." I mean, we didn't have to move right away. I'd have liked to be in there.'

It is unlikely that Sellar would have listened to Livingstone. He was extremely confident that he could secure a higher rent than he had agreed with Transport for London back in 2008. Sellar explained the move in typical style in November 2010: 'We decided that this is one of the most iconic buildings in Europe and that it should be multiletting at upwards of £55 per sq. ft. Separately, TfL accepted that it was perhaps a bit over the top to move there.'[122]

By then, BBC News was using an image of the growing, tapered form of the Shard to illustrate a surge in the economy in the third quarter of 2010. Just as Sellar had predicted, demand for office space in the capital was outstripping supply, a fact that brought plans for around a dozen tall buildings and other major office developments, including the Cheesegrater and the Walkie-Talkie, out of mothballs.

Sellar was so confident in the likelihood that all the space in the Shard would eventually be let – not least because it was the standout project in London – that he decided not even to start marketing it again until 2011, when, as he said, 'the building will be very visible. And then the market will come to us.'

Meanwhile, James Sellar was similarly confident about the residential apartments, which were originally to be serviced by the Shangri-La: 'It is where I would want my apartment rather than certain streets in the back of Kensington. People will be buying into a cultural icon.'[123]

In the end, the Sellars had to turn down increasingly fervent attempts to buy the apartments because the Shard company's board decided that they would be held for leasing: no part of the Shard would be sold.

At the same time, Irvine Sellar was continuously driving the development, pushing the project management team of Bernard Ainsworth and Turner & Townsend, and also having his own meetings with the major players. No matter how large the numbers, and how wealthy he personally has become, money is not an abstract notion to Sellar. When he negotiates or talks about budgets, one gets the sense that he is imagining the money in notes and even coins sitting on the table before him, rather than as figures in a ledger. He strikes me as neither greedy nor mean-spirited, but money is the meter of his success, and he is driven by optimising value.

Reflecting on the meetings in the latter stages of the Shard development, he says, 'Every hour of every day is vital, it's critical, it's money. There were excuses, the weather's bad, this is bad, this is a problem, continuously. So I'd be driving those meetings, saying, "Well, we've got to find a way of making up the time without damaging the quality." I still had faith in Pycroft and Cole during those times. There was a mutual, common desire to make it work. From their point of view, building the Shard was a massive badge of honour.'

I ask him what was the key to keeping everyone on track despite the schedule: 'Aggressive charm.'

In December 2009, during an interview with the *Daily Mail*, Sellar was grumpily dismissing a photographer and saying, 'there's a bloody long way to go and a lot of aggravation still'. Property development is a slow and frustrating business, somewhat at odds with Sellar's character, as he revealed in that interview: 'If I had a choice I would have preferred to have stayed in retail. I like the pace of retail. Property trading can be fast – I find that exciting. But to go through all the detail of building a small town – which is what we are doing here – it is walking through treacle at times.'[124]

The weather was a more than sporadic problem, which contributed greatly to his frustration. It had originally been evaluated that 'winding off', when winds would be too strong to continue construction of the upper storeys, would occur 27 per cent of the time, but that was guesswork as no one had built such a tall building in London before, and the English weather, as everyone caught in a hailstorm while wearing a T-shirt can attest, is difficult to predict at the best of times. As Flan McNamara says, 'The wind records for this height of building did not exist. No one in London had tried to build in the strength of that wind before.' For periods, winding off would reach 70 per cent.

Sellar tells me: 'I was up there in seventy-, eighty-mile-an-hour winds and they could move you sideways.'

The core was topped out in early 2011 and by March the fiftieth floor of the Shard was being built around it, but the weather was becoming an increasing factor. Whenever the wind speed exceeded 40 mph (64 km/h), the craning of materials had to stop, and at the height of 600 feet (183 metres) above ground, high winds were more frequent. The jump lifts may have helped matters, but when the cranes stood idle, lorry-loads of steel and other large key materials would be waiting to be unloaded below, snarling up both progress and traffic.

The temperature often dropped below freezing, making real the threat of frostbitten fingers and toes for the construction workers. The Sellar Property Group solicitor George Josselyn recalls that he made a site visit towards the end of the construction of the core: 'At the bottom it was a cold, rainy, winter day but fairly normal; at the top it was snowing. There were only two people up there, one manning the jump lift and the other trying to bend pieces of steel reinforcement wires with some large pliers. Both looked bitterly cold and were wrapped up as if for the Himalayas. We did not stay very long.'

From January 2011, a three-storey screened platform was used to protect the workers from the high winds, cold and rain as they created each post-tensioned concrete floor, although work still had to cease when winds exceeded 50 mph. The rig was attached to rails fixed to the side of the building so that it could be winched upwards after work was completed on each floor. Because of the building's taper, the size of the rig had to be altered as it ascended.

The screens prevented not only workers from being blown off the building, but also objects. Terminal velocity could easily have led to a terminal conclusion: from that height, even a small bolt could kill an unwitting construction worker or passing pedestrian on the ground.

In February 2011, an elusive urban fox that had climbed to the seventy-second floor – the top of the viewing platform – was captured. It had been living there for days, having climbed stairs and a ladder to be almost 920 feet (280 metres) above the ground. It was surviving off the leftovers from the workers' meals. As the fox had been in the building since at least Valentine's Day, the contractors named it Romeo. Perhaps it thought Juliet had scaled the building too, looking for Europe's highest balcony.

Romeo was taken to the Riverside Animal Centre in Wallingford, and then released close to its own manor around London Bridge. According to Ted Burden, the animal centre's founder, 'as we released him back on to the streets of Bermondsey shortly after midnight on Sunday, he glanced at the Shard and then trotted off in the other direction'.[125]

Three months later, in April 2011, a potentially more serious animal story was related in the 'London Bridge Quarter Construction Update', the regular newsletter through which the construction team kept local residents and office workers informed of developments. It announced that a colony of lesser horseshoe bats had been found roosting in the Shard. As the bats are a protected species, construction of the building

The base of the Shard integrated with the station concourse (© Linda Steward)

could have been suspended for up to a year, but the Update reported that the bat colony had been 'viciously devoured by a pack of foxes'. The quoting of a bat-droppings expert called Guy Guano may have aroused suspicions as to the veracity of the tale, which the story's date confirmed: 1 April.

More seriously, Flan McNamara was able to report in May 2011 that, despite the cold weather earlier in the year, the team had lost virtually no time on the post-tensioned levels. At the same time, the M & E (mechanical and electrical) installation was being completed on the office floors.

While focus on the Shard's progress was, naturally, on the changing skyline, much had been happening at ground level to undertake the massive changes to the public realm.

The new station concourse roof, designed by Renzo Piano to link to the Shard, was in place by August 2011. The construction involved intense negotiation with Network Rail – as William Matthews and Joost Moolhuijzen have pointed out, Sellar was effectively decorating his neighbour's house for them while they were still resident. To minimise passenger disruption, the new station roof was constructed over the old roof, and the old roof was removed only when that operation was complete. Renzo Piano's design of the roof in white steel and glazing was sympathetic to the Shard, and even the new bus shelters carry an obvious aesthetic link. Meanwhile, the pedestrian bridge leading to Guy's Hospital was removed, and exterior escalators, plus other changes to the public realm, reorganised, simplified and prettified the relationship between the railway station concourse level and St Thomas Street.

In March 2012, a 30-metre long reproduction of Canaletto's painting *The River Thames with St Paul's Cathedral on Lord Mayor's Day* was put on a temporary side wall of the new entrance to London Bridge station, emphasising how the artist's renderings of London's spires and the tall ships of the river had first inspired Piano's design of the Shard.

The York Handmade Brick Company was given the contract to supply 70,000 special bricks for the Shard – particularly for the lower levels of the façades of the backpack, which were to conjoin the railway viaducts. William Matthews wrote in 2012:

> It was important that the tower, floating above the city, was also rooted in its *topos*. London Bridge station and the railway viaducts to the east and west are entirely based upon brick structures and it seemed appropriate to use the same material for the foot of the tower. The bricks were handmade in Yorkshire using a clay similar in colour and texture to original London stock.[126]

The result was not dissimilar to the terracotta that is a frequent note of colour in Piano's works.

As the structure neared completion, Irvine Sellar discovered something altogether unexpected about his building. He asked William Matthews when the brightly coloured protective wrappings would be taken off the housing for the blinds, only to be told that there was no protective wrapping: the housing for each of the thousands of motorised blinds, as noted earlier, was a bright red-orange, and formed a strip of colour at the top of each floor, breaking up the monochrome design of the building.

This detail had never been discussed with Sellar. He was not amused: 'I said to Renzo, "This iceberg that I've been talking about for years, and you've been talking about too, you've lost the purity of it." To this day, I don't really understand why he did it, but it doesn't take anything away from the design, as it happens. I would have preferred not to have the colour, but 99.9 per cent of people don't even notice it's there. Renzo likes his primary colours. But there were very few issues I had with him in terms of design.'

He says that 'Renzo is, if not the greatest living architect, then certainly one of them . . . he is the best architect I have ever had the experience of working with.'

Throughout the trials and tribulations of the Shard, Piano and Sellar remained on good terms, as Piano confirmed during the construction period: 'He has never betrayed me . . . We always talk very frankly. If I have to tell him something, I tell him. If he has to tell me something – he does. And even in the difficult moments – and we did have difficult moments, especially during the public inquiry – he was very loyal.'[127]

Renzo Piano's contentment extended beyond his dealings with Sellar. He said in 2012,

> We had a magnificent team on site. We were a large group of nearly 200 people; our own architects; the local architectural firm Adamson Associates; an excellent contractor, Mace Group; the engineers at WSP and Arup; and the client's project team. The site was extremely busy; at its peak there were up to 1,500 workers of 60 different nationalities.[128]

Although the workforce was multinational, around two-thirds of the contractors were UK nationals, and Mace and Sellar attempted to ensure that local residents had a role to play. They appointed a full-time regeneration manager at the site to work with the 'Building London Creating Futures' programme of the London Borough of Southwark and create both training initiatives and construction jobs for people from the area. The aim of the training centre was to deliver 240 construction jobs of six months or longer at the Shard, plus 135 at the sister building, the Place, which would become known as the News Building.[129]

By the end of 2011, the Shard had overtaken the Commerzbank Tower in Frankfurt to becomes the tallest building in the European

Union. By then, Renzo Piano and Irvine Sellar were confident that the building would be exactly what they had always said it would be, back when it was still an abstract idea that few people thought would be raised off the page. Piano said:

> This is about the way cities should go. They should stop and we should not go beyond the green belt. If you do this by going vertical that sends a message about conserving land. The building is not about arrogance and power but about increasing the intensity of city life. Architecture is not neutral, it celebrates something. When we built the Pompidou, it celebrated rebellion against the idea that culture should be intimidating. The Shard will celebrate community, the sense of the city, the sense of exchange. I think the building will become loved in London because it is not arrogant. Normally towers are not loved because they shut down at 6 p.m. and you have a black glass block. This is not about money or power. It is about surprise and joy.

In the same article, Sellar was quoted as saying in his more rambunctious style: 'If we want to get out of this malaise then this is the sort of project that should be done. We think it is a great image. It says, "This is London, this is the Shard and we can kick sand in the face of the Eiffel Tower."'[130]

The crown of the Sellar/Piano vision is the twenty-three-storey, 217-foot (66-metre) white steel spire, clad in the shards of façade that reach different heights and never touch. Pre-assembly would play an important role in the spire's complex construction.

Steel contractor Severfield-Rowen, based at Dalton near Thirsk in North Yorkshire, had much experience of intricate steelwork structures, having recently worked on the Richard Rogers Partnership's Heathrow Terminal 5 (2008) and the roof over the Centre Court of Wimbledon (2009). The spire weighs in excess of 530 tonnes and consists of 800 individual parts – an enormous Meccano set which would have been too complicated to put together in mid-air. 'We're building in the middle of winter,' William Matthews said at the time. 'The danger is very real; so the decision was taken that the spire must be practice-built, prefabricated at the steelworks.'

Consequently, in November 2011, a full rehearsal was staged on the ground at Dalton airfield in Yorkshire, with the entire spire constructed in the dry run so that the crew would be prepared once they were working up in the sky. Mace built three-dimensional models that plotted the progress of the spire's construction during the rehearsal, and developed a detailed, day-by-day construction guide for the London team.

The spire was then dismantled and transported south to the capital. As much of the assembly work as possible was undertaken on the ground at the foot of the Shard. Peter Savoy, a project manager at Mace, said: 'It's all about minimising the work force at the top of the building and taking away as much of the human element as possible. Mistakes can't be made at that height with the level of risk.'[131]

The cantilevered crane came into its own. At its full extension, the cab of the crane was level with the very top of the Shard, over a thousand feet up. 'We can build a two-floor section in five days,' John Young revealed, 'but we are 100 per cent wind-dependent.'

It took three hours for the crew to prepare and hoist the first section of the spire. Each of the modular white steel sections was raised up the entire length of the building over the course of five minutes at the serene pace of one metre per second while passers-by watched from below. A specialist team of steel erectors and industrial abseilers – with their safety ropes clipped onto the built structure at all times – received the sections at the apex and started to complete the jigsaw. The bottom of the spire frames what would become the open-air upper deck of the highest viewing gallery in Western Europe.

One of the abseilers, Guy Hayhow, told the *East Anglian Daily Times*, 'Around 90 per cent of the time being in a harness is very uncomfortable. It can be cold and wet, but then in the summer it's sweaty and itchy. However, it's a beautiful job. I'm in the middle of London and there are peregrines whizzing past me. It's a job with the best view in London.'[132] Hayhow, from his eyrie on high, also saw Apache helicopters flying beneath him and police cars careering after suspects on the streets of London.

On 24 March 2012, the press carried images of three men perched precariously on a skeletal steel outcrop at the top of the Shard as they bolted together elements of the uppermost steel structure. The images were evocative of Charles E. Ebbets's 1932 photograph of construction workers having their lunch on a girder suspended above New York.

On 30 March 2012, the construction crew and abseilers carefully positioned the highest structural element of the building, and the very last of the 516 glass panels that cusp the spire was put securely in place a few days later.

Renzo Piano's concept of a fractured, crystalline shard piercing the sky could finally be seen all around London. After twelve years of challenges, the last three of them spent defying gravity, the Shard was finally structurally complete.

It was a time of celebration. 'We took Irvine and Renzo up to the top together for the first time,' Flan McNamara says. 'I forced them to wear hard hats and hi-vis, which wasn't easy. William Matthews was supposed to have some champagne and glasses ready but he hadn't had time, but I managed to rustle some up. William was there, and Joost was there, and we all felt proud of what we had achieved. I remember looking at Irvine and Renzo, those two men standing together at the top of this building they had dared to build – it was something special.'

Irvine Sellar remembers the moment. 'Renzo turned to me and he said, "You know, if we weren't both a little mad, this would never have happened."'

Piano said that the final months of construction were 'almost unbearable' because he was nervous as to whether the final building would reflect the original intention. He was not disappointed:

> The uppermost shards of glass appear to stop, remaining there as if suspended, and this is precisely the effect that I was hoping to achieve. Another thing that I noticed is that the tower really is weather responsive. I kept my fingers crossed during construction because it was impossible to know exactly how it would end up. [The spire is] the most beautiful thing, responding to changes in light just like the rest of the building. From close up [the building] looks like a crystal, from far away the surfaces are always exceptionally beautiful, even when the weather is grey. And

The Shard in June 2012, with construction of the News Building under way at its base
(© Michel Denancé)

from midway between the two it's amazing to watch when the sun catches one of the faces of the building, making the other sides seem to disappear . . . the interior is very light because the glass is very transparent.[133]

Even before its official inauguration on 5 July 2012, the Shard had become the most famous new building in the world, and its fame would not be fleeting. The building was camera candy, and soon became a media stock image in everything from newspapers to BBC News to films and television dramas: an image of the Shard means that the setting is London, no further exposition required.

By 2016, its height had been surpassed by three buildings in Moscow, but few people outside Russia can name those towers (incidentally, they are the Federation Tower's East Tower, the OKO South Tower and the Mercury City Tower). The Shard's continuing global fame proves, just as Piano had always said, that the design was never solely about height.

In the early days, its fame as the tallest building in Western Europe brought some uninvited guests, including a daredevil base jumper and a group of women from Greenpeace who scaled the tower to protest against Shell's operations in the Arctic.

Irvine Sellar was not pleased by the escapades, despite the fact that they brought his building further international coverage: 'If there had been a death, it would have blighted the building. It would have been contaminated. From a reputational point of view, it wasn't what we wanted.'

Nonetheless, on 3 September 2012, Sellar allowed Prince Andrew to be the next person to hang precariously from the exterior of the Shard.

Caroline Sellar recalls that there was a call from the Palace to her father asking him to see Prince Andrew. There was no indication as to what the meeting would be about, but they assumed it was just to update him on the progress of the Shard.

'We had a nice meeting in Andrew's boardroom in his quarters. He was asking about the building; but then he said: "Right! I'm going to get to the reason why I actually asked you here." My father and I looked at each other, and I thought, "That's a bit strange." He spoke about charities, the Outward Bound Trust, which his father is patron of, and the Duke of Edinburgh's Award. The Trust has been going since the early 1950s, and he described the desperate need to raise some funds. He and his fellow board trustees, including the climber Chris Bonington, were sitting round and wondering, "What can we do?" – and Andrew looked out of a window at the Shard and said, "Why don't we abseil down the Shard?", much to the horror of all the other trustees. "It will never happen," they said, "it's a bonkers idea." That's why we were called in. The blood drained from my father's face. I thought it was hilarious. I also thought, "What a fantastic idea."'

Prince Andrew himself recalled that Irvine Sellar

just looked at me as if he thought I was mad, but he gave it a couple of minutes and said 'yes' for two reasons. One of which is that it will raise the profile of the Shard as well as the Outward Bound Trust, but also because it's a charitable event that will have an impact on the local community. He is trying to involve people to understand that this is their building, their community.[134]

Sellar reveals, 'When Andrew wanted to do his climb, I wasn't too happy about it. That would have been great, wouldn't it – the fourth in line to the throne, as he was at that time, killed on a climb on the Shard? Wonderful publicity!'

I ask him why he allowed it to go ahead.

'Because he assured me it would be professionally managed with specialists, and the training [conducted by the Royal Marines] would be second-to-none, and it was. That gave me enough confidence, and there was a good, charitable reason for doing it – they raised a lot of money.' The abseil raised £2.8 million for the Royal Marines Charitable Trust Fund and the Outward Bound Trust, and part of the funds was used to send 700 young people from Southwark on an Outward Bound course.

Caroline Sellar had a follow-up meeting with Ffion Hague (wife of the then Foreign Secretary William Hague) about the Outward Bound Trust; she was so interested in the organisation's work that she later replaced Ffion as one of its trustees.

A few months later, Prince Andrew was dressed in an all-in-one flying suit, ready to abseil from level 87, just beneath the peak of the ninety-five-storey Shard, down to the twentieth level of the building. He was joined by Ffion Hague and Chris Bonington – more used to scaling Everest – and young people from Southwark. The Prince was first to descend, half abseiling, half sliding down the wet glass.

'Well I won't do that again,' he revealed to the waiting press when he was back on earth. 'It was nerve-racking. I think we were in the clouds when we started. It was scary at the top . . . I slipped down the whole first section.' Ffion Hague, who went next, said, 'It is very disconcerting to see birds flying beneath you . . . Then halfway down the wind kicks in and you can begin to hear the platform announcements at London Bridge.'

The Mac cartoon in the *Daily Mail* on 4 September showed the Duke of Edinburgh, Prince Charles, the Queen, Camilla and three corgis abseiling down the Shard as a window-cleaner shouts, 'Oi, I hope you royals aren't going to make a habit of this. I've just washed that bit.'

When Sellar later met the Queen, who made her own rather more stately visit to the Shard on 21 November 2013, he reminded her, 'Your son climbed down the Shard, Ma'am.'

'Abseiled,' she corrected him. 'Silly boy!'

Chapter 11

The Piano Trilogy

> You could call it an accident. You could call it luck. You could call it
> a miracle. Many things occurred without which this development
> would never have happened. You have to recognise what these
> things are and take the opportunities.
>
> Irvine Sellar

In 2000, when Irvine Sellar decided to build tall at London Bridge, he
was already thinking beyond the red line of the Southwark Towers
site he co-owned and envisaging that the whole area could be
regenerated. Those thoughts moved on apace in 2003 when the New
London Bridge House site opposite the Shard became available. He was
no longer thinking of merely creating the first supertall building in the
United Kingdom: he wanted to create a place.

London Bridge Quarter is a bravura piece of literal map-making
beyond the signpost that is the Shard. A single building, no matter how
vast, could not alter the public realm and texture of the locality to the
extent required. The quarter turned an area of London Bridge into a
place of possibilities rather than an embarrassment through which
travellers would hunch their shoulders and grip their bags more tightly.
Chris Cole of WSP said in 2014:

> The biggest thing that will happen in conjunction with the Shard is that
> in five or seven years' time London Bridge Quarter will be recognised

as one of the great areas of London, with the best train station. It will elevate the financial value of the Shard – not the iconic value, which is there already and always will be. Irvine has put the building up and created the location – usually it is the other way round.

The London Bridge Quarter includes the Shard, the News Building and Shard Place in a £2 billion-plus development. I ask Irvine Sellar why he decided to call the area a quarter, in the manner of the French *quartier*, i.e. to suggest an area of a conurbation with a specific character or use. It's an increasingly used label as it immediately conjures identity and is market-friendly. Sellar is in prosaic mood: 'It was just the fact that it wasn't a square. It's on two levels. You've got the concourse level, with the Shard offices entrance, the News Building, the station and the bus station, but you've got everything else, access to the viewing gallery, the hotel and restaurants and Shard Place, on St Thomas Street.'

The News Building – originally called the Place, somewhat confusingly, but not to be confused with the third building, Shard Place – was built on the site of New London Bridge House and opened in 2014.

Shard Place is currently being built on the sites of two former buildings across from the Shard and adjacent to the News Building. Fielden House, a four-storey 1950s building opposite the Shard on London Bridge Street, had been bought freehold in November 2006 on behalf of Teighmore's then shareholders before Sellar's other partners left the Shard project. The building had 16,365 square feet (1,520 m²) of office space plus street-level retail and vaults beneath London Bridge Street. Sellar later bought a 130-year lease on the building behind it on St Thomas Street, nos 21–27, a 1980s four-storey building separated by a yard from Fielden House. With the Qataris just as positive as Sellar about expanding the concept of the London Bridge Quarter by creating a third building, the two parties formed a joint venture in 2013 to own both buildings and the yard in between them, and in the following year bought the freehold of 21–27 St Thomas Street from Guy's Charity. The resultant Shard Place will open in 2018.

Renzo Piano is the architect of the whole quarter, with Joost Moolhuijzen as the partner-in-charge of all three buildings and Jack

Fielden House (right) with Guy's Tower and Southwark Towers (Sellar Property Group Archive)

Carter taking over William Matthews's role effectively as the project architect for the later buildings.

London Bridge has a 2,000-year-old heritage, much of it as a place for outsiders, but nonetheless with great cultural and social texture. That layering of history can come with consequences for a developer, but Irvine Sellar acknowledges, 'Where we built was at a low point in the Thames, very slightly to the south of where the Romans built the crossing, so we expected quite a bit of Roman history.' The only question was how much, and whether it would forestall the development of any of the three buildings or public areas.

The site of the Shard revealed an array of ancient artefacts, but it was the site of the News Building, it turned out, that had enjoyed a previous life as a piece of prime real estate, at least in terms of land outside the city walls. A first-century Roman villa – built around AD 80 at the point when the city across the water was starting to become the de facto administrative capital of Roman Britain – was unearthed there. The villa was excavated by a team from Museum of London Archaeology (MOLA), coordinated by Derek Seeley, who carefully scraped away to find multiple artefacts and the hypocaust of the building, the size of which suggests it was the home of someone of notable wealth or authority. The skeletons of two Romans were also found. While one body was laid out formally with his hands across his chest, the other, more horrifically, was found sandwiched between two walls.

The sites revealed further gruesome history from a more recent era. The digging around the site of the News Building, where St Thomas' Hospital had been situated from the thirteenth to the nineteenth centuries, revealed a haphazard array of skeletons in what could be more accurately described as a dumping ground rather than a formal burial site. There was no decorum in the way that the bodies were strewn; they were patients who could not be saved by the often-barbaric techniques of medieval surgeons, or, indeed, died because of them. Patrick Williams, a senior project manager at Turner & Townsend, which has worked on all three buildings of the London Bridge Quarter, revealed, 'They're not lined up. Basically, if the doctors got it wrong they were just hoofed out the back door into the garden. When the pit was full, they covered it over.'[135] Having been disinterred, the deceased patients were finally granted some level of respect for the dead when the skeletons were reburied in accordance with modern-day regulations.

Construction director Flan McNamara says, 'I'm proud of our relationship with MOLA. We try not to hassle them and we make conditions as comfortable as we can when the archaeologists are out there in the middle of winter digging stuff out with effectively a spatula. Some developers see them as the enemy but we don't. Standing there screaming and shouting doesn't make the process any quicker, but being helpful does.'

To prevent the archaeological dig at the News Building site from causing severe delays to construction, it was divided into two periods. In October 2010 to March 2011, after Keltbray had demolished New London Bridge House, the MOLA team worked in fourteen pits where the new building's piles would later be sunk, returning in July 2011 for a further three-month dig after the ground-floor slab had been set.

Despite the level of finds and the procedures involved in the digs, Sellar says, 'They didn't cause delays to any of the buildings. We were on budget and on programme.'

Renzo Piano says about the relationship between the buildings of the London Bridge Quarter, 'It's a conversation. It's a case of scale, of course. You have the tall building – that is like Don Quixote, and the others are Sancho Panza. There's a connection and a reverberation between them. It's mainly about what you see when you are on the ground. When you are in the space between those buildings you see the dialogue, mainly through the materials, fundamentally glass. They all play with light. We wanted the scale of the smaller buildings not to challenge the scale of the Shard. They have a dialogue at ground level, up to a hundred metres, but above there the Shard is left to have its conversation with the sky and London. There is a dialogue but that building talks to the rest of the city.'

The News Building is a 270-foot (82-metre), seventeen-storey building with a triple-height entrance lobby, 430,000 square feet (40,000 m²) of office space and floor plates of up to 31,000 square feet (2889 m²). The structure incorporates 8,600 square feet (800 m²) of photovoltaic cells on the roof to improve energy efficiency.

Renzo Piano says that the design of the north side of the building – in which overlaid fractures give way to a sublime curve that follows the sweep of the suspended rail tracks just a few metres away – had an interesting gestation. 'We tried many things. We tried to make that façade segmented, but we found the trains coming quite interesting. It's not just about the shape of the rails, it's about the movement of the train and the people on the train. At that point, going around the bend, the people move with the bend. It's a curve because, firstly, the piece of land was like that, but also because of the people moving like that on the train. We took the train and we felt the movement. This curve was more intelligent anyway because it is taking light in a different, better way.'

Unlike the Shard, which Sellar wanted to be multi-let, he envisaged the News Building to be the headquarters for a single tenant. While there were early discussions with PricewaterhouseCoopers, and the briefly entertained possibility of Transport for London taking up the space once Sellar and the Qataris had bought them out of their pre-let agreement for the Shard, it became the headquarters of one of the leading media companies in the world, News International. Thus the name change from the Place to the News Building.

Mace and WSP teamed up again under the guidance of Sellar as the developer. Flan McNamara, Sellar's director of construction, says, 'We had to ensure that the building didn't detract from the Shard and that it was a unified part of the London Bridge Quarter. It was important to get the right sort of floor plate for the market; big corporate occupiers demand floor plates of 20,000–30,000 foot square.'

There was not a lot of wiggle room to establish the floor plates on the confined site of New London Bridge House. Construction began in August 2010 while the Shard was mid-phase, and it had a very tight building programme of 131 weeks. The News Building shared many of the logistical problems of the Shard. It was hemmed in from all sides and even from below: the boundary of the west and south sides was marked by three Underground ventilation shafts; London Bridge Underground station was to the north; the Northern line escalator was to the north-east; the Jubilee line and its ticket office were underneath and its escalators were on the south-east corner. On top of that, full public access to the Underground, London Bridge railway station and the multiple bus routes had to be maintained throughout construction.

The News Building design has created double the space of the New London Bridge House floor plate by cantilevering, from the third-storey level up, by up to 38 feet (12 metres) over the Underground's infrastructure and the bus station. This made design and construction almost as complicated as it had been for the sky-scraping Shard. Surprisingly, the subterranean support for the News Building runs down through the pre-existing Underground infrastructure.

Kamran Moazami of WSP explained, 'The main thing was to design a system that would allow existing activity to continue and avoid any movement of existing assets.'[136] London Underground usually has a 3-metre exclusion zone around its infrastructure, but that would have made it impossible to support the new building properly. The engineers used 3D finite element analysis to prove to London Underground that the works would not lead to unsafe ground movement. With London Underground assured, they could use two piles to straddle the escalator to the Northern line, with another pile propping the end of the building, just 1.5 metres away from the Jubilee line. Once again, Sol Data monitored all movement.

Sellar took the radical decision to have one less basement level to reduce the amount of time necessary for the archaeological dig. Consequently, Piano and his team worked with WSP to remodel the design, reducing the space given over for plant, and thereby saving floor space equivalent to the lost basement level.

The length of the building running along London Bridge Street meant that, unlike the Shard, the News Building has twin cores. As they had with the skyscraper, the team used top-down construction and jump-started the cores, building them upwards on plunge columns while the basement levels were still being excavated. The basement core walls were then cast around the plunge columns. The first core was finished by the end of September 2011, allowing the building to progress upwards, while the basement slab was not cast until June 2012.

Sellar, as usual, was driving the team forward to meet deadlines that pushed the realms of possibility. Gordon Gray of Mace said, 'At one stage we had demolition, archaeology, piling and the core all going on in a very small footprint because the programme was so demanding.'[137]

The News Building presents itself as a series of angled façades opposite the Shard. The façades are stepped outwards on the south side so that you do not sense the full weight of the building. The lightness is helped by the asymmetric, double-pointed front cantilever, meaning that there is more public space at ground level and the entrance is set well back from the perimeter. In fact, the building is also set back along the two longer sides, either as a cantilever or supported by columns, increasing the public realm and allowing broader pavements. Rather than matching the angled white steel of the Shard's perimeter columns, the columns are rounded and clad in smooth concrete, and are sympathetic to the Shard's supporting columns in the railway concourse, as well as those supporting the railway tracks.

There are three columns along the north side, where the angularity of the façade planes resolves to the curve that draws on that of the rail

The almost structurally complete News Building at the
foot of the Shard, December 2012 (© John Safa)

tracks. 'It is an eccentrically loaded building,' says Flan McNamara.
'To use more than three columns on that side, we would have had to
dig through the middle of the station underneath.'

The News Building's entrance façade has hand-riven Italian marble
on the exterior (complementing the office reception area and core
cladding of the Shard), and the same marble, but smooth polished,
within. The pale, light, triple-height reception is fronted by glazing and
dominated by News Corp's large-letter legend, 'Telling the stories that
matter, seeding ideas and searing emotion, capturing moments, meaning
and magic . . .' which runs to many lines and is somewhat at odds with
Sellar's rather more concise maxims for life.

The building shares the double-skin, floor-to-ceiling glazing concept
of the Shard, while the blind housing behind the outer skin is

The News Building reception, prior to the hanging of
News Corp's enormous legend along the marble wall (© Michel Denancé)

yellow-orange, rather than the red-orange of the Shard. The idea of the
wing walls seen on the taller building has been extended. As well as
over-shooting the stepped fissures between the façades of the building,
they hang down into the cantilevered and column-supported recesses,
and also overshoot the top floor of the building.

The growing Piano motif of breaking down indoor/outdoor boundaries, even in high-rises, is borne out by the large, south-facing, protected
roof garden on level 14, which has a marvellous view of the Shard, plus
naturally ventilated winter gardens inside the offices on levels 3 to 12.

Although the News Building is large and has its own presence, it is
a surprisingly unobtrusive building. 'It could so easily be a monstrosity
sitting there over the top of the bridge,' William Murray says. 'You
would never know that as a development, the London Bridge Quarter

has a million square feet of office space, and many people would barely even know that there is an office building there.' This is testament to Piano's skill at creating light and space around the base of a building.

On 19 May 2013, the *Sunday Times* was somewhat gleefully reporting that the Shard was the 'tallest white elephant in the world' due to the lack of leased office space. Three years later, I raised the story with Irvine Sellar. He laughed as he said, 'The fact is that those journalists are now in my offices right next to the Shard.'

Within a couple of months of that negative article, the owners of the *Sunday Times* announced that it would be moving its headquarters into the companion building. In typically sanguine style, Sellar gives a wry smile. 'Bad news sells. That's just the way it is,' he says and waves the memory away.

News International signed a thirty-year lease on the News Building. The publishers of *The Times*, the *Sunday Times* and the *Sun* began moving from Wapping in June 2014, with the remainder of the staff transferring in September. There are now 4,000 staff in the building covering the twelve News UK businesses, including HarperCollins and the UK division of the *Wall Street Journal*. As a gesture of its desire to be a good, community neighbour, News UK donated eighty-eight Nexus and iPad tablets to eight local libraries in Southwark.

At the opening ceremony on 16 September 2014, Mayor Boris Johnson said: 'The London Bridge Quarter has helped to spearhead a renaissance in this important part of the capital, attracting scores of new businesses and creating thousands of jobs . . .' Johnson then scanned his lexicon for a new description of the Shard: 'Nestled next to the giant cosmic spear that is the Shard, I can think of no better place for some of Britain's most prominent and historic titles to base themselves.'[138]

Sellar says of Fielden House and 21– 27 St Thomas Street, 'We always had development in mind for the two buildings to make the development complete for the Renzo design. It was a joint venture with the Qataris – we'll develop it, and they'll fund it with nearly £300 million.'

The resultant twenty-six-storey residential building, announced in January 2014 and due to be completed four years later, will 'float' on white steel pillars above the public space connecting London Bridge Street and St Thomas Street at the foot of the Shard. It is a glazed rectangular tower, so there is a marked difference in form within the Piano trilogy. Yet again, there are construction issues; the Underground runs across the corner of the site, which has influenced the design as it limits the placement of piles.

The tower is suspended 30 feet (9 metres) above the upper station concourse level, and 52 feet (16 metres) above St Thomas Street, creating room for new public seating and landscaping in the London Bridge Quarter, along with a ground-level bar and retail outlets. The raising of the building will create a balcony overlooking St Thomas Street. The 165,000-square-foot (15,300 m²) building will contain 148 apartments in what are effectively conjoined towers of twenty-six floors and sixteen floors. As with the News Building, much effort has gone into ensuring that Shard Place will not interrupt prime local views of the Shard.

A grand public stairway, inspired by the Spanish Steps in Rome, will run down the side of the building to connect the concourse level with the lower level and lead to Guy's Quad and the new Science Gallery, thereby transforming the relationship between London Bridge Street and St Thomas Street. The franchise of the Science Gallery Dublin opens in 2018 and is expected to attract 300,000 visitors a year to join the near million who visit the View from the Shard. The capital cost of building the gallery has been supported by the Wellcome Trust, Guy's and St Thomas' Charity and the Shard owners themselves.

At Shard Place, WSP are once again the engineers, with Skanksa undertaking the pre-construction work while a fixed-price contract is out for tender. Demolition was completed in April 2016 and piling was under way by summer 2016.

As for the name Shard Place, Sellar says, 'What I have realised is that the Shard is globally known. You talk to people in New Zealand or Colombia or anywhere else, they know the Shard. I can't think of another new building in London – except maybe the Gherkin – that has that. You can say, "I live in Shard Place." You won't need to give any other explanation of your address.'

Even though the News Building and Shard Place are more or less single-use buildings, Sellar's intent was to ensure that there was variety

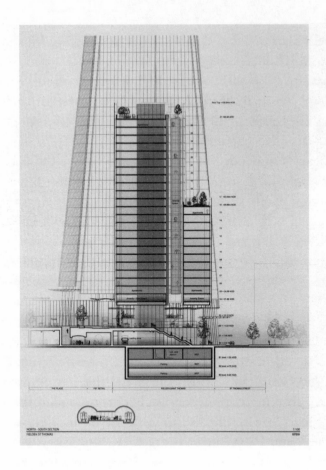

North–south section of Shard Place in front of the Shard (© RPBW)

within the London Bridge Quarter – this is a man who once said that he had come to realise what the 'c-word' meant: consolidation. 'We had very little residential in the quarter so Shard Place provides the balance. We have a very powerful office building in the News Building, and the Shard is totally unique, as I've said many times, because it is the vertical city, so we have a balance between the three buildings.'

'The appeal of the apartment building,' he explains, 'is that it has all that the Shard delivers – the hotel, the restaurants and bars – and all the connectivity benefits. It's an area in which we and our partners have pumped in £2 billion.' It will also benefit from the rail masterplan at London Bridge finally coming to fruition. 'Network Rail are pumping in another £2 billion in transforming the rail station into probably one

View from the piazza towards the base of the Shard and the station (© Michel Denancé)

of the best stations in Europe, so you've got £4 billion of assets and you are right in the centre of this dynamic, globally recognised address.'

Beyond the address, Sellar and his team have sought to make it a building that stands out in a climate where there are a great many luxury residential apartments on the market. 'There will be a lot of good facilities – a private gym, a playroom for kids, a great outdoor space.' The latter will be a south-facing residents' garden on level 16 (the roof of the lower section of the tower), aligned with the roof terrace of the News Building. The apartments, which will have either multiple aspect or duplex configurations, will be naturally ventilated, and like the offices in the sister buildings, they will have single-glazed winter gardens, with naturally generated heating and cooling for year-round use.

'It will be a Renzo Piano special,' Sellar says, relaxing into salesman mode. 'It will be different and distinctly residential but still compatible, and recognisable as being the same DNA as the News Building and the Shard. They will be the top-quality residences – five-star – from which you can get around London in no time at all.'

He says that not only will the building enhance the streetscape in Joiner Street and St Thomas Street – pushing forward his long-held ambition to improve the public realm – but the pedestrian flow will be improved by lifting the building 9 metres off the ground.

Renzo Piano agrees: 'By working on all three buildings, we have made the area of the station better. The concourse level, the new station and the combination of the Shard, the News Building and Shard Place altogether create a place of dignified urbanity. It is a bit frustrating that those things take a long time.'

In 2015, Sellar said, 'We have the sister building and the fact that we built a new station concourse which has completely transformed London Bridge station – it's placemaking. And a tower should not be in splendid isolation, it should be part of the immediate facility, it should embrace it.'[139] He also uses the phrase 'placemaking' in my interviews with him, and it is no accident that he wanted the office building in the London Bridge Quarter to be called the Place, before News Corp gave the building its own stamp, and he consequently named the residential building Shard Place.

The word 'placemaking' has had strong currency among planners, developers and architects for the last few decades (and has become so overused now that some practitioners shy away from its usage, rather in the same way as they might avoid 'iconic'). It is used, in broad terms, to describe the creation of public areas, such as piazzas, parks, gardens and waterfronts, that are of interest or give pleasure: they are spaces to which people are attracted and where they wish to spend time, rather than thoroughfares – a place rather than betwixt.

The socio-architectural concept started to become refined in the United States in the late 1950s, particularly through the work of the writer Jane Jacobs and her editor at *Fortune* magazine, William 'Holly' Whyte. In works such as *The Death and Life of Great American Cities* (1961), Jacobs wrote of the consequences of the homogenisation and the mechanisation of urban areas, and de-pedestrianisation through the removal of pavements. She highlighted that the top-down placement of major highways and mass high-rise social housing leads to the ruination of community and a sense of place. Her thinking was a forerunner to that of Irvine Sellar and Renzo Piano, especially in her belief that high density is good for placemaking, as is mixed use. As the Project for Public Spaces, the American organisation that today pursues policies partly inspired by Jacobs' philosophy, explains:

> Jacobs advocated for 'mixed-use' urban development – the integration of different building types and uses, whether residential or commercial, old or new. According to this idea, cities depend on a diversity of buildings, residences, businesses and other non-residential uses, as well as people of different ages using areas at different times of day, to create community vitality. She saw cities as being 'organic, spontaneous, and untidy', and views the intermingling of city uses and users as crucial to economic and urban development.[140]

I doubt that Sellar, who is always extremely neatly dressed, was ever seeking to create an 'untidy' environment for the London Bridge Quarter, but much of that summation holds true to his vision. Jacobs may have been a liberal-left theoretician who believed in community intuition as a basis for planning, a standpoint almost necessarily at odds with the intention of a commercial developer who projects a scheme onto a site, but nonetheless there is at least some shared sensibility about what makes a good place.

While research is being undertaken by the likes of the Centre for Advanced Spatial Analysis and Space Syntax to provide scientific evaluation of contentment with a space (Space Syntax's early research showed that people were willing to walk much further just to have a sandwich in the public space at Broadgate[141]), it is hard to define what makes a good place. The Project for Public Spaces has produced a wheel diagram under the heading 'What Makes a Great Place', breaking it down into quarters: Sociability, Access & Linkages, Uses and Activities and Comfort & Image.[142] The London Bridge Quarter development scores highly in some categories, not least because it has open public spaces and it offers leisure activities, as well as transport connections. It has an identity and a point in its orientation.

The literary academic Vybarr Cregan-Reid, while running along a path through Prince Charles's Poundbury estate for his book *Footnotes*, hit upon one of the many reasons why Poundbury fails to be a place:

> I am furious at the idiocy of this design. It is a path to nowhere, that no one can possibly need. The developers must have thought that this tidy triangle would look lovely from the road, that the path would look walked, peopled, inhabited. The path's design prioritises those that will never step on it, and instead pass by it in their cars or watch it from a distance as they do the washing up. Does development really have to be so myopic and halfwitted?[143]

Terry Farrell has identified the area around the Euston Road and Marylebone flyover in London as somewhere a sense of place was clearly undone by infrastructural imposition. The same could be said about the way the rail infrastructure and road systems voided the area between Tooley Street and St Thomas Street in London Bridge. The post-war mini-cluster created further problems in terms of both aesthetics and pedestrian-friendliness.

On a grand scale, top-down imposition is very much at the centre of the social problems surrounding the manufactured super-quarter of Canary Wharf as it continues to bed down. We are increasingly conscious that London, with all its outrageous beauty and opportunity, has closed its doors to much of its own population. In some areas, Londoners themselves are a diminishing part of the fabric.

Canary Wharf is focused on its tall towers for bankers, and though it does have some level of mixed use with integrated bars, restaurants and retail, and a periphery of residential development, it is representative of an inward-looking Superlondon where, too obviously, capital rather than community is the original motivation behind planning and development.

Canary Wharf is bizarrely claustrophobic and hard to navigate considering the clean slate that was given to the developers. The atmosphere has improved markedly in the last decade, but once the commuters have left, it is still something of a non-place, lacking vitality, because it is a machine; when the operatives have left for the weekend, it is as stationary and forlorn as a forgotten Fleet Street printing press.

It is difficult to see how the success of the Docklands development has significantly aided the Underlondoners in the shadows of its towers. Beyond it lies an anti-pedestrian mass of roads and depressed, shambolic areas where local people live. The cusp of the Docklands has been populated with seemingly unplanned streets and estates of barely designed little box-houses. It is the piss-stenched back alley to the rear of the Wharf's theatrical façade; the residents are a few miles from the bankers and a million miles from their advantages. Tower Hamlets, the borough in which the headquarters for so many global corporate businesses sit, has high rates of long-term illness and premature death, the second-highest unemployment rate in London, and 'Life expectancy is lower than average for both sexes and levels of drug misuse, violent crime and new cases of tuberculosis are high . . . Tower Hamlets has the highest level of children living in poverty in England.'[144] Isolation and exclusion are made worse by proximity.

This is not to say that there has been no attempt by the Canary Wharf Group to engage with its poorer east London neighbours. But when you walk around areas of Mudchute, it is hard to see even minor trickle-down benefits.

Londoners intuit natural fabric; we do not like the feeling that a place has been wholly created, plonked down from a CAD package to a cold reality without an organic gestation.

One could claim that despite its mixed use and the Shard's viewing gallery, the London Bridge Quarter is just as much for Superlondoners as is Canary Wharf. London Bridge Quarter, however, does not have Canary Wharf's problem: it exists within the fabric of the city because it was literally built upon it, integrating with its existing structure.

Sellar's detractors may take the moral high ground, but the true moral purpose in architecture is to create the best possible environment for living, and not to be a relic of a past where life was, on balance, worse. Yet neither should new development eradicate wholesale the cultural identifiers that generate a sense of belonging or pleasure. Sellar, I have discovered over the course of our conversations, intuitively knows this, as does Piano.

Sellar always claimed that the creation of the London Bridge Quarter would enable him to follow through the sort of changes to the public realm that CABE wished to see implemented when they protested against planning permission for the Shard at the public inquiry in 2003. At the same inquiry, Sellar's team made it clear that the building of the Shard would in no way inhibit the Railtrack/Network Rail masterplan for London Bridge station – which had been mooted since the end of the previous century – if indeed it ever came into being.

In autumn 2016, a large part of that masterplan became bricks and mortar (plus some rather fetching wood panelling), providing a good opportunity to assess whether the London Bridge Quarter, as it stands so far, has been beneficial when it comes to placemaking and integrating with infrastructure.

What is immediately apparent in the piazza, as the space between the Shard and the News Building is somewhat grandly called, is the successful synthesis of the buildings and the transport infrastructure, with the bus stops now relocated to the north of the space, the entrance to the Underground close to the entrance to the News Building, and the rail station's upper concourse physically linked to the Shard. The subtle design links in the use of white steel and glazing between the buildings, the bus shelters and the canopies reveal an identifiable 'quarter' but without the danger of veering into corporate-style homogeneity.

When I sit in the piazza, it is half-past twelve. Many other people are sitting on the benches or on the edge of the large planters that bring greenery to the space. Some people are standing, waiting for friends or colleagues, using the biggest signpost in London as a reference point. Others are walking straight from the buses into the station concourse, and are able immediately to see both the platform indicators and some of the platforms themselves before crossing the threshold, something formerly impossible before Sellar and Piano took the matter in hand as part of the Section 106 agreements for the two completed buildings.

The people within the station who pop into M&S Simply Food or Nero Express may not realise that they are actually within the structure of the Shard. Likewise, it is clear that some people who leave the station concourse and come out into the piazza have no idea that the columns that they weave between are within the Shard's perimeter, that they are within its space, and it is only when they look back that they realise that they have been walking underneath the tallest building in the country. That its volume takes people by surprise, even when they have been within its footprint, is testament to the way that Sellar and Piano made the building relate to the public realm: they wanted it to be permeable in its boundaries rather than looming and blocking out both the street and the light, and they have succeeded.

Other people are less surprised by the presence of the building: tourists are taking photographs and looking up with obvious joy. Others still are walking to or from the almost perpetually moving doors of the busy News Building.

The piazza is a place of activity, but it is by no means choked. The road that swerves through the space is virtually traffic-free, with the exception of the occasional bus or taxi, enabling the people on the benches to have a relatively peaceful, outdoor lunch. The idea of willingly coming to sit outside London Bridge station, enjoy a little autumn sunshine and a quiet sandwich in the days before the London Bridge Quarter would have been simply ridiculous. Your fellow diner would most likely have been a rat.

The workers having their lunch are not bothering to look up because the London Bridge Quarter and the Shard are already part of the fabric of their lives, and they seem happy to sit at the foot of the monster without feeling any threat.

The success of the quarter on the upper concourse level has been there to gauge since the News Building opened in 2014. The question as to whether the St Thomas Street section of the quarter works too can only be answered now that the first stage of the Network Rail masterplan is complete, and the mass of street-narrowing hoardings has been removed.

The work has finally made for better orientation between the two series of railway platforms at London Bridge station, access to, which, for historical reasons that are too complicated to unpick, is on different levels and some distance apart. Those who enter under Renzo Piano's concourse roof can immediately see one set of platforms in front of them and an escalator that will take them down to the spacious new lower concourse. Vast improvement has come with the additional station entrance on St Thomas Street where, after years of being behind boards, the railway arches are exposed.

St Thomas Street has been opened up and runs from Borough Market through the London Bridge Quarter, right down to meet Bermondsey Street, which has been resuscitated over the last decade or so to be a creative, slightly alternative neighbourhood known for its cafés, bars, restaurants and artisan shops. As St Thomas Street beds in, the London Bridge Quarter will undoubtedly become the centrepiece of a chain of three linked, vibrant, destination areas.

The brickwork all along the viaduct arches on St Thomas Street and the brickwork at the base of the backpack of the Shard are sympathetic to each other, courtesy of the choice of York handmade bricks for the tower. The same bricks are used next to the entrance to the View from the Shard and form a prime feature of the façade on the lower floors of the News Building, both along London Bridge Street and on the north side, revealing an integrity and sympathy for the urban texture. There is much more cohesion to the area in terms of orientation and design, but not at the cost of heterogeneity. It will be a dynamic area for different adventures. This is the benefit of mixed use, bringing people to the area day and night for offices, residence, retail and entertainment: it helps to create a place.

Sellar played a part in helping to change street-level appreciation of design and retail through Carnaby Street and Mates, and something of that sensibility has helped change North Southwark for the better.

Sellar says, 'I think London Bridge Quarter has become an important district that will match Covent Garden and Mayfair in years to come and will match any other district. London is made up of a thousand villages and this village will expand and grow. London Bridge was historically important and when we acquired our first building there it was very downbeat, very forgotten and very sad. It has been rejuvenated as a result of what we're doing and as a result of what Network Rail is doing.'

Despite Sellar's optimism, more work clearly needs to be done, at this point, on Joiner Street, connecting St Thomas Street to the Underground Station and Tooley Street. On the upper level, the above-ground rail infrastructure on the north side and the space underneath the rail tracks are the most visible scars of the former dark days of London Bridge. At night, this is the place where revellers urinate in a perhaps unconscious reckoning that, if the place won't respect itself, then they won't respect it either.

As what is fast becoming a cultural quarter evolves, it will become imperative to resolve this area, as it should be a welcoming gateway from the bridge into the regenerated district. In the end, it may take a joint effort from Network Rail, the London Borough of Southwark, and Sellar and his Qatari partners to complete the jigsaw. Otherwise, though, there is undoubtedly a germ of truth in what Sellar says: it is an area people will actively seek out.

The final work on the station masterplan will be completed in 2018, the same year that Shard Place and the Science Gallery also open, but London Bridge has already been given orientation and articulation. Finally, London Bridge is a place rather than an accident of infrastructure.

Chapter 12

Vision into View

Persistence is omnipotent. There are unrewarded geniuses on every street corner and intellectual derelicts in the dole queues; the element that makes things happen is persistence.

Irvine Sellar

Be true to yourself. Don't kid yourself. You might want to kid the rest of the world, but know yourself.

Irvine Sellar

In an interview in 2015, Irvine Sellar was asked why he had persevered with the development of the Shard:

Because I'm persistent. I always had hope . . . There was every possible obstacle that you could imagine that got in the way of the process – this should have been a five- or six-year programme, not twelve or fourteen years – but we had minor things that interrupted us like the largest planning inquiry that ever took place in London, that was one, like the worst financial crisis in living memory, that was two, and a few other issues that took place along the way that slowed down the process. It wasn't great but we saw our way through that . . . Look, if you are swimming the Atlantic and you happen to be halfway across, you might as well carry on. There's no point in turning back, is there?[145]

Just as the Shard was having its inauguration, Gerald Ronson, whose Heron Tower remains the tallest building in the City, said about Sellar: 'He's the most persistent man I know, next to myself. You have to give him 11 out of 10 for this.'[146]

When I ask Renzo Piano about the difficulty of bringing something new into the fabric of a city, he says, 'When we had our first meeting, in Berlin in 2000, my son was one year; by the time we finish and the station is completed, he will be over eighteen. But this gives you the sense that cities are organic. They are like an elephant with a slow metabolism. They don't move fast but change slowly. Architecture relies on the long term to become loved, to become part of the city, to be adopted by time. You need the patina.'

Yet before the Shard had even been inaugurated on 5 July 2012 by Sheikh Hamad bin Jassim bin Jaber Al Thani and Prince Andrew in the lead-up to the evening dinner and the light show that attracted 300,000 onlookers, it was apparent that London, a city apparently deeply averse to tall buildings, had adopted its new landmark almost without reservation. The Shard very quickly became part of the fabric of the city.

After construction had been completed, Piano travelled to London to witness the reaction to the building for himself: 'I spied. I walked against the crowd on St Thomas Street, watching the faces of the people coming towards me looking up at the Shard.' He does something similar whenever he completes a building, hiding behind pillars or pretending to make a phone call so he can assess the reactions of passers-by without obviously staring at them. 'And I saw them approaching me distracted, chatting amongst themselves or simply looking away, and then stopping for a moment and looking upwards. And the expressions that I observed were not negative, but rather full of surprise and delight.'[147]

The delight extended to leading architectural writers and architects. Peter Murray wrote in the *Financial Times* that the Shard 'generates wonderful surprises in the cityscape . . . It is also, quite simply, one of the most beautiful tall buildings in the world. We have become so used to lumpen orthogonal blocks or contorted icons that the triangular simplicity of the Shard is boldly refreshing.'[148]

One the country's most eminent architects, Sir Terry Farrell, designer of the supertall KK100 tower (2011) in Shenzhen, was similarly laudatory: 'It's got style and it's a phenomenon. If we come back in ten years, people will feel affectionate towards it.' He also said that the Shard was an example of the positive results of building tall: 'That's what tall buildings do. They create a massive amount of demand and that brings in revenues and taxes that allow the council to sort out the immediate area.'[149]

Murray and Farrell might be expected to respond positively to a well-designed and innovative skyscraper, but the Shard also elicited acclaim from more unlikely quarters. Clive Aslet, an architectural writer and former editor of *Country Life*, was drawn to the Shard despite his conservatism when it came to tall buildings: 'I can't help it, I love the Shard. Let's hope it kicks off an architectural revolution in London. On the whole I'm not one for tall buildings, but the sheer scale of this mighty, heaven-soaring spike overwhelms my better instincts . . . There is an energy about it, which, in these dark days, makes me glad for London.'[150]

Sir Norman Rosenthal, formerly in charge of exhibitions at the Royal Academy, joined the applause: 'I cannot now imagine London without the Shard and would go so far as to say that it is arguably the greatest and most beautifully skyreaching building to be erected in London since St Paul's Cathedral.'[151] While decrying other tall buildings such as Centre Point and Tower 42, he wrote, 'Finally, along comes something that is genuinely magnificent to look at . . . I don't care about its function or who built it, or even who financed it. It is a masterpiece of visual design by one of the great living architects, Renzo Piano.'

'The first thing about development of a tall building,' Irvine Sellar said in 2015,

> is that it's there to be enjoyed by the public. In our case, we happen to believe that tall buildings are not fortresses, they shouldn't be impenetrable, they should be enjoyed by the public, which means that they are vertical towns that form part of the city and the immediate cityscape . . . they can view from our building, they can eat in our building, because we've

got restaurants, and they can work there. And what does it do? It creates jobs. It's got to be compatible but not exactly fit the [history of the] immediate area because in our case that would take us back to the Roman era and that wouldn't work! It's got to look good. It's got to be pleasing, and it's got to be accessible.[152]

The key to accessibility, established in that very first meeting with Renzo Piano in 2000, is the viewing gallery: Londoners feel that they own the view of the Shard – they have calibrated it into their personal psychogeography of the capital – but the gallery offered them the chance also to own the view from it.

Two viewing galleries, in fact, are marked on very early Piano drawings, one halfway up the building and another at the top. In the end, having two areas fulfilling the same function did not make sense, and the lower platform would have been regarded as inferior in any case. While the prime, narrow space at the top of the building was reserved for the public gallery, the space lower down was given over to restaurants.

In October 2011, it was announced that Andy Nyberg, who worked on the 'At the Top' attraction at the Burj Khalifa in Dubai and the Sears Tower Skydeck in Chicago, would develop the viewing gallery at the Shard. There was a great deal of anticipation about the quality of the views the building would provide, not solely because of its height, but because of its siting near the river, allowing panoramas that cover the spread of the city north and south. The views extend to 35 miles in the unlikely event that there is a clear day.

Some people anticipated the opening of the viewing gallery by Boris Johnson on 1 February 2013 with a charged nervousness unrelated to vertigo. Within seconds of the attraction opening its doors, one visitor, James Episcopou, got down on bended knee and proposed to girlfriend Laura Taylor. Another engagement followed within minutes.

The architect John Pawson was also an early visitor:

Driving to the Shard from my home [in Notting Hill], my destination was constantly in view, which intensified the excitement of arrival . . . I could, and did, spend years looking at the geometries of the building in plan and the sweeping coils of the train tracks. This is exactly the view

I've been trying to get for years: the right height to see the river snaking away, but low enough to feel an intimacy with what you are looking at.[153]

In terms of the interior, the View from the Shard experience begins much further down. The welcome area before the lift is low lit with dark grey walls, so the experience of coming into the light at the top of the building and the view is all the more heightened. The glazing outside the lifts at the top is opaque though – a late alteration that arose after the organisers noticed that as soon as the lift doors opened, visitors would rush to the windows rather than going up the short flight of stairs to the proper View from the Shard platforms.

There are two observation decks: one enclosed, with wooden flooring and wood-clad core, and preserved from the elements; and a higher one for the slightly more adventurous where one can feel the cool air filtering through the open shards of glass and the lattice of the steel spire. It is there that you feel the true height of the Shard as it fractures into the sky. A million people visited the View from the Shard in its first year, matching the number for the Houses of Parliament.[154] The attraction reported a record day of sales on Valentine's Day 2015, with 6,161 visitors, who between them drank 2,414 glasses of champagne. A marriage proposal took place on average every 30 minutes.

Below the viewing gallery sit the thirteen levels of apartments – the least publicly accessible part of the building. In the show apartment, designed before the Shard's board decided not to put the residences on the open market, everything is bespoke, from a 103-inch television behind motorised, custom-designed metal doors to a three-ton marble bath, which had to be carried up the stairs as it would not fit into the apartment lifts; an interior wall had to be removed for its installation. Despite the luxury and attention to detail that has gone into the furniture, kitchen and lighting, the eye is perpetually drawn to the changing exterior vistas that unfold from room to room.

The Shangri-La, on levels 34 to 52, opened a year after the View from the Shard on 6 May 2014, and a decade after the hotel chain's former chief Giovanni Angelini had stood alongside Irvine Sellar at the top of Southwark Towers. In that time, as the progress of the Shard hit hurdle after hurdle, the chain doubled from forty-six to ninety hotels

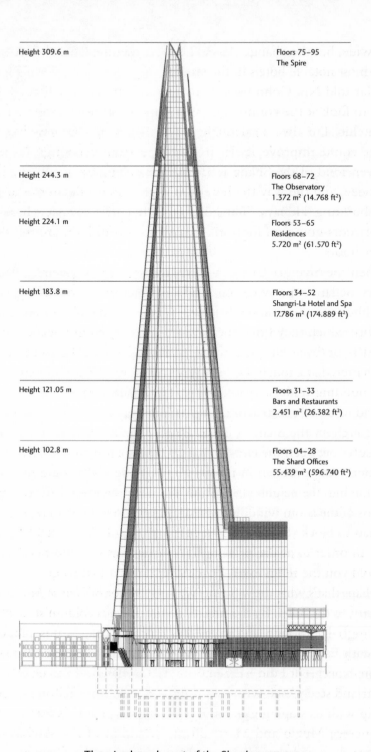

Height 309.6 m — Floors 75–95
The Spire

Height 244.3 m — Floors 68–72
The Observatory
1.372 m² (14.768 ft²)

Height 224.1 m — Floors 53–65
Residences
5.720 m² (61.570 ft²)

Height 183.8 m — Floors 34–52
Shangri-La Hotel and Spa
17.786 m² (174.889 ft²)

Height 121.05 m — Floors 31–33
Bars and Restaurants
2.451 m² (26.382 ft²)

Height 102.8 m — Floors 04–28
The Shard Offices
55.439 m² (596.740 ft²)

The mixed-use layout of the Shard (© RPBW)

worldwide, but the Shangri-La At The Shard immediately became one of the most notable hotels in the stable.

Sellar told Nik Cohn back in 1971: 'Unfortunately, wherever I go I tend to look at the commercial aspects. When I'm in a restaurant or a nightclub, I'm always calculating to see if it's run business-like and how it could improve itself. It stops me from relaxing.'[155] He is, however, fond of the Shangri-La, its restrained luxury and emphasis on service, and the way the hotel rooms are circumfluent to the core of the building. He says, 'The hotel is not like *The Shining*, where you see corridors going on forever. There is beautiful light around those smaller floors.'

When the Shangri-La encountered problems with their own contractors, Sellar Property Group itself took over the fit-out of aspects of the public areas of the hotel. Michael Donnelly remembers the trepidation with which they fitted the two huge decorated glass panels in the ground-floor foyer. Each is composed of non-laminated glass that could have shattered at a touch. Donnelly, who has thirty years of experience in the building trade, says it was the single most difficult thing he has ever had to do in construction.

Throughout the Shard, the wing walls of the outer skin overshoot the fissures between the façades, but this design feature initially caused a disconcerting problem in the hotel: the wing walls could provide a reflection into the neighbouring suite. The solution was relatively simple: the glass of the room windows was polarised. Donnelly also reports that they had to block the space between the panes of glass that adjoin two rooms in order to assure privacy: 'The view was so good that I could have told you the religion of the man in the next bathroom.'

Perhaps that's what drew Shane Watson, author of *How to Meet a Man after Forty*, to the hotel. By the time the *Sunday Times* columnist reviewed the Shangri-La, though, and assessed its rooms of pale creams, blues and greys with Eastern touches, all privacy problems had been rectified.

'You expect – or I did – the interior of the Shangri-La to be cool and angular and steely,' she wrote, 'but instead it has the feel of a graceful tall ship with its sloping glass walls and internal pillars that slant.'[156]

Francesca Muzio and Maria Silvia Orlandini of FM Architettura d'interni designed the signature suite interiors at the Shangri-La on levels 37–9. Piano may have approved of the choice, as Muzio previously worked at the Renzo Piano Building Workshop, and Orlandini used to be a philosophy student. 'Everyone knows the Shard from the outside . . . Renzo Piano created a panorama of the city,' Muzio said. 'It's like a living wallpaper and so interesting, because the buildings are part of people's imaginations and memories.'[157] While there is an emphasis on interior luxury, the vistas are the focus.

The designers partially clad the structural columns with mirrored glass to angle the views into the room, and kept the windows clear of furniture, although there are baths right by the windows in a third of the 202 rooms. If a guest is not allocated one of those rooms, on level 52 there is a blue-tiled infinity pool where they can see the view over the lip of the water.

London has belatedly started to appreciate rooftop bar culture – a bacchanalian side effect of global warming. The Shangri-La has the highest bar in Europe. Designed by André Fu of AFSO, Gŏng, the intimate bar, also on level 52, draws on Eastern inspiration with gloss-lacquered walls in cinnabar.

The hotel's restaurant is Tīng, where marriage proposals are so frequent that the art of innovative ring-placement on plates and in cocktails is *de rigueur* for the waiting staff. The floor is dark wood and the volume is broken up by fragile wooden screens, lending an air of sedateness frequently broken by the – one would hope joyful – cries of surprise from the ring-finders.

The Shangri-La assumed that the London outpost primarily would be a business hotel for executives and would be empty at the end of the week, but the rooms are booked continuously at weekends, especially by those on honeymoon or celebrating anniversaries. It has become a destination hotel because of the uniqueness of the building and its views.

Beneath the hotel on levels 31–3, the three high-end restaurants – Hutong (Chinese), Aqua Shard (contemporary British) and Oblix (rotisserie and grill) – opened in summer 2013. Each has an entirely different design while making use of the view and running popular bars.

The property sector had long suggested that the offices of the Shard were going to be hard to lease, following Sellar and the Qataris' decision to buy out the deal with Transport for London and the extended recession.

In early 2012, the Barclays Capital 'Skyscraper Index' report presented information that suggested that the Shard would be seeking tenants in a time of doom: 'Often the world's tallest buildings are simply the edifice of a broader skyscraper building boom, reflecting a widespread misallocation of capital and an impending economic correction.' The suggestion was that skyscraper booms coincide with recession, and there is historical evidence for this, with the Equitable Life Building in New York, which was completed in 1870 and considered by some to be the first skyscraper, marking a five-year recession; the Golden Age in New York and Chicago coinciding with the advent of the Great Depression; and, in the United Kingdom, completion of the NatWest Tower in 1979 and One Canada Square in 1991 both signalling an 'unhealthy correlation' between skyscraper building and recession.[158]

In spring 2012, there were ongoing reports of new tall buildings failing to attract occupiers, but Sellar remained calm, saying, 'We are not depending on pre-lets, but expect to be leased up within a sensible timeframe.' Sellar was playing the long game, and his relationship with the State of Qatar and the quality of the offices meant that he could await developments from a secure position.

When the building was inaugurated, Sellar appeared calm and unfazed even though only six floors were leased in preparation for the opening of the offices section of the building in summer 2013. He told *The Times* on 6 July 2013, 'We want to make sure we have the right compatibility and so we are going to have asset managers, energy companies, lawyers and many more. We want a broad mix.' And when one looks at the tenants towards the end of 2016, that is exactly what he has, with twenty-nine tenants from fourteen different sectors: Al Jazeera, Gallup, Campari, Tiffany, HCA Healthcare, investment, consultancy and financial services, a marketing agency, lawyers, a business school, energy companies and more. In a link to Sellar's days in fashion retail, the Shard is the headquarters of MatchesFashion.com.

Peter Murray, when discussing the mixture of tenants at the Shard, says, 'One of the more interesting things about the Shard is that if he had been a more conventional developer, it wouldn't have been like that.

I remember sitting in the offices of Sir Peter Levene, when he was chairman of Lloyd's, and he looked out over the Shard and was very rude about it, largely because he had just moved from Canary Wharf where the philosophy was that every floor had to be same, with the same shape all the way up the building so you end up with an orthogonal building, so he just thought the Shard was incredibly inefficient as a building, difficult to build, expensive, wrong location, all the sorts of things the traditional developer would be saying. Irvine had this vision that he just doggedly pursued, which is why we [at New London Architecture] made him our New Londoner of the Year.'

Other awards followed, both for the building and the man. The Shard was awarded first place at the 2013 Emporis Skyscraper Awards, which considers buildings throughout the world that are over 328 feet (100 metres) tall. The judges called the Shard 'a skyscraper that is recognized immediately and which is already considered London's new emblem'.

In 2013, *Building* magazine's Project of the Year went to the Shard, Construction Client of the Year went to the Sellar Property Group, Project/Construction Management Firm went to Mace, and Construction Consultant went to Turner & Townsend. During one of my interviews with Sellar, he laughs when he tells me that *Property Week* has just inducted him as a 'Legend' into its Hall of Fame, and grins with pleasure when he reports that Steven Norris has referred to him as 'the godfather of The Shard'.[159] *The Godfather* is his favourite film.

Despite the accolades for the architecture, the popularity of the viewing gallery, hotel and restaurants, and the commercial success of the building, Renzo Piano always doubted that the praise would be universal because the Shard works against established ideas.

'Architecture makes cities,' he says. 'I have an example in the work I did with Richard Rogers at the Centre Georges Pompidou. It took ten years to be loved, but now it is part of the city. Buildings like the Pompidou and the Shard show a change, a shift in history. At a certain moment in May 1968 in Paris, something had to happen to the museum. It needed young bad boys like me and Richard Rogers to say enough is enough: a place for art should be open, accessible, unpretentious, not for the elite, not a place for intimidation.' He then talks of his opportunity to work in Berlin in the 1990s, and 'another shift' as the wall came down, and he was able to use architecture to knit East and West back together at Potsdamer Platz.

'Architecture shows a change and the Shard shows the change that cities should not be about buildings that are closing their doors; the buildings should be more open, they should breathe. An architect does not change the world, but we can witness the change and express the change. That's why sometimes it's not easy to be loved immediately. That's why when you make something like the Shard you have to accept that someone doesn't agree. Changes are frightening for people. The future is mysterious, but, still, it is the only place we can go. As an architect you have a duty to do what you know is good. A good doctor doesn't tell the patient what he wants to hear. A good doctor tells the truth, and a good architect tries to tell the truth, even if the truth is uncomfortable and creates some trouble.'

That trouble, personified by the Queen's Counsels of English Heritage and Historic Royal Palaces at the public inquiry, was far from dispersed by Inspector Gray's positive conclusions back in 2003. The day before the Shard's inauguration, Simon Jenkins was reminding the readers of the *Guardian* that the praise was not universal, and that buildings could be dangerous for our culture and society.

At the time of the opening, Islamist militants were attempting to destroy ancient shrines and a fifteenth-century mosque in Timbuktu. Jenkins believed that an equal desecration was occurring on his own shores: 'This is planning in the age of Barclays, an oligarchy of wealth, a financial fanaticism every bit as selfish and destructive as the religious fanaticism of Timbuktu. But there is a difference. Timbuktu's shrines can and surely will be rebuilt. The Shard has slashed the face of London for ever.'[160] Elsewhere, he also claimed that 'the Shard served no public, civic or social function'.[161]

Jonathan Jones, the *Guardian*'s art critic, had already made a similar point in August 2011, calling the Shard 'an architectural catastrophe for London . . . self-evidently a monument to wealth and power run way out of control. It screams with dazzling arrogance that money rules this city and says money inhabits a realm way above our heads.'[162] He believed the building to be 'a vision of the financial sector floating above the proletarian streets, living by different rules and shaping events below it with icy ease'.

There is little point in attempting to convince either Jenkins or Jones of the aesthetic merits of the Shard, as there can be no scientific measure and they are both highly intelligent men who know their own minds – but their criticisms also have a political basis: that the Shard is bad for society. Their viewpoints, perhaps, do not take into account the multi-tenant nature of the Shard – Campari may not be to my taste but it does not strike me as particularly representative of the 'oligarchy of wealth' and 'financial fanaticism' – but the critics' opinions must be taken seriously.

Tall buildings have been expressions of wealth, power and ego since the building of the pyramids, and the Shard is no different. The Shard is a commercial building, constructed, as Sellar has always stipulated, to maximise value. It is representative of the mercantile city – it is not a charity, not a hospital, nor a community centre, and no such buildings were ever going to be built on the Southwark Towers site. The state, as a builder, is long deceased; a typical London borough can barely afford to construct a new public lavatory.

As Helen Castle, the editor of *Architectural Design* (*AD*), has pointed out, 'At a time when private partnerships have become a requirement of any kind of development, at the large scale requiring injections of capital from overseas, commercial concerns have become the driving force.'[163]

Like it or not – and I say this as someone with an inclination towards the left – there is little new building of significance in London without the catalytic principle of extraction of value from land: in the twenty-first century, even the social/affordable housing and transport infrastructure sectors are fundamentally commercial enterprises. The state is evaporating. Increasingly, the invisible hand is the only hand.[164]

While it is fair to ask what the London Bridge Quarter gives back to London beyond subjective aesthetics, its social or cultural consequences really should only be assessed in the light of our times and in the light of it being a commercial development. So, has this venture resulted in a trickle-down benefit beyond the already healthy bank balances of Irvine Sellar and the State of Qatar?

The highly regarded design and architecture critic Deyan Sudjic was very critical of the Shard project even after Renzo Piano came on board, but by 2014, with the building by then a reality, he had reconsidered its worth because of the cultural and social effect of the building: 'For centuries powerful London lived north of the river alongside its cathedral and palaces, its parliament, its law courts and its stock exchange. South of the river was something else. It was where London went to misbehave. Of all the changes in London since the turn of the millennium, none have been more profound than the end of that division.' He called the completion of the Shard 'an even more dramatic step in reordering the city's geography' than Tate Modern or the Millennium Bridge. 'Renzo Piano's distinctive design . . . has become an essential part of the urban landscape, a marker that demonstrates in the most unmistakeable way that the long-neglected segment of the South Bank of the Thames has come back to life.' He concluded by saying that the Shard is 'a turning point for London'.[165]

The story of the Shard is a uniquely London story, and it is born of someone who is driven by pride in this city. The story of Irvine Sellar – from north London market trader to Carnaby Street to developer of a new city quarter – is a uniquely London story, too.

The location of the site at London Bridge was elemental to Sellar's decision to build tall, so the best organisation to assess the effect of the development is the London Borough of Southwark itself. While Jones, Jenkins, Sudjic and myself can theorise as to whether the Shard is a good or bad building beyond aesthetic terms, those at the borough have an involved and continuous interaction with its social, cultural and financial consequences at ground level.

When I mention to Sellar that I am going to speak to someone at the borough, he says: 'Speak to the leader of the council, Peter John. He's said it himself: the Shard has put Southwark on the map from America to Australia, where they didn't even know how to pronounce Southwark before the Shard came along.' Indeed, while the Shard was still being constructed, John said, 'The Shard is helping to kick-start a whole swathe of regeneration, which has the potential to ripple down through the borough.'[166]

I did not go to see Peter John, not solely because I'm contrary, but because I wanted to speak to council officers rather than an elected councillor, in the hope that they would give me an honest appraisal without the possibility of political posturing or cauterisation.

The man who opened the door for the development of the Shard was Fred Manson, and the man best positioned to know whether that was a wise decision is his successor as regeneration director at Southwark, Stephen Platts, along with the programme manager Dan Taylor, who has been involved in the development of the London Bridge Quarter since 2003, almost right from the start.

Neither of the men are the sort of pen-pushers stereotypical of council planning departments. They are physically unalike, with Taylor in his thirties, tall and lean, and Platts, slightly older, shorter, with a welcoming grin, but they are both insightful, keenly intelligent, and passionate about driving Southwark forward. It soon becomes clear that, like Fred Manson and Ken Livingstone back in 2000, they know from experience that in these cash-deficient times for councils, the only remaining way forward for social regeneration is to harness the potential for improvements that can be a side effect of a good development.

I ask them whether the London Bridge Quarter has improved the area at ground level.

'The public realm has improved massively,' Taylor replies. 'As a pedestrian all you would see was a wall of buses, and you couldn't see the train station beyond. The reorientation of the bus station means that as you are walking up from the bridge you can now see the concourse, you can see the transport interchange. Before, it was somewhere where you might get a train, get a bus, but the idea of wanting to walk into the London Bridge area would have been crazy. Sellar took on the responsibility of working with Network Rail, TfL and ourselves to deliver both the station concourse improvements and the bus station, and the public square next to the News Building. That was a massive task, involving reams of legals that they had to go through. Network Rail and TfL needed everything to be risk assessed to death, and the costs, which were massive, went up. Renzo Piano and Irvine Sellar decided unilaterally to effect the works themselves – they could have paid us £25 million and left us potentially to do a botched job of the bus station, but they said that we've got to get this right at the ground floor otherwise the building will just sit in a squalid public realm.'

Stephen Platts: 'That was critical. Before, we used to have a pedestrian bridge going over to the hospital, which was awful. The whole of St Thomas's frontages were closed off when the Pricewaterhouse building was there. Really, I think the transformation of St Thomas Street is just starting. We have huge aspirations for that street, which the Shard has been key to delivering. Now we have got Fielden House, which Sellar is developing, which again readdresses St Thomas Street, and we have the Science Gallery going into St Thomas Street, which will involve a new public square.' Platts points out that the money the Shard owners have put into the building of the Science Gallery has not come from a Section 106 requirement: 'They have just decided to chip in and help fund it.'

He adds, 'The aspiration for St Thomas Street is to turn it into a really high retail and leisure destination. The key to that has been the Shard, and its rethinking of what St Thomas Street could be rather than a back street.'

Platts says that an ordinary but high-quality development would not have transformed the location in the way the Shard has. He reveals that Southwark's policy matches Sellar's own preference for multi-use: 'The range of uses means that it's operating from early in the morning to late at night, and it drives the footfall, drives the interest, and creates broad opportunities for the residents of Southwark. In the City, for many years it was proportionately mostly offices, and in the evenings and at weekends it was like a ghost town. If you speak to the leisure retailers, they say that to get a high-quality offer, you need a daytime trade and an evening trade. Culturally significant buildings are also important to drive footfall and bring revenue into the area.'

'And Londoners can get in the Shard,' Taylor adds. 'There are not many buildings in the City that Londoners can get in. I know the View might seem expensive at the moment, but when it opened, Irvine gave away 10,000 tickets to all our schools. And you can get into that building for a special occasion such as a birthday or an anniversary, and share that high quality, which means that Londoners can relate to it.'

As for the commercial benefits of having the Shard in Southwark, Taylor says, 'We've always been the wrong side of the river and the wrong side of the railway tracks. We call ourselves the missing quarter of central London, but now the City is moving across to Southwark and some people do not like that.'

Platts says North Southwark has been redefined in terms of the commercial property sector. Prior to the Shard and More London, the area was seen as secondary to the City, the West End and midtown. Office buildings tended to be of low quality and many buildings were empty.

'The Shard has been a major part of establishing North Southwark as part of central London but with its own identity. The rents in the Shard are the same as in the City, and we now have more extremely high-quality developments coming through in Southwark, which are on a par to any other developments whether in the City, Canary Wharf or the West End. North Southwark is no longer secondary, and companies are willing to come here because it provides something that is a little more unique than other parts of London. We have the history, we have a broad spectrum of uses – we have culture, we have residential, we have commercial, and a good leisure offer in terms of restaurants and bars, plus the transport infrastructure.'

His thoughts tie in with those of William Murray, whose own offices are in London Bridge and who previously told me, 'London Bridge was very much a second-class location, but there is an edge, a buzz to this place, which is different from other places. I think now it's a place that people really want to go to because it has so much more character than other places in London and the Shard has given it a gilded edge.'

Platts continues: 'One of the biggest impacts of the News Building, which we didn't see coming, has been the supply chain required to service an organisation like News International. The sub-contractors are now wishing to come to North Southwark to be near News International, and that ripple effect has driven demand for office space. We now have one of the lowest void rates in terms of offices anywhere in London. And that drives the leisure activity in terms of restaurants and bars, and it is buzzing in the evening.'

The two men say that the Shard has defined North Southwark in terms of location and provides aspiration for its younger residents. I ask what that means in real terms.

'This is not solely because of the Shard,' says Taylor, 'but in 2003 we were the twelfth most deprived place out of 326 boroughs in the country, and now we are forty-first. Obviously we have a long way to go, but the Shard is part of that improvement, bringing the opportunities.'

Platts: 'There was a time when people would say that all Southwark residents would be was cleaners or caretakers in those buildings, and that is absolutely not the case.'

James Sellar said in May 2011, that 'This sort of project is really successful when it grounds itself in the local neighbourhood and we want to make sure that local people in the area relate to it', but, just as the Shard was opening a year later, a *Guardian* journalist claimed that 'The only working-class Londoners will presumably bus in at night from the outskirts to clean the bins.'[167]

Peter John was forced to point out in a letter to the newspaper,

> The development has not only paid for much-needed improvements to London Bridge station and the public realm, but has also brought construction jobs and £5m of vocational training for local residents . . . Instead of just seeing the Shard as a tall building, sceptics should look a little harder to see the genuinely deep and positive impact that it will have on the local area.[168]

I ask whether the £5 million put into training by Sellar and his partners has had a genuine rather than notional effect.

Taylor: 'Apart from the training courses, one of the most important things that happened was that, within the building, Sellar appointed a social enterprise called Good People. Their job was to create a relationship with all the tenants, the restaurants, the hotel, and then work with our own Southwark Works who network with the employment agencies, and they deal with people who have barriers to work, such as mental health issues and single-parenting issues. That approach has created hundreds of jobs for people in Southwark.'

Taylor: 'And when the View from the Shard opened, about 70 per cent of the employees were local residents. We have 300-plus case studies. It was the same case during construction.'

Platts: 'You get developers who just tick the boxes and do the minimum to fulfil the legal requirement. With the Shard there was a genuine desire to achieve a good outcome for Southwark residents.'

Castle has written, 'When so much lip service is paid to the concept of regeneration, there is a very real chance that it is becoming devalued and may come to mean everything and nothing': indeed, it may have no value to the original residents of an area.[169] Among all this positivity about the improvements to the social realm and bringing investment, jobs and footfall into North Southwark, I ask Platts and Taylor about the disadvantages that regeneration may have brought through driving up affordable rents and driving out lower-end retail.

Platts: 'We still have a substantial amount of social housing in North Southwark and that's not going to change. If you speak to a pensioner on social housing, they might say all this is great, but I can't afford to go to restaurants in the Shard, I'm not interested in Tate Modern, all I get is more and more people on the streets. And some of the local services I enjoyed – let's say the old ladies' hair stylist, cut and blow dry for £8 every week, has now turned into Toni & Guy for £80. That pensioner says, what's it brought me? We are conscious of that. We own some retail parades in North Southwark and we are trying to protect some of the retail offer that serves a large percentage of the population from all becoming trendy coffee shops or bakers selling a loaf of bread for £3.50. However, you would hope that for the younger generation, regeneration has brought them aspiration, that they are part of central London.'

Taylor: 'As part of the station redevelopment, we will have five new, affordable retail spaces on St Thomas Street. And we have gone in and spent council money on people's shops, doing them up, to safeguard them. We have been able to create job opportunities and the ability to get involved in the job programmes, and everyone accepts that London Bridge station, and the whole public realm around the Shard, is so much better than it was.'

I ask whether the Shard has damaged the urban grain of Southwark.

'Before,' Platts says, 'we didn't realise that [commercial developers] would want to build tall in Southwark. The economics weren't there to build beyond a certain height in Southwark and the Shard changed all that. What's quite interesting now in London Bridge is that we are protecting the profile of the Shard, so we are restricting the height to around that of Guy's Tower.'

In Southwark today, a key element in planning a tall building is the design, and the impact on the Southwark and the London skyline. This is a response to the realisation, courtesy of the Shard, that the beleaguered borough should be deemed worthy of world-class architecture. 'Our policy won't be about designating areas,' Platts says, 'but about good architecture, about public transport and about the relationship with the neighbourhood, and about local views as well as long-vista views. Planning can still be a bruising process for developers but it has to be, because you are changing the skyline with, hopefully, something that will be there for centuries.'

Taylor concludes: 'The Shard will probably be listed soon, which would no doubt delight Irvine.'

His words echo those of Ken Livingstone: 'The Shard was a brilliant scheme for London; my real regret is that we had to waste two years with English Heritage trying to sink it. And you know what's going to happen – not while Irvine and I are alive, but thirty years down the road? It will be listed.'

In the commentaries of Jenkins and Jones, developers such as Sellar come across as Machiavellian egomaniacs raping the land in the pursuit of personal greed, but Ken Livingstone believes that there are exceptions: 'There are some rapacious capitalists. But Irvine is different – he's in for the long haul. The Australian who put up the Westfields in Stratford and West London, he was the same. If you look at the two Westfield sites in London, they may not make a profit for a long time – they are really well designed and built, tasteful, no squalid crap, no junk food. That means it cost him more to build them; it might be longer before he and Irvine can turn a profit, but they don't mind too much, they have that long-term view; whereas with so many people in the property world, it's just "Get in, get out, make as much money as you can." With Irvine, the Shard is there to achieve something.'

At my next interview with Irvine Sellar, I raise the subject of the local job initiatives connected to the London Bridge Quarter. I wonder whether he will take the opportunity to bolster his public image.

Instead, he tenses up immediately, his blue eyes darting with wariness.

'I'm not a saint. I'm not going to take much credit for that. We've always been in favour of employing the unemployed, of course. That was a methodology we applied. If you create offices, hotels or restaurants you need staff, and if you build them in areas where there is under-employment then you partly deal with the problem. It just happens that for us, this is done on a massive scale because 12,500 people are employed between the Shard and the News Building. Not all of those come from Southwark, but a decent proportion do.'

He picks up a pen with his left hand and starts tapping it repeatedly against the table.

'That's what development does: it brings employment. It should be expected. The only way in which we've performed out of the box is the scale and size, and helping to make Southwark a much more widely known borough.'

When I raise the fact that, in the assessment of the planners at Southwark, he stepped beyond the requirements of his Section 106 agreements to improve the public realm, he says with a face as stern as if he were going into battle, 'When we make a commitment, we make a commitment. I don't need to have a medal round my neck for saying that's what I've done. It's part of the deal. We as developers or as entre-preneurs, we create wealth and that can have a good side effect. I'm not a saint, but if I give my word, it's done.' He swipes his right hand as if he's clearing away the old station concourse, the battered bus station, the much-abused pedestrian bridge. 'It's the hardest thing to get me to give my word in the first place, but once I've given it, it's done.'

The beat of the pen in his other hand grows faster. 'I will work hard screwing the price down, but if people behave properly, then I want fairness, but never mistake kindness for weakness. Don't take the piss or you'll see the other side.'

He throws the pen down and looks at me aggressively as if I, rather than some imaginary contractor, have just foolishly attempted to take him for a ride.

And then he breaks into a smile and looks like a charming, relaxed family man.

So, Dark Lord of Development or Left-Leaning Lily-Livered Liberal? A greedy developer or a visionary with a keen sense of social responsibility?

Sellar has often been caricatured into one-dimension, but he has long been just as multi-faceted as the Shard. He has been accused by journalists of merely paying lip service to social and ethical considerations, but, incompatibly, he is also described as a tough, straight talker. My experience is that when Sellar, impatient and sometimes direct to the point of rudeness, goes to the effort of opening his mouth, he means what he says.

He calls himself determined, while Renzo Piano says that his defining characteristic is obstinacy, but the architect believes that is a virtue: 'Irvine is one of the few people I have met who knows about obstinacy. If you are obstinate in the wrong place you are just silly, not intelligent. You are like the fly that keeps beating its head against the glass of the window. Plenty of people are obsessed with pushing their ideas, but he spent enough time thinking about the right idea first. Before defending, understand what is right and what is wrong. We can spend hours talking about the famous Irvine Sellar obstinacy, and we can spend hours talking about my obstinacy – I'm quite well known for this, too – but it's not enough. First you have to be sure that you have a good idea.'

As well as obstinate, Sellar is ambitious and he is proud. In my final interview with him, he tells me, 'I was at a dinner last night, and 80 per cent of the room were Lord this, Lady that, Sir that, but they only want to talk about one thing: the Shard. "Oh, you're the man who built the Shard." Who wants a title? I've got my title. I'm the man who built the Shard. That's the accolade. And don't forget, this is a private company, not a huge public company where there are massive teams of people. Those lords and ladies know how impossible it was and they want to know how I did it. Well, I'll tell you. When I was a kid, when I was running those fairground games in my backyard, there was always a dot some distance before my eyes, but when I covered the distance, the dot would still be just as far away before my eyes, so I would carry on, and that dot hasn't gone away even now. I want to be where I'm not, and that's called the drive factor. I need to be able to look myself in the eye, in the mirror, and say I've achieved what I wanted to achieve. The result: the Shard couldn't have happened without me. I made it happen against the odds.'

Sellar is obstinate, but he is an agile rather than fixed thinker. He is a listener and an absorber of what is going on around him, and he is willing to learn. Ever since he started on his first market stall, one of his passions has been for creative innovation. A developer will always try to get the best possible deal for himself, but in his case he is also driven to create something that is the best per se, and that drive brings good side effects.

Fran McNamara says, 'Irvine wanted to build a building that had style, not just quality. I think that there is a link back to Mates and his pursuance of style in the fashion industry, right through to his decisions about architecture.' He adds, 'The Shard was built in elegance. It could have been dumbed down. We could be sitting in an ordinary building now, but we're not. The cost of this building is a benchmark against any other building, yet every detail is elegant. All that is down to his determination. And he has fought those fights for the News Building and Shard Place as well. He didn't want one proper jewel and some costume jewellery around it.'

To repeat one of Sellar's favourite maxims, with which I began the first chapter: 'What is the first rule of salesmanship? Sell yourself. The buyer has to like you and trust you. Then you'll be able to sell them something of value because you've built up that trust.'

He is neither the first nor the last salesman to understand this, but it is elemental to his character that he uses the words 'something of value' rather than the anticipated brag of 'anything' in the explanation. To him, success lies not in kidding the buyer: the sale is a moral contract and a promise of quality.

To return to Freud and the threat of the new neighbour, the way that the neighbour is finally accepted is through trust and by giving back to society, whether to the individual, the community or the environment. The Shard gives back, partly due to its permeability, partly due to its aesthetics, partly due to its involvement in the regeneration of the area and the transport infrastructure, partly due to the attempts made to ensure that it is not a monster within its environment. Despite its vastness, for the majority it is a good neighbour and a good leader for London – a totem that manages to evince pride.

There are very few developers that go out of their way to deliver buildings of great architectural merit. If Sellar had constructed a high-rise fridge, he would probably have made more money, and the making of that money would not have involved the myriad challenges he faced. He struck the balance between fine architecture – and its intrinsic, long-term cultural value – and commercial value. The Shard, as Piano has intimated, is a lesson in fighting for what is right.

Sellar's ambition and obstinacy, throughout his career, have been entwined with a quest for quality, innovation and a sense of self-worth.

That is why the Shard is a work of outstanding architecture, why Southwark and London at large both benefit, and why, when most people look at this huge new neighbour on the skyline, they smile.

In the late afternoon of 24 February 2017, not long before this book was scheduled to go to press, the publisher Andreas Campomar, members of his team and I met Irvine Sellar in his Mayfair offices. It would be Irvine's last ever meeting.

He had recently achieved a council resolution to grant planning approval for a scheme that would enhance the setting of Paddington, an area of London that, like London Bridge, has evolved as an accident of infrastructure with little sense of place. His solution would be another Renzo Piano building, but a cube this time rather than a shard. Further plans he and his son James had for Southwark were also coming to a head, so he was busy as ever, doing deals, plotting the future, putting his stamp on London.

Nonetheless, he had agreed to our meeting in which we wanted to request permission to use some images from his personal archive in this book. That afternoon, he said that he felt like he had caught a virus during a flight from Qatar but, flanked by his daughter Caroline and his lawyer George, he was still his gregarious, amusing and 'aggressively charming' self, filling the room with his vivaciousness. When I happened to mention that the photographer of some other images we wanted to use was asking for an unusually high fee, he gave his familiar, dangerous but paternal smile: 'Just send him in here,' he joked. 'I'll sort him out for you.'

Irvine Sellar died two days later on Sunday, 26 February 2017. He was eighty-two, still with that unreachable dot on the horizon before his eyes, still trying to do something new and still chasing perfection.

Afterword: A Sense of Place

To be culturally assimilated, a tall building must be known beyond the fact of its presence on the horizon or in the data; it must be permeable. People do not travel to the top of the Empire State Building just for the view, whether they express this consciously or not. They want to be part of the building, part of the structure, to know it, to sense its height from its innards, to feel it with their feet. When they see it again from afar or on film, dominating the skyline, they feel ownership, as the relationship is no longer abstract but tactile: they have related the monster back to the human scale. Philippe Petit famously high-wired between the Twin Towers on the morning of 7 August 1974; exponents of parkour bridge the impossible gap; the same desire to scale the unscaleable keeps the limbs moving despite numbness and frostbite up the north face of Everest. The world is not ours until we feel it physically, through our feet, and leave behind a trace of ourselves, a scent.

I have decided to walk the seven miles from my home all the way to the base of the Shard and then, if permitted, up every one of its 306 flights of stairs to the viewing gallery and the top of the tower. Walking to the top of the Shard is my poor man's Everest: I want to understand it's height through my physicality, through my own scale.

I live in Upper Norwood in south-east London, a mile from the other famous tapering tower in London, the Crystal Palace transmitter. Built in 1950 and reaching 720 feet (219 metres), it was the tallest structure in London before the rise of One Canada Square in 1991, and it is still in fifth place. Starting at the foot of the transmitter would provide neat symmetry, but my purpose is to walk from my own home so my starting point is Crown Point.

This is an intersection whose name few people would register as a place; its supposed lack of identity is underlined by being split down the middle by the borough border of Lambeth and Croydon. The words Crown Point flicker for a few seconds as the name of a stop on a couple of bus routes, but for most travellers it is a non-place, a hinterland of a few shops that merely fills a gap en route.

To the few people who live and work at the crossroads, though, it is a place and they shout it out: its name is incorporated into so many shop signs to be almost comical. When I first moved here, the shops included Crown Bathrooms, Crown Beauty, Crown Bakery, Crown Point Post Office, Crown Kebab, Crown Cuts (a thoroughly good name for a hairdresser's), Crown Point Food & Wine and the Point-less Crown Food & Wine, all on a little crossroads parade.

Some of those shops have closed, but the civic pride and sense of belonging remain. The intersection has recently been the focus of a planning war, not on the scale of the Shard, but pretty fierce: the local shopkeepers, their livelihoods under threat, battled to prevent a Lidl budget supermarket opening, and, failing that, at least to make sure that the building was better designed and a better neighbour in terms of its setting. I signed the baker's petition because I do not want her bakery to disappear, even though I do not like her bread, but the German company won the day. English Heritage did not feel the need to intervene.

Crown Point is a good place to start not just because it is very near my home. It is on Beulah Hill, a clay ridge that is one of the highest places in London and affords panoramic views of the centre of the city. The Shard is nearly exactly magnetic north from Crown Point and the almost straight road from one to the other would bring much happiness to an orthodox crow.

Within a few metres of my starting point, at 9.30 in the morning, I have my first sight of the Shard, a building I see from afar almost every single day.

Most buildings give definition to light, but the Shard is defined by it. Some days it is crisp and sharp and slices the sky, sometimes it fuzzes into the cloud and almost disappears. Sometimes it is pale blue, sometimes it gleams white, sometimes gold; sometimes it is light grey, gun-metal or dun; it changes with the weather and with the movement of the earth in relation to the sun. As I walk downhill from Crown Point, I can see two façades and the edge of a third. Today, as the morning sun shines, the larger façade is pale grey and the sliver is a true, sure line dark enough to have been drawn by a 2B pencil. In between them, there is a surprising spear of the purest white.

The building, the beacon for my journey, sits just to the left of the City cluster, most notably the Walkie-Talkie with its comic outline, the Cheesegrater and the Gherkin, which I am always relieved to see still has a good profile from here. You could not guess that a broad river separates the Shard from those buildings, but the gap is large enough to let you know that the tapered building is not a member of that family of unlikely cousins.

As I walk, I try to keep the Shard in view at all times, crossing the road whenever necessary, and have the pleasure of seeing it twin itself with the spire of the late-Regency clock tower of St Luke's Church, reaching exactly the same height from my angle. The Shard is lost once I reach the bottom of the hill and walk through West Norwood and then Tulse Hill and Herne Hill, the centres of which, despite their names, are not on the hills themselves. These poor lowlanders lack the visual connection to the city afforded by the Shard.

These places along the route have their individual identities, grains and textures: every place is still different even as the tide of homogeneity makes every place more and more the same. The restaurants, cafés, shops and houses of worship respond to the very particular social, racial and religious mix. The jerk shops fade away, the number of chicken shops and halal butchers increases and decreases, the signs of gentrification come and go. Just these few miles of walking inform the pedestrian that London is not an amorphous mass, and any new building, from the enormous Shard to a beverage stand, must be rooted in the particular.

On Denmark Hill, I think that I should be able to find at least the tip of the Shard again, but I cannot see it for trees and buildings. I cross the road, and there it is – just the peak, the fracture against a mostly blue sky. I lose sight of it quickly as the road bends, so I cross back again, but the tallest building in Western Europe is playing hide and seek.

I stand and crane, and the top of the maligned Strata at Elephant & Castle pops into view instead, announcing that I am crossing the border from the London Borough of Lambeth to Southwark. The building was winner of the 2010 Carbuncle Cup for the ugliest new building in the United Kingdom, and is often denigrated by architects and critics as a toy-town structure that has no relationship to its setting. When Stephen Platts and Dan Taylor from Southwark said they wanted to make sure that the borough is a destination for world-class architecture, the Strata was the white elephant in the room.

I walk through King's College Hospital, transplanted from Holborn at the beginning of the twentieth century as a result of the explosion in the numbers of poorer people in Southwark and Lambeth. The mammoth hospital buildings give way to a little pocket of gentrification, with shops and cafés – no doubt run by artisanal adventurers reinventing the cupcake. The shops entitle themselves 'Love Walk . . .' after a little side street on which they are not located, rather than 'Camberwell . . .'

Once in Camberwell proper, I am firmly in Southwark and the Shard becomes a constant, peaking up above the trees and buildings, and harder to lose than to find. The building has changed since my view near Crown Point. Now it is more clearly broken up and fractured, more reminiscent of the mast and rigging of a tall ship, and there are variants of blue and grey dappling its surfaces. The gleaming spear of white has become a pale strip barely noticeable within the variations of tone.

I walk through undeveloped Walworth, with its tattered window displays and faded façades, where a tired café has attempted to go all al-fresco with two small tables on the noisy, fume-belched street. There are people sitting at those tables, and they don't look unhappy.

I reach Elephant & Castle, the symbol of the post-war identity of Southwark, famous for failed social experiments in the sky, a depressing shopping centre, and a monstrous road system. A massive mixed development is in the process of being layered on top of the memory of the vilified Heygate Estate, which has been wiped from the map despite the protests of some of its supplanted residents. Whatever the run-down estate was like as a home, it gave rise to the finest piece of political graffiti I have ever seen: the largest tower was adorned with the ten-foot-high words 'NOW' and 'HERE', separated by a huge expanse, but the brain would dutifully collapse the two words into one.

As I follow the curve of the roundabout, I wonder whether, as the story of the Shard is also the journey of Irvine Sellar from market boy to famous entrepreneur and developer, I should have walked from Wood Green in north London to the Shard, a distance that is also exactly seven miles. My current route feels right, though, as the story of the Shard is also a story of Southwark and the land south of the river, and a story of how we can have a personal relationship with an immense new building.

Finally off the main road, I walk among the five-storey brick buildings of the social housing Rockingham Estate. Here, there is a clear view of the upper storeys and fractured spire of the Shard. The top of the building is so translucent that I can see the floors of the partially open storeys above the viewing platform and, like Michael Donnelly, I'm glad that the radiator – in aesthetic rather than environmental terms – is not there to spoil the effect. It is this transparency that allows the building to disappear into the sky.

On occasion, when some of the blinds on the same façade of the Shard are variously raised, lowered or half-mast, there is a confusion of texture that reminds me of the cluttering on the balconies of 1960s residential high-rises, a careless dabbing of finger-paint over the architect's careful plans. There will come a point when glass technology advances to the point where blinds are not necessary, and even white glass will completely regulate both light and radiation. Today, though, the south façades appear uncluttered and serenely beautiful, and offer a softened impression of the growing clouds.

I pass through tranquil Trinity Church Square, a surprising enclave of Georgian houses, and I cross Long Lane, where social and affordable housing blocks abut newer, private residential developments, no doubt expensive due to their proximity to central London, a proximity underlined by the Shard.

I am a few hundred yards from the foot of the building. It does not look huge when close because it retreats from the base. It has none of the loom of an orthogonal slab – a fridge. At street level, the Shard is as close to humble as a thousand-foot building can be.

I lose sight of it as I walk along Great Maze Pond, through Guy's Hospital campus. The curve of the road reveals the stuttered façades of the News Building first, followed by the top of the Walkie-Talkie and the Gherkin, and then there it is.

I stand still. I have come on a good day. The light is right. The Shard is grey-blue, muzzied by the impression of cloud, and its surface is slowly changing. I can see two façades at once, and the edge of two more, creating the desired image of a fractured shard. The building is serene. I try to ignore Guy's towers.

I emerge from Great Maze Pond and walk between the building's exterior escalators and canopies on one side and what will become Shard Place on the other, and towards the entrance to the View from the Shard on Joiner Street.

I have been trying, for some time, to negotiate permission to walk up all 306 flights of stairs to the top. I have been told that I am likely to be denied permission as I am, apparently, a security risk (even though my idea of aggressive action is to not over-tip a waiter who has been rude), but there is still a sliver of hope. All the time I have been walking the seven miles from my home, I have been hoping for a last-minute reprieve, and outside the entrance, I check my phone for a final time.

Nothing.

I look up the length of the Shard, the monument to Irvine Sellar's persistence, its size representative of the challenges he faced: the impossibility of constructing such a tall but elegant skyscraper here, supposedly the wrong person building in the wrong place, at the wrong height, and at the wrong time.

Perhaps it is best that I cannot walk up it after all. There is every chance that I would have required medical assistance halfway up the stairs.

The lift – or rather, the two lifts it takes to get to the top of the building – will have to do. The staff are very courteous as they show me and the other visitors to and from the elevators. Today, every single one of them has a south London accent.

The lower deck of the viewing gallery is on level 69, which is a calm place whatever the crowds, but, whenever I visit, I soon head up to the less-populated open-air Skydeck on level 72. The reasons why I prefer it up here have little to do with the extra dozen or so metres of height. At the fissures between the façades, the glazing only reaches up to normal height, and there is no enclosing ceiling above, so you can feel the air and the sunshine directly on your face. There is no sanitisation of the experience, nor of the structure. I can see at close hand the tapering steel of the spire, the beams riveted together, and the exposed, diminishing steel floor plates of the few levels above.

The Shard offers what is probably the best view in the world, not just because of its height – the observation deck at the Burj Khalifa is far higher – but because of what it reveals: the history of London, its texture, its patterns and its lack of patterns. It allows us to understand London in a way that has previously been obscured: the unique, organic nature of the metropolis becomes obvious from on high. It is easy to imagine the ancient, Roman-paved Watling Street running from the ports of Kent across the site of the bridgehead just below me and onwards over Ludgate Hill and ever northward. Within the patchwork of buildings, roads and railway tracks, there is a surprising amount of greenery, from lines of trees to the residential squares to formal parks and the rougher Hampstead Heath.

I look down at the City and its medieval chaos of narrow streets near the Bank of England, at Tower 42 and the groundscrapers from the late twentieth century, and the parade of giants from recent years. There is an irony that, after all the complaints of English Heritage about the Shard harming the view of St Paul's, the building provides a better view of the breadth and magisterial balance of the cathedral than has ever before been possible. What is just as absorbing is the thick band of railway tracks that snake from the foot of the tower over the railway bridge, and the broad Thames sweeping left and then right towards the towers of Canary Wharf. One can detect the layers of city-making across 2,000 years.

It is eleven-thirty, and some people are already drinking champagne as they circle the building's core at leisure, but this is not an elitist place. The price of admission is quite steep, but an advance ticket is only a few more pounds than a premium seat to see a film at the Odeon Leicester Square. London is an expensive city, but cheaper for overseas tourists since the value of the pound collapsed in June 2016. A couple to whom I talk are from Granville, Ohio, here because 'you can't come to London and not see it from up here'. I then talk to a family of four in T-shirts and shorts, whom I had thought would be American too. It turns out that they are from Camberwell. It is their third visit. The youngest child drags the parents away, back to the glass, back to the view.

I step forward again and indulge myself. I look for the Strata because I know I can orientate from there, but although it is a mostly clear day, there is a blue haze and I cannot pick out Beulah Hill. I cheat and find, first, the Crystal Palace transmitter and then its slightly shorter sister, the Croydon transmitter, and convince myself that, within the indistinct greenery between them, I can detect exactly where my home sits on Beulah Hill.

There is a tracer line of myself all along the roads from Crown Point to Knights Hill, Norwood Road, Herne Hill, Denmark Hill, Camberwell Road and on to the Elephant, a trail of unseen atoms along every little twist and turn through the estates and hospital buildings, reaching to the base of the Shard. I have not felt the height of the building through aching legs, but the tracer line runs up the lift shafts in the core of the building, and circulates the glazed perimeter until it reaches where I am standing right now.

The line of connection allows me to believe that this is my London out there, among those streets, and this is my London right here, a thousand feet above the ground, where I can feel the cool air on my skin and hear the soft growl of the city.

Bibliography

Aaronovitch, David, 'The man who made the London skyline',
   Sunday Times (11 June 2016).
Acharya, Dipal, 'High art', *Evening Standard* (25 January 2013).
Adam, Robert, 'Power and status in the city', *Spectator* (6 July 2002).
Ascher, Kate, *The Heights: Anatomy of a Skyscraper* (New York:
   Penguin, 2013).
Attack the Block, dir. Joe Cornish (2011).
Bailey, Martin, 'The Bilbao effect', *Art Newspaper* (20 February 2002).
Ballard, J. G., *High-Rise* (London: Fourth Estate, 2012 [reprint]).
Bar-Hilel, Mira, 'Prescott orders planning probe into London's
   1000ft "shard of glass" tower', *Evening Standard* (24 July 2002).
Benzine, Adam, 'Changing of the Shard', *Property Week*
   (11 August 2006).
Bill, Peter, 'Piano's forte', *Estates Gazette* (6 September 2008).
Bill, Peter, *Planet Property* (Kibworth Beauchamp: Matador, 2013).
Billingham, John (ed.), 'Topic: tall buildings – a new era', *Urban
   Design* (spring 2004).
Binney, Marcus, 'Towering spike is blunted to pacify its critics',
   The Times (5 April 2003).
'BLP ousts Nabarros on "Shard of Glass" planning', *Legal Business*
   (September 2002).
Booth, Robert, 'London's Shard: a tower of power and riches looking
   down on poverty', *Guardian* (21 December 2011).

Bradbury, Dominic, 'The only way is up', *Telegraph Magazine* (19 November 2011).

The Bridges that Built London with Dan Cruikshank, BBC4 (June 2012).

'Bringing down Southwark Towers, *Building* (7 September 2007).

Bunkers, Brutalism and Bloodymindedness: Concrete Poetry, BBC4 (April 2016).

Burgess, Anthony, *A Clockwork Orange* (Harmondsworth: Penguin, 1972 [reprint]).

Castle, Helen, 'Editorial', *Architectural Design* (January/February 2012), no. 215.

Chakrabortty, Aditya, 'The Shard is a perfect metaphor for modern London', *Guardian* (26 June 2012).

Chatham, Jennifer, 'KONE jump lifts installed in the Shard', *Elevator World* (March 2011).

Cohn, Nik, *Today There Are No Gentlemen: The Changes in Englishmen's Clothes since the War* (London: Weidenfeld & Nicolson, 1971).

Commercial Property Register (May–September 2009).

Cregan-Reid, Vybarr, *Footnotes: How Running Makes Us Human* (London: Ebury, 2016).

'CTBUH Height Criteria', Council on Tall Buildings and Urban Habitat (no date), http://www.ctbuh.org/TallBuildings/ HeightStatistics/Criteria/tabid/446/language/en-US/Default.aspx.

Cuthbertson, Anne, 'Interview – the last word: Irvine Sellar', *London Magazine* (June 2016).

Davey, Jenny, 'Heron Tower joins Erotic Gherkin', *The Times* (23 July 2002).

Drayton, Guy, 'London love story', *Building Design* (28 November 2003).

Dupré, Judith, *Skyscrapers: A History of the World's Most Extraordinary Buildings* (New York: Black Dog and Leventhal Publishers, 2013).

Eisele, Jonathan and Ellen Kloft, *High-rise Manual: Typology and Design, Construction and Technology* (Basel: Birkhäuser, 2003).

Ellis, Bret Easton, *American Psycho* (New York: Vintage, 1991).

Fairs, Marcus, 'Interview: Renzo Piano on the Shard', *Dezeen* (18 May 2012), http://www.dezeen.com/2012/05/18/ interview-renzo-piano-on-the-shard.

Farrell, Terry, *Shaping London: The Patterns and Forms that Make the Metropolis* (Chichester: Wiley, 2010).

Fickling, David, 'Shard reaches for the sky amid office sector gloom', *Financial Times* (16 March 2009).

Field, Marcus, 'Shard times: the glittering symbol of London's future', *ES Magazine* (13 May 2011).

Finch, Paul, 'Letter from London', *Architects' Journal* (24 September 2009).

Flack, Shirley, 'Another barrier falls: with a boutique for him and her together', *Daily Sketch* (7 October 1966).

Forshaw, Alec, *New City: Contemporary Architecture in the City of London* (London: Merrell, 2013).

Foster, Mike, 'Sellar spies opportunities in adversity', *Wall Street Journal* (20 April 2009).

'Fox lived in the Shard skyscraper at London Bridge', *BBC News* (24 February 2011), http://www.bbc.co.uk/news/uk-england-london-12573364.

Freedman, Lisa, 'Tower power', *The Business: Financial Times Weekend Magazine* (24 March 2001).

Freud, Sigmund, *Civilization and Its Discontents* (London: Penguin, 2014 [reprint]).

Gates, Charlie, 'Shard developer lines up Piano for new site', *Building Design* (19 September 2003).

Gates, Charlie, 'Shard takes all', *Building Design* (21 November 2003).

Gibson, Robert, '"Taliban" slur upsets EH', *Estates Gazette* (17 November 2001).

Glancey, Jonathan, 'Trust me', *Guardian* (29 March 2002).

Gray, John L., 'Report to the First Secretary of State: London Borough of Southwark Application by Teighmore Limited' (Bristol: The Planning Inspectorate, 23 July 2003).

Grayson Perry: All Man, 'Rational Man' episode, Channel 4 (May 2016).

Hammond, Ed, 'Sellar tops out his towering ambition', *Financial Times* (4 July 2012).

Hardman, Robert, 'So that's how it feels to be a pigeon', *Daily Mail* (9 June 2012).

Heathcote, David, *Barbican: Penthouse over the City* (Chichester: Wiley-Academy, 2004).

High-Rise, dir. Ben Wheatley (2016).

Hillier, Bill et al., *Broadgate Spaces: Life in Public Spaces* (London: Unit for Architectural Studies, Bartlett School of Architecture and Planning, 1990), http://www.spacesyntax.com/project/broadgate-spaces-life-in-public-places.

Hipwell, Deirdre, 'Sellars' market', *Property Week* (18 July 2008).

Holloway, James, 'The Shard's bleeding edge: anatomy of a 21st-century skyscraper', *Ars Technica* (5 December 2011), http://arstechnica.com/gadgets/2011/12/the-shards-bleeding-edge-anatomy-of-a-21st-century-skyscraper.

Hosken, Andrew, *Ken: The Ups and Downs of Ken Livingstone* (London: Arcadia Books, 2008).

Huxley, Aldous, *Brave New World* (London: Chatto & Windus, 1932).

'Irvine Sellar', CTBUH Interview Series, Council on Tall Buildings and Urban Habitat, New York (27 October 2015).

Jacobs, Jane, *The Death and Life of Great American Cities* (New York: Random House, 1961).

Jameson, Angela, 'Fashion king aims to tower over rivals', *Daily Mail* (9 December 2010).

'Jane Jacobs', *Project for Public Spaces* (undated), http://www.pps.org/reference/jjacobs-2.

Jenkins, Simon, 'Ken falls victim to Big Apple envy', *Evening Standard* (18 January 2001).

Jenkins, Simon, 'Paddington Pole may be dead but the vanity of architects lives on', *Evening Standard* (19 July 2016).

Jenkins, Simon, 'Save our skyline from the Spike', *Evening Standard* (17 April 2003).

Jenkins, Simon, 'The Shard has slashed the face of London forever', *Guardian* (3 July 2012).

John, Peter, 'Letters and email', *Guardian* (30 June 2012).

Johnson, Boris, 'A global city bounces back', *Newsweek* (7 December 2009).

Jones, Jonathan, 'The Shard is a broken society's towering achievement', *Guardian* (19 August 2011).

'Keep out of it, Ken', *Daily Mirror* (18 May 2001).

Koestler, Arthur, *The Act of Creation* (London: Hutchinson and Co., 1964).

Lane, Thomas, 'Civil Stars', *Building Magazine* (5 March 2010).

Lane, Thomas, 'The Place to be', *Building Magazine* (25 January 2013).

Lawrence, Andrew, 'Skyscraper Index' (Hong Kong: Barclays Capital, 2012).

London Bridge Quarter Section 106 Project Board, 'London Bridge Quarter Section 106 Project Board performance report' (London: London Borough of Southwark, 28 November 2012).

London First and Savills, *Redefining Density: Making the Best Use of London's Land to Build More and Better Homes* (London: London First/Savills, 2015), http://research.euro.savills.co.uk/pdfs/redefining-density-joint-report-with-london-first.pdf.

Low, Valentine, 'Mother doesn't worry . . . she's used to it', *The Times* (21 August 2012).

'The march of the skyscrapers', *Evening Standard* (20 July 2000).

Martínez Mindeguía, Francisco, 'Bruno Taut, Architecture in the Alps, 1919', *Arquitectura an Dibuixos Exemplars* (accessed 27 July 2016), http://www.etsavega.net/dibex/Taut_Alpine.htm.

Mathieson, Nick, 'The higher they climb . . .', *Observer* (10 September 2000).

McMeeken, Roxanne, 'Bernard Ainsworth interview: Shard man', *Building* (13 June 2008).

Meades, Jonathan, *Bunkers, Brutalism and Bloodymindedness: Concrete Poetry*, BBC4 (April 2016).

Merrick, Jay, 'The tower and the glory', *Independent* (26 March 2001).

Miller, Sarah (ed.), *Shangri-La London* (London: Shangri-La, 2014).

Moore, Rowan, 'Save us from this poke in the eye with a sharp stick', *Evening Standard* (10 April 2000).

Moore, Rowan, 'Save us from these heights of bad taste', *Evening Standard* (12 April 2000).

Moore, Rowan, 'Piano tunes in to London', *Evening Standard* (18 July 2000).

Moore, Rowan, 'Tower set to raise the stakes in London', *Evening Standard* (9 November 2000).

Moore, Rowan, *Slow Burn City: London in the Twenty-first Century* (London: Picador, 2016).

Moore, Rowan and Clair Weaver, '1,000ft skyscraper gets the go-ahead', *Evening Standard* (19 November 2003).

Morrison, Richard, 'High society', *The Times* (28 November 2001).

Morrison, Richard, 'According to Lord Rogers, the London skyline is "unbelievably boring"', *The Times* (17 March 2003).

Mount, Harry, 'Time to end blue-sky thinking?', *The Times* (11 April 2012).

Murray, Peter, 'The building dividing London', *Financial Times* (26 May 2012).

Norman, Paul, 'High ambitions', *Estates Gazette* (6 November 2010).

Norman, Paul, 'Qatar and Sellar buy new London Bridge Quarter site', *CoStar News* (18 April 2013), http://www.costar.co.uk/en/assets/news/2013/April/Qatar-and-Sellar-buy-new-London-Bridge-Quarter-site.

Norris, Steven, 'What's not to like about Irvine Sellar's "shard of glass"?', *Property Week* (11 April 2003).

Norris, Steven, 'Business as usual in London as the experts take charge', *Property Week* (22 April 2016).

Orwell, George, *Nineteen Eighty-four* (London: Secker & Warburg, 1949).

Parsley, David, 'Heavenly inspiration', *Sunday Express* (17 August 2003).

Pearman, Hugh, 'High societies', *Sunday Times* (16 July 2000).

Phillips, Mike, 'Modern-day miracle', *Property Week* (2 March 2012).

Piano, Lia (ed.), *The Shard: London Bridge Tower* (Genoa: Fondazione Renzo Piano, 2012).

Piano, Renzo, *Renzo Piano: The Complete Logbook* (London and New York: Thames & Hudson, 2017).

Pickard, Jim, 'Failure to fill Gherkin casts shadow on high-rises', *Financial Times* (4 October 2004).

'Plan for Shard square ditched', *Building Design* (30 April 2004).

Powell, Kenneth, *21st Century London: The New Architecture* (London: Merrell, 2011).

Powell, Kenneth, *The Shard: The Official Guidebook* (London: Thames & Hudson, 2013).

'Probe into "Shard of Glass" plan', *Evening Standard* (23 July 2002).

Prynn, Jonathan, 'Carnaby cool', *Evening Standard* (4 February 2010).

Randit, Mukund, 'A Sellar's market?', *Director* (March 2001).

'Renzo's Shard proves too good to turn down', *Building Design* (21 November 2003).

Roberts, Dan, 'Business fears over "Big Chill"', *Sunday Telegraph* (19 August 2007).

Robinson, James, 'Towering ambition', *Sunday Business* (12 November 2000).

Rose, Steve, 'Renzo and the great glass elevator', *Guardian* (14 June 2012).

Rosenthal, Norman, 'The Shard is a St Paul's Cathedral of our time', *Guardian* (7 August 2012).

Russell, Jonathan, 'Market wipes £200m off British Land's shop sale', *Sunday Telegraph* (19 August 2007).

Russell, Jonathan, 'Economic downturn means London skyscrapers may not reach completion', *Daily Telegraph* (16 August 2008).

Scudamore, James, *Heliopolis* (London: Harvill Secker, 2009).

Sellar, Irvine, 'The way I see it', *Men's Wear* (5 October 1978).

'Sellar "committed" to £350m Piano skyscraper', *Property Week* (March 2001).

'Sellar reaches for the skies', *Financial Times* (17–18 March 2002).

Shah, Oliver, 'My epic battle to build the Shard', *Sunday Times* (1 July 2012).

'Shard rakes in £5 million from visitors to viewing platform in first year', *Evening Standard* (21 March 2014).

Shepherd, Rob, 'Cutting edge', *ECA Today* (1 July 2011).

Simpkins, Edward, 'Tall tower or tall tale?', *Sunday Telegraph* (12 November 2000).

Slater, Lydia, 'Touching the void', *Evening Standard* (7 October 2005).

Smith, Adam, *The Theory of Moral Sentiments* (London: Andrew Millar/Edinburgh: Alexander Kincaid and J. Bell, 1759).

Smith, Kristina, 'Mace aims high with the Shard', *Contract Journal* (11 March 2009).

SOM Thinkers, *The Future of the Skyscraper* (New York: Metropolis, 2015).

'Square dropped from "Shard of Glass" plans', *Regeneration & Renewal* (May 2004).

Sudjic, Deyan, 'Don't come to me with your storeys', *Observer* (19 November 2000).

Sudjic, Deyan, 'Who says the only way is up?', *Observer* (17 March 2002).

Sullivan, Louis H., 'The tall office building artistically considered', *Lippincott's Magazine*, no. 57 (March 1896), pp. 403–9.

Sylvester, Felicity, 'Woodbridge: abseiling down London's famous Shard is all in a day's work for former Suffolk school boy', *East Anglian Daily Times* (9 July 2012).

The Tallest Tower: Building the Shard, directed by Colin Campbell, Channel 4 (2013).

'TfL's 30-year Shard deal starts to look like a bargain', *Evening Standard* (date unknown; August 2006).

Thompson, Paul, 'Shard's giant core shoots up', *Construct Yearbook 2010–11* (London: Construct/Construction News, 2011).

Thorpe, Vanessa, 'Egos "a threat to skylines"', *Guardian* (27 May 2007).

The Towering Inferno, dir. John Guillermin (1974).

Wallace, William, 'New rise of London', *Los Angeles Times* (12 May 2003).

Waller, Martin, 'Sellar's market for PwC', *The Times* (18 September 2004).

Watts, Peter, *b.there!* (1 March 2012).

Weaver, Matt, 'Prescott approves disputed "shard of glass" tower', *Guardian* (20 November 2003).

Wehner, Piers, 'Ken attacked for "secret garden" planning talks', *Estates Gazette* (8 June 2002).

Wells, Matthew, *Skyscrapers: Structure and Design* (London: Laurence King, 2005).

'What makes a great place', *Project for Public Spaces*, http://www.pps.org/reference/what_is_placemaking (undated; accessed 6 September 2016).

Willoughby, Michael, 'Archaeology in London: what lies beneath', *On Office: Architecture and Design at Work* (16 February 2011).

'Works starts on Renzo Piano's monumental London Bridge tower', *Building* (7 September 2007).

Wright, Emily, 'I don't do interviews', *Building* (6 February 2009).

Yandall, Paul, 'Sellar ready to tell PwC to vacate Shard of Glass site', *Estates Gazette* (11 September 2004).

Acknowledgements

I am indebted to all the following who agreed to be interviewed or supplied helpful material:

Steve Ayton, Francesca Bianchi, Stefania Canta, Helen Castle, Chris Cole, Michael Donnelly, David Goldberg, Alan Grieve, David Hartwell, Jan Hillier, George Josselyn, Christopher Katkowski, Tony Leyland, Calver Lezama, Ken Livingstone, Francesca Manfredi, Fred Manson, William Matthews, Flan McNamara, Mel Morris, Peter Murray, William Murray, Barry Ostle, Baron Phillips, Renzo Piano, Stephen Platts, Stephen Pycroft, Derek Seeley, Caroline Sellar, Irvine Sellar, Maurice Sellar, Danielle Swift, Dan Taylor, John Young, and staff at the British Library, Constable/Little, Brown, Renzo Piano Building Workshop, Sellar Property Group and the London Borough of Southwark. RPBW and DCD Rights Ltd were extremely helpful in the provision of images.

With thanks to Bevis Hillier, who conducted a series of interviews about Irvine Sellar, quotes from which have been used in this book, and to the archivist Carly Eck for her knowledge of Irvine Sellar's early career and willingness to act as a sounding board for the project.

Thanks to all those journalists and critics who trailed the story of the Shard and the London Bridge Quarter over the course of nearly two decades. It is impossible to list all their many thousands of articles in the Bibliography, but without their efforts to record the twists and turns of the Shard's development, this book would not have been possible.

At Constable, particular thanks to the publisher Andreas Campomar, the great Renaissance man who allowed me to pursue this story and kept me on the straight and narrow, and to the brilliant Claire Chesser, press officer Helen Upton, designer Bekki Guyatt, picture editor Linda Silverman, copy-editor Nick Fawcett, proofreader Kim Bishop and lawyer Meryl Evans, all of whom played significant roles in the life of this book.

Endless gratitude to Miranda Harrison.

Notes

Introduction

1   Richard Nordquist, 'Icon, iconic and other overworked words', *About Education* (21 June 2013), http://grammar.about.com/b/2013/06/21/icon-iconic-and-other-overworked-words.htm.

2   Jonathan Meades, 'Iconic: the adjective of the age', *Economist: Intelligent Life* (March 2009).

3   Including *New Blood*, BBC, Series 1, Episode 4 (2016), and the entirety of *Marcella*, ITV, Series 1 (2016).

4   Jay Merrick, 'The tower and the glory', *Independent* (26 March 2001).

5   Ed Hammond, 'Sellar tops out his towering ambition', *Financial Times* (4 July 2012).

Chapter 1: Changing the Landscape

6   Terry Farrell, *Shaping London: The Patterns and Forms that Make the Metropolis* (Chichester: Wiley, 2010), pp. 39–40.

7   See *The Bridges that Built London with Dan Cruikshank*, BBC4 (June 2012).

8   The full text of *Planning Policy Guidance 1: General policy and principles* (1997) can be found at http://www.leics.gov.uk/ppg01_general_policy_and_principles_1997.pdf.

9   *The Tallest Tower: Building the Shard*, Channel 4 (2013).

10 'Land Securities: Annual Report 2015', http://annualreport2015.landsecurities.com/pdf/Full_Report.pdf.

11 Shaw's original is 'The reasonable man adapts himself to the world: the unreasonable one persists in trying to adapt the world to himself. Therefore all progress depends on the unreasonable man.' George Bernard Shaw, 'Maxims for Revolutionists', *Man and Superman* (London: Constable, 1903).

Chapter 2: Tall Stories

12 See 'CTBUH Height Criteria', Council on Tall Buildings and Urban Habitat (no date), http://www.ctbuh.org/TallBuildings/ HeightStatistics/Criteria/tabid/446/language/en-US/Default.aspx.

13 See Professor Banister Fletcher and Herbert Fletcher, *London Building Acts 1894 to 1909*, fifth edition (London: Batsford, 1914), p. 50, https:// archive.org/stream/londonbuildingacoofletrich#page/50/mode/2up.

14 Rowan Moore, 'Save us from this poke in the eye with a sharp stick', *Evening Standard* (10 April 2000).

15 Rowan Moore, 'Save us from these heights of bad taste', *Evening Standard* (12 April 2000).

Chapter 3: A Lunch in Berlin

16 Renzo Piano, *Renzo Piano: The Complete Logbook* (London and New York: Thames & Hudson, 2017), p. 26.

17 Marcus Fairs, 'Interview: Renzo Piano on the Shard', *Dezeen* (May 2012).

18 Hugh Pearman, 'High societies', *Sunday Times* (16 July 2000).

19 Anne Cuthbertson, 'Interview – The Last Word: Irvine Sellar', *London Magazine* (June 2016).

20 Lisa Freedman, 'Tower power', *The Business: Financial Times Weekend Magazine* (24 March 2001).

21 Shirley Flack, 'Another barrier falls: with a boutique for him and her together', *Daily Sketch* (7 October 1966).

22 Nik Cohn, *Today There Are No Gentlemen: The Changes in Englishmen's Clothes since the War* (London: Weidenfeld & Nicolson, 1971).

23 Cohn, *Today There Are No Gentlemen*.

24 Lia Piano (ed), *The Shard: London Bridge Tower*, (Genoa: Fondazione Renzo Piano, 2012) p. 183.

25 Piano, *The Shard*, p. 13.

26 Peter Bill, 'Piano's forte', *Estates Gazette* (6 September 2008).

Chapter 4: Big Thinking in a Little Space

27 Rowan Moore, 'Piano tunes in to London', *Evening Standard* (18 July 2000).

28 Piano, *The Shard*, p. 13.

29 Francisco Martínez Mindeguía, 'Bruno Taut, Architecture in the Alps, 1919', *Arquitectura an Dibuixos Exemplars* (accessed 27 July 2016), http://www.etsavega.net/dibex/Taut_Alpine.htm.

30 Piano, *The Shard*, p. 185.

31 See 'Census Information Scheme GLA Intelligence: Demography', London Datastore, http://data.london.gov.uk/census/infographic-demography (accessed 28 July 2016).

32 'Sellar reaches for the skies', *Financial Times* (17–18 March 2002).

33 See Andrew Hosken, *Ken: The Ups and Downs of Ken Livingstone* (London: Arcadia Books, 2008).

34 London First and Savills, *Redefining Density: Making the Best Use of London's Land to Build More and Better Homes* (London: London First/Savills, 2015), p. 3, http://research.euro.savills.co.uk/pdfs/redefining-density-joint-report-with-london-first.pdf.

35 James Robinson, 'Towering ambition', *Sunday Business* (12 November 2000).

36 Edward Simpkins, 'Tall tower or tall tale?', *Sunday Telegraph* (12 November 2000).

37 Rowan Moore, 'Tower set to raise the stakes in London', *Evening Standard* (9 November 2000).

38 'Keep out of it, Ken', *Daily Mirror* (18 May 2001).

39 Simon Jenkins, 'Ken falls victim to Big Apple envy', *Evening Standard* (18 January 2001).

40 Simon Jenkins, 'Paddington Pole may be dead but the vanity of architects lives on', *Evening Standard* (19 July 2016).

41   Deyan Sudjic, 'Don't come to me with your storeys', *Observer* (19 November 2000).

42   Simpkins, 'Tall tower or tall tale?'

Chapter 5: The Fear of Neighbours

43   Sigmund Freud, *Civilization and Its Discontents* (London: Penguin, 2014 [reprint]), Chapter 5.

44   Jonathan Meades, *Bunkers, Brutalism and Bloodymindedness: Concrete Poetry*, BBC4 (April 2016).

45   Quoted in Judith Dupré, *Skyscrapers: A History of the World's Most Extraordinary Buildings* (New York: Black Dog and Leventhal Publishers, 2001 edition), p. 7.

46   Richard Morrison, 'High society', *The Times* (28 November 2001).

47   Anthony Burgess, *A Clockwork Orange* (Harmondsworth: Penguin, 1972 [reprint]), pp. 19–23.

48   J. G. Ballard, *High-Rise* (London: Fourth Estate, 2012 [reprint]), p. 66.

49   James Scudamore, *Heliopolis* (London: Harvill Secker, 2009).

50   Quoted in Piers Wehner, 'Ken attacked for "secret garden" planning talks', *Estates Gazette* (8 June 2002).

51   Robert Adam, 'Power and status in the city', *Spectator* (6 July 2002).

52   Jonathan Glancey, 'Trust me', *Guardian* (29 March 2002).

53   Deyan Sudjic, 'Who says the only way is up?', *Observer* (17 March 2002).

54   As quoted in the *Morning Star* (25 July 2002) and elsewhere.

55   Quoted by Robert Gibson, '"Taliban" slur upsets EH', *Estates Gazette* (17 November 2001).

56   'Probe into "Shard of Glass" plan', *Evening Standard* (23 July 2002).

57   Robert Booth and Tim Hyman, 'Shard splits design tsars', *Building Design* (9 May 2003).

58   Quoted in Booth and Hyman, 'Shard splits design tsars'.

59   Jenny Davey, 'Heron Tower joins Erotic Gherkin', *The Times* (23 July 2002).

60   David Millward, 'Donald Trump is the new John Prescott', *Daily Telegraph* (27 April 2016).

Chapter 6: The Inquiry

61 Piano, *The Shard*, p. 186.

62 Richard Morrison, 'According to Lord Rogers, the London skyline is "unbelievably boring"', *The Times* (17 March 2003).

63 For a brief explanation of Section 106 and the related Community Infrastructure Levy, which began in 2010, see the Planning Advisory Service website, http://www.pas.gov.uk/3-community-infrastructure-levy-cil/-/journal_content/56/332612/4090701/ARTICLE.

64 Piano, *The Shard*, p. 19.

65 Marcus Binney, 'Towering spike is blunted to pacify its critics', *The Times* (5 April 2003).

66 Steven Norris, 'What's not to like about Irvine Sellar's "shard of glass"?', *Property Week* (11 April 2003).

67 Simon Jenkins, 'Save our skyline from the Spike', *Evening Standard* (17 April 2003).

68 William Wallace, 'New rise of London', *Los Angeles Times* (12 May 2003).

69 Throughout this chapter, quotes from the public inquiry are taken from John L. Gray, 'Report to the First Secretary of State: London Borough of Southwark Application by Teighmore Limited' (Bristol: The Planning Inspectorate, 23 July 2003).

70 Wallace, 'New rise of London'.

71 Martin Bailey, 'The Bilbao effect', *Art Newspaper* (20 February 2002).

72 Quoted in J. A. L. Waddell, *Bridge Engineering* (New York: Wiley, 1916); Joseph Aloysius Hanson, 'All downhill from here', *Building* (31 July 2015).

73 Piano, *The Shard*, p. 186.

74 Matt Weaver, 'Prescott approves disputed "shard of glass" tower', *Guardian* (20 November 2003).

75 Piano, *The Shard*, p. 186.

76 'Renzo's Shard proves too good to turn down', *Building Design* (21 November 2003).

77 Charlie Gates, 'Shard takes all', *Building Design* (21 November 2003).

78 *Regeneration & Renewal* (28 November 2003).

Chapter 7: A Frantic Lull

79 'Square dropped from "Shard of Glass" plans', *Regeneration & Renewal* (May 2004); 'Plan for Shard square ditched', *Building Design* (30 April 2004).

80 Components of the description here are drawn from various articles including Jenny Davey, 'Legal row engulfs plan for the "Shard of Glass"', *The Times* (15 November 2005); Jim Pickard, 'Shard of Glass dispute settled out of court', *Financial Times* (9 December 2005); John Mulligan, 'Irish Nationwide wins judgment of E4.2 million against Halabi firms', *Irish Independent* (31 March 2014); Christian Metcalfe, 'Sellar makes further allegations in £55 million Shard wrangle', *Estates Gazette* (13 November 2007); Wikipedia, 'The Shard' (last modified 8 March 2017).

81 Simon Thurley, *Cornerstone* (May 2007); quoted in Vanessa Thorpe, 'Egos "a threat to skylines"', *Guardian* (27 May 2007).

82 Jim Pickard, 'Failure to fill gherkin casts shadow on high-rises', *Financial Times* (4 October 2004).

83 Piano, *The Shard*, p. 45

84 Paul Yandall, 'Sellar ready to tell PwC to vacate Shard of Glass site', *Estates Gazette* (11 September 2004).

85 Lydia Slater, 'Touching the void', *Evening Standard* (7 October 2005).

86 The quotes from both Barry Ostle and Hamish McKenzie come from Adam Benzine, 'Changing of the Shard', *Property Week* (11 August 2006).

87 'TfL's 30-year Shard deal starts to look like a bargain', *Evening Standard* (date unknown; August 2006).

88 Deirdre Hipwell, 'Sellars' Market', *Property Week* (18 July 2008).

Chapter 8: The Crash

89 Mike Phillips, 'Modern-day miracle', *Property Week* (2 March 2012).

90 Dan Roberts, 'Business fears over "Big Chill"', *Sunday Telegraph* (19 August 2007); Jonathan Russell, 'Market wipes £200m off British Land's shop sale', *Sunday Telegraph* (19 August 2007).

91 Mike Foster, 'Sellar spies opportunities in adversity', *Wall Street Journal* (20 April 2009).

92 Robert Hardman, 'So that's how it feels to be a pigeon', *Daily Mail* (9 June 2012).

93 Nick Mathieson, 'The higher they climb . . .', *Observer* (10 September 2000).

94 *Evening Standard* (16 November 2005).

95 Oliver Shah, 'My epic battle to build the Shard', *Sunday Times* (1 July 2012).

96 Paul Norman, 'Qatar and Sellar buy new London Bridge Quarter site', *CoStar News* (18 April 2013), http://www.costar.co.uk/en/assets/news/2013/April/Qatar-and-Sellar-buy-new-London-Bridge-Quarter-site.

97 Hipwell, 'Sellars' Market'.

Chapter 9: Breaking Ground

98 The nine 150-plus-metre buildings completed between 2002 and 2008 are HSBC Tower, Citigroup Centre 2, 30 St Mary Axe, Broadgate Tower, Beetham Tower Manchester, 1 Churchill Place, 40 Bank Street, 25 Bank Street and 10 Upper Bank Street. The four pre-existing buildings over 150 metres are One Canada Square (1991), Tower 42 (1980), BT Telecom Tower (1966) and BT Tower Birmingham (1966).

99 Jonathan Russell, 'Economic downturn means London skyscrapers may not reach completion', *Daily Telegraph* (16 August 2008).

100 See 'CTBUH Height Criteria', Council on Tall Buildings and Urban Habitat (no date), http://www.ctbuh.org/TallBuildings/Height Statistics/Criteria/tabid/446/language/en-US/Default.aspx.

101 Hipwell, 'Sellars' Market'.

102 *The Tallest Tower: Building the Shard*, Channel 4 (2013).

103 Roxanne McMeeken, 'Bernard Ainsworth interview: Shard man', *Building* (13 June 2008).

104 David Fickling, 'Shard reaches for the sky amid office sector gloom', *Financial Times* (16 March 2009).

105 Piano, *The Shard*, p. 50.

106 Piano, *The Shard*, p. 185.

107 David Parsley, 'Heavenly inspiration', *Sunday Express* (17 August 2003).

108 Piano, *The Shard*, pp. 18–19.

109 James Holloway, 'The Shard's bleeding edge: anatomy of a 21st-century skyscraper', *Ars Technica* (5 December 2011), http://arstechnica.com/ gadgets/2011/12/the-shards-bleeding-edge-anatomy-of-a-21st -century-skyscraper.

Chapter 10: The Impossible Made Possible

110 Bill, 'Piano's forte'.

111 *The Tallest Tower: Building the Shard*, Channel 4 (2013).

112 *The Tallest Tower: Building the Shard.*

113 Jennifer Chatham, 'KONE jump lifts installed in the Shard', *Elevator World* (March 2011).

114 For the concrete-pump geeks among us, they used a SP8800 Schwing portable pump, which was 8 metres long and 3 metres high and had a 17-litre engine, capable of producing 243 bar of concrete pressure and pumping 3,180 cubic feet/90 m³ of concrete per hour.

115 Paul Thompson, 'Shard's giant core shoots up', *Construct Yearbook 2010– 11* (London: Construct/Construction News, 2011).

116 Kristina Smith, 'Mace aims high with the Shard', *Contract Journal* (11 March 2009).

117 Thomas Lane, 'Civil Stars', *Building Magazine* (5 March 2010).

118 Paul Norman, 'High ambitions', *Estates Gazette* (6 November 2010).

119 Paul Finch, 'Letter from London', *Architects' Journal* (24 September 2009).

120 Boris Johnson, 'A global city bounces back', *Newsweek* (7 December 2009).

121 *The Times* (21 December 2009); *Commercial Property Register* (May– September 2009).

122 Norman, 'High ambitions'.

123 Hipwell, 'Sellars' Market'.

124 Angela Jameson, 'Fashion king aims to tower over rivals', *Daily Mail* (9 December 2010).

125 'Fox lived in the Shard skyscraper at London Bridge', *BBC News* (24 February 2011), http://www.bbc.co.uk/news/uk-england-london -12573364.

126 Piano, *The Shard*.

127 Bill, 'Piano's forte'.

128 Piano, *The Shard*, p. 187.

129 London Bridge Quarter Section 106 Project Board, 'London Bridge Quarter Section 106 Project Board performance report' (London: London Borough of Southwark, 28 November 2012).

130 Robert Booth, 'London's Shard: a tower of power and riches looking down on poverty', *Guardian* (21 December 2011).

131 *The Tallest Tower: Building the Shard*, Channel 4 (2013).

132 Felicity Sylvester, 'Woodbridge: abseiling down London's famous Shard is all in a day's work for former Suffolk school boy', *East Anglian Daily Times* (9 July 2012).

133 Piano, *The Shard*, p. 188.

134 Valentine Low, 'Mother doesn't worry . . . she's used to it', *The Times* (21 August 2012); 'Halfway up he was neither up nor down', *The Times* (4 September 2012).

Chapter 11: The Piano Trilogy

135 Michael Willoughby, 'Archaeology in London: what lies beneath', *On Office: Architecture and Design at Work* (16 February 2011), http://www. onofficemagazine.com/features/item/1090-archaeology-in-london.

136 Thomas Lane, 'The Place to be', *Building* (25 January 2013).

137 Lane, 'The Place to be'.

138 'News UK completes move from Wapping to new London Bridge HQ', News UK (16 September 2014), https://www.news.co.uk/2014/09/ news-uk-completes-move-from-wapping-to-new-london-bridge-hq.

139 'Irvine Sellar', CTBUH Interview Series, Council on Tall Buildings and Urban Habitat, New York (27 October 2015).

140 'Jane Jacobs, *Project for Public Spaces*, http://www.pps.org/reference/ jjacobs-2 (undated; accessed 4 September 2016).

141 Bill Hillier et al., *Broadgate Spaces: Life in Public Spaces* (London: Unit for Architectural Studies, Bartlett School of Architecture and Planning, 1990), http://www.spacesyntax.com/project/broadgate-spaces-life -in-public-places.

142 'What makes a great place', *Project for Public Spaces*, http://www.pps. org/reference/what_is_placemaking (undated; accessed 6 September 2016).

143 Vybarr Cregan-Reid, *Footnotes: How Running Makes Us Human* (London: Ebury, 2016), p.139.

144 'Health Profile 2015: Tower Hamlets', *Public Health England* (2 June 2015), http://www.apho.org.uk/resource/item.aspx?RID=171849.

Chapter 12: Vision into View

145 'Irvine Sellar', CTBUH Interview Series.

146 Shah, 'My epic battle to build the Shard'.

147 Piano, *The Shard*, p. 189.

148 Peter Murray, 'The building dividing London', *Financial Times* (26 May 2012).

149 Peter Watts, *b.there!* (1 March 2012).

150 Clive Aslet, *Daily Mail* (5 July 2012).

151 Norman Rosenthal, 'The Shard is a St Paul's Cathedral of our time', *Guardian* (7 August 2012).

152 'Irvine Sellar', CTBUH Interview Series.

153 Dipal Acharya, 'High art', *Evening Standard* (25 January 2013).

154 'Timeline', *The Shard* (2015), http://www.the-shard.com/shard/the-vision; 'Shard rakes in £5 million from visitors to viewing platform in first year', *Evening Standard* (21 March 2014).

155 Cohn, *Today There Are No Gentlemen*.

156 Shane Watson, 'Beyond the class ceiling', in Sarah Miller (ed.), *Shangri-La London* (London: Shangri-La, 2014), p. 12.

157 Lisa Johnson, 'Suites of one's own', in Sarah Miller (ed.), *Shangri-La London* (London: Shangri-La, 2014), pp. 33–7.

158 Andrew Lawrence, 'Skyscraper Index' (Hong Kong: Barclays Capital, 2012).

159 Steven Norris, 'Business as usual in London as the experts take charge', *Property Week* (22 April 2016).

160 Simon Jenkins, 'The Shard has slashed the face of London forever', *Guardian* (3 July 2012).

161 Murray, 'The building dividing London'.

162 Jonathan Jones, 'The Shard is a broken society's towering achievement', *Guardian* (19 August 2011).

163 Helen Castle, 'Editorial', *Architectural Design* (January/February 2012), no. 215.

164 'The rich . . . are led by an invisible hand to make nearly the same distribution of the necessaries of life, which would have been made, had the earth been divided into equal portions among all its inhabitants, and thus without intending it, without knowing it, advance the interest of the society.' Adam Smith, *The Theory of Moral Sentiments* (London: Andrew Millar/Edinburgh: Alexander Kincaid and J. Bell, 1759), Part IV, Chapter 1.

165 Deyan Sudjic, preface, in Sarah Miller (ed.), *Shangri-La London* (London: Shangri-La, 2014).

166 *Southwark*, no. 8 (winter 2011/12).

167 Aditya Chakrabortty, 'The Shard is a perfect metaphor for modern London', *Guardian* (26 June 2012).

168 Peter John, 'Letters and email', *Guardian* (30 June 2012).

169 Castle, 'Editorial'.

Index

Page numbers in *italics* refer to illustrations